*Managing Quality in Projects*

*To the memory of my parents*

# *Managing Quality in Projects*

RON BASU

GOWER

Published by
Gower Publishing Limited
Wey Court East
Union Road
Farnham
Surrey, GU9 7PT
England

Gower Publishing Company
110 Cherry Street
Suite 3-1
Burlington
VT 05401-3818
USA

www.gowerpublishing.com

Ron Basu has asserted his moral rights under the Copyright, Designs and Patents Act, 1988, to be identified as the author of this work.

**British Library Cataloguing in Publication Data**
Basu, Ron.
  Managing quality in projects. -- (Advances in project management)
  1. Project management. 2. Quality control. 3. Project management--Case studies. 4. Quality control--Case studies.
  I. Title II. Series
  658.4'04-dc23

  ISBN: 978-1-4094-4092-5 (pbk)
  ISBN: 978-1-4094-4093-2 (ebk – PDF)
  ISBN: 978-1-4094-8462-2 (ebk – ePUB)

**Library of Congress Cataloging-in-Publication Data**
Basu, Ron.
  Managing quality in projects / by Ron Basu.
    p. cm. -- (Advances in project management)
  Includes bibliographical references and index.
  ISBN 978-1-4094-4092-5 (pbk) -- ISBN 978-1-4094-4093-2 (ebook) 1. Project management. 2. Quality control. 3. Project management--Case studies. 4. Quality control--Case studies. I. Title.
  HD69.P75B387 2013
  658.4'013--dc23

2012029740

MIX
Paper from
responsible sources
FSC
www.fsc.org
FSC® C018575

Printed and bound in Great Britain by the
MPG Books Group, UK

# CONTENTS

# LIST OF FIGURES

# LIST OF TABLES

# ACKNOWLEDGEMENTS

I acknowledge the help and support from my colleagues and students at Henley Business School, Essex Business School in England and SKEMA Business School in France.

In particular I acknowledge the encouragement and support of Abby Ghobadian (Henley Business School), Stephen Simister (Henley Business School), Darren Dalcher (Middlesex University), Jay Mitra (Essex Business School) and Rodney Turner (SKEMA Business School)

I am most grateful to the many contributors to the case examples and diagrams included in the book with special mentions to Chris Little (BAA) and Daniel Keeling (Crossrail).

The illustrations in Chapters 8 and 9 are developed from original work undertaken during the projects in question and I am grateful to the contributing organizations for permission to use them.

Every effort has been made to credit the authors, publishers and websites of material used in this book. I apologise if inadvertently any sources remain unacknowledged and if known I shall be pleased to credit them in the next edition.

My sincere thanks go to the staff of my publishers, especially to Jonathan Norman for getting this project off the ground.

Finally the project could not have been completed without the encouragement and help of my family, especially my wife Moira, daughter Bonnie and son Robi.

Ron Basu

# ABOUT THE AUTHOR

Ron Basu is Director of Performance Excellence Limited and a Visiting Fellow at Henley Business School, England. He is also a Visiting Professor at SKEMA Business School, France. He specialises in operational excellence and supply chain management and has research interests in performance management and project management.

Previously he held senior management roles in blue-chip companies like GSK, GlaxoWellcome and Unilever and led global initiatives and projects in Six Sigma, ERP/ MRPII, supply chain re-engineering and total productive maintenance. Prior to this he worked as management consultant with A. T. Kearney.

He is the co-author of *Total Manufacturing Solutions, Quality Beyond Six Sigma, Total Operations Solutions* and *Total Supply Chain Management* and the author of *Measuring e-business Performance, Implementing Quality, Implementing Six Sigma and Lean, FIT SIGMA* and *Managing Project Supply Chains*. He has authored a number of papers in the operational excellence and project management fields. He is a regular presenter of papers in global seminars on project management, Six Sigma and manufacturing and supply chain topics.

After graduating in Manufacturing Engineering from UMIST, Manchester, Ron obtained an MSc in Operational Research from Strathclyde University, Glasgow. He has also completed a Ph.D. at Reading University. He is a Fellow of the Institution of Mechanical Engineers, the Institute of Business Consultancy, the Association for Project Management and the Chartered Quality Institute. He is also the winner of an APM Project Management Award.

Ron lives with his wife Moira in Gerrards Cross, England and has two children, Bonnie and Robi.

# INTRODUCTION
# WHY MANAGING QUALITY IS ESSENTIAL
# IN PROJECT MANAGEMENT

## WHY PROJECT QUALITY?

We all agree and accept that as an end user of a product or service we would like what we order, when we want it and on the basis of good value for money. In a competitive world of consumer choice, we also expect it to last. We understand the benefits of a market-driven economy and need for appropriate product and service quality. This is the domain of operations, services and supply chain management. And we define our expectations as 'quality is what customer expects as a lasting experience' (Basu, 2011a). However, in the field of project management the importance of quality is not so clear-cut. Project managers appear to accept the 'iron triangle of cost, budget and quality' (Atkinson, 1999) but focus more on 'on time and budget' delivery as the success factors. Quality in projects is often relegated to mere 'lip service' and to tick-box compliance.

Project managers also appreciate the risk of a project on the basis of its uniqueness, complexity and deliberate design but appear not to connect the outcome of risks with the root causes underpinned by the dimensions of project quality. As a consequence we find many examples (as described later) of projects which were delivered on time and within budget but failed to meet the expectations of end users in the longer run. We need to ask ourselves 'how diligent are we in terms of project processes to deliver project objectives'? This is the minimum requirement to meet the customer needs. Furthermore we should also investigate 'how good is our project management … as a vehicle for delivering the longer-term outcomes and benefits as required by the sponsors and end users'. This is an element of the additional requirements of sustainable quality leading to project excellence. The relationship between *project quality* and *project excellence* will be discussed in more detail later.

Let us have a look at the current thinking and practices around these questions. The extant project management literature (Turner, 1999; Atkinson, 1999: Meredith and Mantel, 2003; Morris and Hough, 1997) identifies and supports three criteria or objectives for assessing the success of a project known as the 'iron triangle 'of time, cost and quality. The first two objectives are relatively simple to define and measure (Morris and Hough, 1997). Project quality as the third objective or dimension of the iron triangle is more difficult to define and assess, although it has received some attention in the academic literature (Turner, 2002; Heisler, 1990). Turner (2002) is among the few authors who attempts to more clearly define project quality comprising two dimensions as product quality and process quality. The guidelines for project quality in the project management bodies of knowledge (Association of Project Management, 2007; Project Management Institute, 2008) also reflect procedures of design and process requirements. These definitions and guidelines appear to suffer from two important limitations, viz. a lack of clarity in the definition (Whitty and Schulz, 2005) and the exclusion of organisational learning practices (Kotnour, 2000).

The lack of clarity around quality is often the source of project disputes and there are plenty of examples in the business world, as illustrated in the box, documenting the link between inadequate attention to quality management and unsuccessful major projects.

---

### CASE EXAMPLE THE MILLENNIUM DOME

'The Millennium Dome project was one of the most controversial public works projects ever undertaken' (National Audit Office, 2000). The National Audit Office report also stated that the New Millennium Experience Company experienced severe financial difficulties. The main cause of these difficulties was the failure to achieve the visitor numbers: other contributing factors included the quality of project delivery and the contents within the dome.

### CASE EXAMPLE WEMBLEY STADIUM

'The company that built the new Wembley Stadium, which opened after years of delays and almost tripling its cost, is suing the engineering consultants behind the project for £253m, claiming that their services were unsatisfactory' (*The Observer*, 16 March 2008). A preliminary search of legal cases (British and Irish Legal Information Institute, http://www.bailii.org, accessed 26/11/08) indicated several instances (2512 hits) of litigations because of 'poor quality' in projects. For example, in the recent Wembley Stadium project, there were eight major litigations related to project quality and three of these litigations were related to the definitions of project quality. In the case between Multiplex Construction Ltd and Honeywell Control Ltd (both being the contractors of Wembley Stadium) the dispute was to resolve the statement in the contract, 'It will have extensive, high-quality corporate hospitality facilities and a state of the art communications system (installed by Honeywell).' (Neutral Citation Number: [2007] EWHC 447 (TCC), www.bailii. org, accessed 26/11/08).

## CASE EXAMPLE WEST COAST RAIL UPGRADE

The rail line between Glasgow and London was undergoing an £8.6bn upgrade from 2003. The modernisation of the West Coast Main Line will deliver the following enhancements:

- 125mph route capability for tilting trains delivering much faster journey times.
- Capacity for significantly more long-distance passenger and freight trains than today.
- Better and more resilient performance in travel time and safety measures.

The National Audit Office said it might not be able to cope with current levels of growth beyond 2015. The auditors' report on the West Coast Line warned that electronic signalling equipment might become obsolete significantly earlier than expected. The auditors were also concerned about the ineffective communications between key stakeholders (Government, Network Rail, Rail Track and Virgin Trains). To sustain train operations, the line's operator, Virgin Trains, was paid £590m more in subsidy in the period 2002–06 than envisaged in its franchise agreement, their report said. In January 2008, an over-run on work results in one of the worst delays yet. Network Rail is fined £14m.

## CASE EXAMPLE HEATHROW TERMINAL 5

'Thousands of suitcases are being sent to Milan by British Airways to try to help clear a backlog of 19,000 bags at Heathrow's new Terminal 5' (*The Guardian*, April 2 2008). The conclusions of the House of Commons Transport Select Committee Report (2008) highlighted that insufficient communication between the owner of the new terminal, BAA, and its operator, British Airways, was a major factor in the ensuing complications with the baggage system and security searches. As it will be discussed later, communication could be an essential component of people-related quality.

The above examples of major project failures appear to focus on the quality of design, the quality of execution processes and the quality of communications between stakeholders. Many papers and studies in the 1990s (Belassi and Tukel, 1996; Tam, 1999; Kirby, 1996) highlighted project failures, but the problems still exist (MPA, 2003). Recent academic publications (Jamieson and Morris, 2008; Ling, Liu and Woo, 2008; Zou, Zhang and Wang, 2007; Abdelsalam and Gad, 2008) also suggest that causes of project failures include inadequate risk evaluation and quality management. These papers also highlight that there is a lack of clarity regarding the dimensions of project quality and its application with key stakeholders.

When you look at the domain of operations management you may observe some proven paths to follow. Operations management enjoys some success stories (along with the occasional failure) in terms of the application of quality-based operational excellence concepts such as total quality management, Six Sigma, lean and supply chain management (Oakland, 2003). The application of operational excellence concepts are now extended to non-manufacturing processes.

> *Firms such as Motorola, General Electric ... successfully implemented Six Sigma. Motorola saved $15 billion in an 11 year period. General Electric saved $2 billion in 1999 alone ... Although Six Sigma initiatives have focused primarily on improving the performance of manufacturing processes, the concepts are widely applied in non-manufacturing, administrative and service functions. (Weinstein, Castellano, Petrick and Vokurka, 2008)*

Even though operational excellence concepts (such as Six Sigma) are often driven by the objective of cost-effectiveness the enablers of these concepts are rooted to the fundamentals of quality management (Oakland, 2003).

In the domain of operations management, the dimensions and definitions of quality have been identified by some authors (Garvin, 1984; Parasuraman, Zeithamel and Berry, 1984). The early leaders of total quality management (TQM) (Deming, 1986; Juran, 1989; Feigenbaum, 1983) emphasised the importance of people-related issues as a dimension of quality. On the other hand, the dimensions and definitions of quality appear to be wanting in publications related to project management. Project management standards (e.g. PMBOK, 2008; PRINCE2, 2009) focus primarily on processes in the project life cycle with some references to quality management systems. Turner (2002) appears to agree with Wild's (2002) dimensions of product quality and process quality. Kotnour (2000) points out the lack of clarity in the definition of project quality and the role of organisational learning in project management. There are publications regarding the success criteria and success factors of projects (Pinto and Slevin, 1988; Grude, Turner and Wateridge, 1996) but their implications in the dimensions of project quality are not clear. The application of excellence models in projects appears to be limited (Westerveld, 2003). Unlike operations management, the tools and concepts of operations excellence (Basu, 2008), such as lean and Six Sigma, are rarely being applied in project management (Pinch, 2005).

As summarised in Table I.1, the publications for the manufacturing and service sectors are more focused on the definitions of quality with distinctive dimensions and also encompass operational excellence concepts. The publications for the project management sector include success criteria and success factors, but these in turn appear to show a gap with their link with the dimensions of project quality. There is also an apparent gap between the application operational excellence concepts in project management.

**Table I.1**    **Classification of publications on quality and excellence**

| Publications | Dimensions and definitions of quality Product process people | Success criteria and success factors | Excellence models | Operational excellence concepts SCM/ TQM/6Sigma | Application sector |
|---|---|---|---|---|---|
| Gravin (1984) | x* | | | | Manufacturing |
| Parasuraman, Zeithamel and Berry (1984) | x | | | | Service |
| Wild (2002) | x x x | | | | Manufacturing |
| Deming (1986) | x x | | | x | Manufacturing |
| Juran (1989) | x x | | | x | Manufacturing |
| Feigenbaum (1983) | x x | | | x | Manufacturing |
| Whitty and Sculz (2005) | x | | | | Projects |
| PRINCE2 (2009) | x | | | | Projects |
| Turner (2002) Kotnour (2000) | x x x | | | | Projects Projects |
| Pinto and Slevin (1988) | | x | | | Projects |
| Grude, Turner and Wateridge (1996) | | x | | | Projects |
| Westerveld (2003) | | | x | | Projects |
| **This book** | **x x x** | **x** | **x** | **x x** | **Projects** |

* x denotes the presence of the topic in the publication.

On the basis of this summary there appears to be a knowledge gap in project management related to the benefits achieved by quality management when compared to the manufacturing and service operations. This book investigates the impact of all aspects of quality management in project management (see Table 1.1). The aim of the book is to contribute to this knowledge gap in project management and take the status of subject matters a step forward.

Furthermore, this preliminary review also indicates that there should be a clearer definition of project quality to establish some key dimensions. If you cannot define, you cannot measure, and if you cannot measure, you cannot control, assure or improve. First, what are the dimensions of project quality? Is it meeting specifications, timescales, budgets, achieving its purpose, producing happy project teams and stakeholders? Or does project quality constitute a combination of all these?

Secondly, what tools or models can be effectively used in the quest for achieving and sustaining project excellence? What factors and processes are important in assessing the maturity and performance of projects?

Thirdly, how can the successes of operational excellence concepts, such as supply chain management, lean thinking and Six Sigma, be gainfully deployed in enhancing project quality and excellence?

## THE AIMS AND PURPOSE OF THIS BOOK

This book aims to examine how quality should be defined and measured in the management of projects, and how the best practices of operations management can be applied to improve the likelihood of achieving project excellence. The investigation focuses initially on defining the dimensions of quality in project management and identifying sources of measurement for project excellence. Although there are a number of tools that measure excellence such as the balanced scorecard (Kaplan and Norton, 2004) or the EFQM model (2003) in operations management, it could be argued that the jury is still out (Association of Project Management, 2007) as how to apply these tools to achieve the level of longer-lasting performance in projects. An in-depth analysis will critically evaluate the assertions behind why it is important to include the dimensions of quality, excellence models and operational excellence methodologies in delivering sustainable outcomes of projects. The subsequent data collection phase of the field research will be validated by a causal research model, and further examined by case studies. These case studies are expected to open opportunities for further research in applying the best practices in different types of projects and programmes in construction, information technology and change management.

The purpose of this book is to go beyond the traditional measures of risk assessment, cost and time management in a project. It has been argued by Westerveld (2003) and Wateridge (2002) that although there have been significant publications on both project success criteria and critical success factors for projects, there has not been adequate research to define a concept that can link the two. There are also signs of visible efforts by IPMA (International Project Management Association) (e.g. the 'project excellence' model) and PMI (Project Management Institute) (e.g. the 'OPM3' model) to assess a project organisation's maturity and capability leading to project excellence. However, there appear to be no practically grounded and academically robust links between project excellence processes and project quality dimensions.

ISO 10006, in spite of its title – *Quality management - guidelines to quality in project management* – appears to provide the opposite effect in managing quality in projects (Stanleigh, 2007). If more attention were given to the items of written procedures at the expense of other critical people-related elements, then the project could become unsuccessful, although in theory it may remain compliant with standards. Other documents of project methodology also appear to offer little more than mere lip service regarding quality management. For example, BS6079 (2002) does not cover quality (other than project control) and PRINCE2 (2009) methods provide limited guidelines for quality planning and quality control within the process 'planning quality' module and reflect internally focused design and process requirements.

In summary, you may understand the role of quality in project management, but this alone is not sufficient. There is a far greater need to appreciate how one can define and measure the dimensions of quality – especially the people-related sustainable criteria – and then apply them towards the goal of achieving project excellence.

Against this backdrop, this book will fill the gaps in measuring project quality and project excellence.

Based on the initial review and apparent gaps identified, the key research question in this book has been formulated as: *How can project quality enable major projects deliver sustainable outcomes to key stakeholders leading to project excellence?* For the purpose of a focused enquiry in the literature, this overall research question has been broken into four supplementary areas:

1. What are the current processes of measuring the dimensions of quality in various stages of the project life cycle and what are the sustainable criteria?
2. What are the current models and approaches of assessing project excellence and what are the links between project success criteria and critical success factors?
3. Can a holistic model measure the dimensions of quality of a project and also assess the overall effectiveness of a project and project organisation?
4. How practically are the operational excellence approaches likely to be used in project management and how do we relate the outputs of such approaches to project excellence?

## MAJOR PROJECTS

The case examples presented earlier in the chapter underline the importance of project quality more significantly attributed to major infrastructure projects. The infrastructure includes highways, railways, ports, tunnels, bridges, power plants, mass transits, municipal facilities or a combination of similar public facilities with the primary purpose of serving public needs, providing social services and promoting private economic activities (Algarni, Adriti and Polat, 2007). According to the recent UK Infrastructure Report (BMI, 2008):

> As one of the most robust economies in the world, the UK boasts of a large and highly developed construction industry, currently valued at over £80 billion. The UK construction industry is characterised by a small number of large players that have access to huge capital reserves and world-class technology, enabling them to undertake massive infrastructure development projects. Recent major infrastructure projects include the planned development of the Crossrail in London at an estimated cost of £18 billion, the £5.8 billion development of the Channel Tunnel Rail Link, and the £4.3 billion construction of Terminal 5 at Heathrow Airport.

In comparison to other major undertakings, the major infrastructure projects in the UK may have to face additional technical and management challenges, such as wide range of stakeholders including consumers, multifunctional features in building, roads, rails, tunnels and systems and above all, a long public review period before it can take off. The demand on project quality management is also likely to be more challenging in keeping with the complexities of a major infrastructure project.

With the above rationale, the research, particularly the case studies, will focus primarily on the issues, challenges and opportunities in project quality and excellence in major infrastructure projects in the UK. The infrastructure initiatives also cover systems to deliver sustainable logistics service requirements of a community and country as part of local and global requirements.

It is intended that conclusions and recommendations from this book will provide a foundation to extend the definition and implementation of project quality and excellence to all types of projects in all parts of the world.

Furthermore, the scope of this research is restricted to quality-related issues given that the effect of other project management parameters (such as time, cost and risk) are considered as separate areas of further research.

## PROJECT QUALITY, PROJECT EXCELLENCE AND SUSTAINABILITY

The title of this book highlights project quality as the primary theme of the book, but as indicated previously, a sustainable outcome also leads to project excellence. In this section the scope and parameters of project quality and project excellence are explained.

The success criteria of a project are the metrics and longer-term (or sustainable) outcomes which determine the degree of a success achieved by a project. The success factors are the enabling conditions and processes embedded in the project culture to ensure the success criteria of a project. For example 'on time' completion is one of the success criteria and stakeholder management is a success factor.

The initial literature review (Westerveld, 2003; Wateridge, 2002) indicates that there has not been adequate research to define concepts that can link projects success criteria to success factors. The concepts of project quality and project excellence are intended to link success criteria with success factors. *Project quality* is the philosophy of the adherence of standards throughout the life cycle of a project. *Project excellence* is the delivery of sustainable outcomes to key stakeholders during the life cycle of the project, particularly during the final closure stage. Project quality relates to the success factors and enablers and Project excellence relates to the success criteria and outcomes of a project. It will be demonstrated later that the dimensions of project quality are necessary but not sufficient contributors to project excellence.

It is also important to understand the span of project excellence and its interface with operational excellence. The life cycle of a project typically goes through four stages: initiation, design, execution, finalisation and follow-up (Turner, 1999). It is important to note, as shown in Figure I.1, that the span of project excellence follows the project life cycle although its effectiveness is enhanced at the final stage. Following the closure when the project is managed as operations by the operations team, it is the role of operational excellence to ensure, improve and sustain the outcomes delivered by the project beyond the project life cycle.

Another important and relevant area of understanding is sustainability in the context of managing quality in projects. I aim to examine key aspects of managing quality in major projects and to identify the major elements that contribute towards

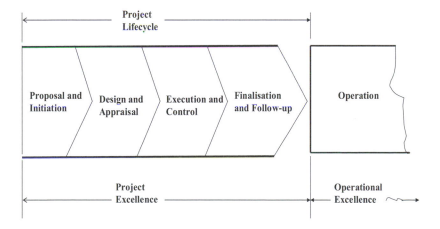

**Figure I.1    The span of project excellence**

making the outcome of such projects sustainable. Sustainability, in a general sense, is the capacity to maintain a certain process or state indefinitely and in the context of preserving the environment, it relates to meeting 'the needs of the present without compromising the ability of future generations to meet their own needs' (United Nations, 1987). The sustainability of project outcomes, in the context of this research, is not environmental, it is the longer-lasting stability of the deliverables and processes derived from the PDCA cycle (Deming, 1986), as illustrated in Figure I.2.

An empirical study in operational management by Gallear et al (2000) supports the proposition that the longer-lasting outcomes of quality initiatives such as TQM are 'dependent on the integration of its underlying concepts with the normal business processes'. The sustainability of project outcomes, in the context of this research, is comparable to the stability of a process. Stability involves achieving consistent and, ultimately, higher process yields defined by a metric or a set point through the application of an improvement methodology and continuous review. The stability is ensured by minimising the variation of the set point. The approach of the plan, do, check, act cycle (PDCA) (Deming, 1986) enables both temporary and longer-term corrections. The temporary action is aimed at fixing the problem and the permanent corrective action consists of investigating and eliminating the

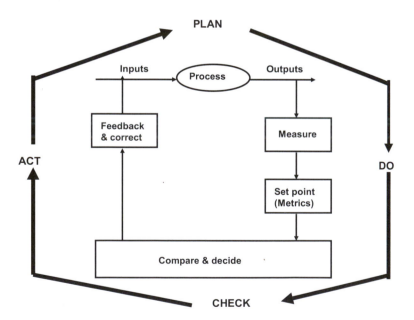

Figure I.2    **A model showing a process towards a longer-lasing outcome in project management (developed from Deming, 1986)**

root causes and thus targets the sustainability of the improved process. Thus, in the context of project management and the scope of this book, a sustainable project is expected to deliver long-lasting outcomes of acceptable quality performance criteria (Mengel, 2008). When a project achieves defined criteria of sustainability (Edum-Fotwe and Price, 2009) in the context of this research, a project achieves project excellence (Abidin and Pasquire, 2007). This research will attempt to address these criteria of sustainability.

The above explanation of sustainable outcome in the context of major projects is also in agreement with the following definition of sustained success in British Standards. 'The sustained success of an organization is the result of its ability to achieve and maintain its objectives in the long-term. The achievement of sustained success for any organization is a complex and demanding challenge in an ever-changing environment' (BS EN ISO 9004: 2009).

## THE PRACTICAL SIGNIFICANCE OF THIS BOOK

Phillips and Pugh (2000) distinguish research from what they call gathering of facts, and suggest that the significance of a research project should be demonstrated by practical and theoretical outcomes in seeking to explain a phenomenon and to analyse relationships. This section addresses the practical significance of this book.

The rationale behind selecting the topic of project quality in this book was partly influenced by the author's association with the Major Projects Association and thus has a strong practical significance. The theme is highly topical in view of the chequered history of a number of major projects in the UK, including the Dome Project, the Channel Tunnel, the new Wembley Stadium, Heathrow Terminal 5 and the expectations of outcomes from the London Olympic Games 2012 and the Crossrail project. A recent paper by Kaplan and Norton (2004) has concluded that measuring the value of sustainable criteria including intangible assets, although difficult to measure, is the Holy Grail of organisational culture, and these are worth far more to many companies in their longer-term performance than their immediate tangible results. This conclusion encourages the study on the role of organisation culture in the longer-term outcome of projects.

This book aims to be practically valuable to the furtherance of research-based operational information within the major projects sector, the critical evaluation of quality-related thinking on current project management practice and the objective application of this in a challenging sector of the economy. It also aims to develop a practical tool to assess and monitor the constructs contributing to project excellence.

The research in this book is predominantly an applied research but it also contains its theoretical significance. The primary theoretical significance of this research is to reduce the aforementioned gap in academic research in defining the dimensions of project quality, and identifying the tools and processes to sustain longer-term outcomes leading to project excellence. From a theoretical point of view, the topic is important for several areas of academic study. First, a critical review of the literature relevant to research questions will develop propositions concerning the definitions and applications of quality and excellence in project management. A detailed review of the publications on research methodology will also bolster the appropriate mixed methodology for conducting research on social science topics such as project quality and excellence.

The theoretical focus of this research is on two dependable variables as units of analysis, viz, project quality and project excellence. The study aims to provide a theoretical underpining to link project quality relating to success factors and enablers and project excellence relating to the success criteria and outcomes of a project.

## SUMMARY

This chapter serves as an introduction to the book and a broad understanding of the nature and importance of project quality. A preliminary literature review included in this chapter identifies a gap in the definition and application of project quality leading to some high-profile project failures. The analysis in this chapter correlates the poor outcomes of projects with the limited perspective that seems to be given to project quality. The commentary in this chapter also explains how the text and structure of this book will fill this gap and differ from the comparable publications on project quality.

# CHAPTER 1

# FUNDAMENTALS OF PROJECT MANAGEMENT

## INTRODUCTION

The theme of this book addresses two broad and apparently isolated areas of business management. One is quality management and the other is project management. Quality management appears to enjoy a higher priority in operations management as compared to project management (Grude, Turner and Wateridge, 1996). According to Arunasalam, Paulson, and Wallace (2003) most concepts of defining and measuring quality have been derived from operations management. Hence, it is considered useful to outline the domains of both operations management and project management in order to structure the discussion related to quality management in both of these fields. It is also important to position the role of quality management amongst the fundamental processes applied in managing projects.

'Operations management has expanded from treating only the core production processes in manufacturing organisations to include service organisations and non-core operations and processes in other functions such as marketing, finance and human resources' (Slack, Chambers, Johnston and Betts, 2006, p. 6). The methodology of implementing a quality management and improvement programme has been well accepted in the environment of operations and process management and also in supply chain management (Dale, 2007). The applications can be varied and the programme is likely to have a different name or label, such as TQM, Six Sigma, Lean Sigma, BPR (business process re-engineering) or operational excellence. Some authors in quality management (Deming, 1986; Juran, 1989; Oakland, 2003) are viewed as key specialists in their areas of expertise.

The PMI (Project Management Institute, 2008) has defined a project as 'a temporary endeavour undertaken to create a unique product or service'. This concept of a project being a temporary and one-time undertaking is perceived as different from operations which comprise permanent or semi-permanent ongoing functional activities. The management of these two disciplines is often very different and requires varying technical skills and philosophies, hence the need for the development of the discipline of project management.

Project management is the discipline of organising and managing resources in such a way that these resources deliver all the work required to complete a project within defined scope, time and cost constraints. Meredith and Mantel (2003, p. 1) describe project management as a social science and comment, 'Project Management has emerged because the characteristics of our contemporary society demand the development of new methods of management.' The Body of Knowledge (Association for Project Management, 2006) also defines project management as 'the most efficient way of introducing unique change'. Bodies of knowledge have been compiled by professional organisations such as the Association for Project Management (APM), and the Project Management Institute (PMI). Specific journals have emerged, such as the *International Journal of Project Management* and *Project Management Journal*. These periodicals, viewed as publications for academic papers in project management, appear to encourage a demarcation between the disciplines of project management and operations management.

Due to the perception of the one-off and unique nature of a project versus the repetitive nature of operations, the traditional approach of project management has been consciously different to that of operations management. Supply chain management is inextricably linked with operations management (Slack, Chambers, Johnston and Betts, 2006, p. 208). A primary objective of both supply chain management and operations management is to ensure optimum customer service by balancing cost, time and quality (Wild, 2002). However, the mindset of project managers appears to exclude the principles and objectives of supply chain management (Ala-Risku and Karkkainen, 2006). This may explain why quality has been a lower priority in project management as compared to time and budget (Grude, Turner and Wateridge, 1996). However, the primary objectives of project management – scope, time, cost and risk – are beginning to include quality as another parameter of objectives (Turner, 2002). Accordingly, the so-called 'iron triangle' of cost, time and quality has emerged. Hence, it can be argued that the primary objectives of project management (with the exception of scope and risk) are closely comparable to those of operations management, that is, quality, cost and time.

## THE IMPORTANCE OF PROJECT MANAGEMENT

The product/market matrix of Ansoff (1987) is a sound framework for identifying market growth opportunities. As shown in Figure 1.1, the x-axis shows the dimensions of the product, and the y-axis represents the current and the new market.

There are four generic growth strategies arising from Ansoff's grid. These are:

1. *Current product/current market*: the strategy for this combination is 'market penetration'. Growth will take place through the increase of market share for the current product/market mix.
2. *Current product/new market*: in this situation the strategy for growth is 'market development'. The pursuit will be for exploring new markets for current products.
3. *New product/current market*: the strategy of 'product development' is followed to replace or to complement the existing products.
4. *New product/new market*: the strategy of 'product diversification' is pursued when both the product and market are new in the business.

If we analyse the four quadrants of Ansoff's product/market matrix it is evident that only the quadrant of 'current product/new market' relates to operations management: the other three quadrants relate to entrepreneurial management and project management. Even in operations management change management is inevitable. Therefore in any form of business strategy the application of project management disciplines is essential. A review of literature addressing the current thinking in innovation and new product development (NPD) initiatives (Cooper, 2001, 2009; Mankin 2006; Feng and Gonslaves, 2010) strongly supports the 'stage gate' process. This basically comprises the stages of a project life cycle and thus recommends the adoption of project management principles for NPD initiatives.

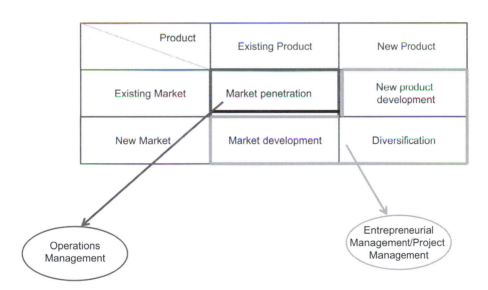

**Figure 1.1     Product/market matrix (based on Ansoff, 1987)**

Over the past several decades, more and more work has been accomplished in business through the use of projects and project management (Mantel, Meredith, Shafer and Sutton, 2001). However, despite the strong growth in project management literature and bodies of knowledge, projects continue to fail in terms of scope (i.e specification) and outcome (quality) in spite of the commonly used measures of cost and time (Thomas and Mengel, 2008). With increasing globalisation, competitive pressures, uncertainties (Atkinson, Crawford and Ward, 2006) and the resultant scope (specifications) creep, the emphasis in improving project planning and stakeholders and people management has grown considerably (Perminova, Gustafsson and Wikstrom, 2008).

People issues, including their expertise, are key factors in the successful delivery of a project's end products, and are often considered the most difficult of the many variables related to planning and implementation activities. This view is supported, at least in principle, by project management bodies of knowledge, such as the PMBOK Guide (2008) and the PRINCE2 system (OGC, 2009). In the context of this book, 'people issues' is defined as the 'organisation quality', scope (product breakdown structure) and specifications are 'product quality' and planning processes are 'process quality'. These three dimensions of project quality and their significance will be developed further in succeeding chapters of this book, but it is important to discuss the fundamentals of project management to ascertain the vital role of project quality in the successful delivery of projects.

This chapter investigates the fundamentals of project management, beginning with project management definitions and processes, followed by project supply chains and project life cycle and then project management characteristics relevant to project quality

## PROJECT MANAGEMENT DEFINITIONS AND CONTROLS

The size, scope, duration and complexity of projects vary widely from a small one-person project of a few days duration to a highly complex multidisciplinary engineering construction or new product-development project spanning multiple years and requiring hundreds of people (Ives, 2005).

The Association of Project Management (APM) in the UK produced the APM *Body of Knowledge* (BOK) in 2006, which provides the following definition of project management:

> *The planning, organisation, monitoring and control of all aspects of a project and the motivation of all involved to achieve the project objectives safely and within agreed time, cost, and performance criteria. The project manager is the single point of responsibility for achieving this.*

*The Project Management Body of Knowledge* in the USA (PMBOK Guide 2008) described:

> *A project is a temporary endeavor undertaken to create a unique product, service or result.*

> *Project management is the application of knowledge, skills, tools and techniques to project activities to meet project requirements. This is accomplished through the application processes.*

The uniqueness of a project is also stated in PRINCE2 (2009) as:

> *A project is a temporary organization that is created for the purpose of delivering one or more business products according to an agreed business case.*

> *Project management is the planning delegating monitoring and control of all aspects of the project, and the motivation of those involved, to achieve the project objectives within the expected performance targets.*

The expected performance targets are primarily focused on the iron triangle of costs, times and quality (Turner, 2002; Heisler, 1990; Atkinson, 1999). Another version of iron triangle (Seaver, 2009) shows scope, schedule and budget at three corners of the triangle. It is important to note that the latest versions of PMBOK (2008) and PRINCE2 (2009) have basically done away with the project triangle. The reason for this is that a project has many more constraints to be observed other than the scope, schedule and budget or costs, times and quality. There are six variables of project control suggested in PRINCE2 (2009):

1. **Costs**: The project has to be affordable and delivered within the budget
2. **Timescales**: Arguably the next most important area of concern of a project manager is the delivery on time.
3. **Quality**: The project's deliverables must be fit for purpose.
4. **Scope**: Exactly what will the project deliver? Often scope and quality are misconstrued as synonymous. Scope defines what is included and what is not included in the deliverable.
5. **Risk**: The uncertain characteristic of a project entails risks, but how much risk are we prepared to accept?
6. **Benefits**: Perhaps most often overlooked question, 'why are we doing this?'. Benefits are determined by the outcome of the project perceived by the customer, not just the return on investment.

The role of quality in the control objectives of a project, in PRINCE2 terms, appears to be in the specification and functionality of the deliverable and overlaps with scope and benefits.

## PROJECT MANAGEMENT PROCESSES

In PMBOK (2008) project management processes (identified as 44 processes) are grouped together in five process groups:

1.  Initiating process group; for defining a project.
2.  Planning process group; for establishing the scope and plan of the project.
3.  Executing process group; for executing the plan and completing the work.
4.  Monitoring and controlling process group; for tracking and reviewing the project work.
5.  Closing process group; for formally closing a phase or a project.

PMBOK (2008) also suggests nine knowledge areas to support the processes. Typical project management process groups and knowledge areas are illustrated in Table 1.1.

Table 1.1 maps 44 project management processes into five process groups and nine knowledge areas. These are often interrelated, and factors like 'scope creep' affect many of them. However, there are often uncertainties associated with producing unique project outputs, implying constant challenges and opportunities for the practitioners in managing decision making. Project planning without sufficient recognition of uncertainty generates inferior planning decisions. Many of the uncertainties can be minimised by sufficient or complete (neither over nor under but just right) planning and effective decision making to deal with major planning problems like 'Create work breakdown structure (WBS)' and others shown in Table 2.1. The process groups are linked with the objectives they produce. The output of one process generally becomes an input to another or is a deliverable of the project. For example, the planning process group provides the 'executing process group' a documented project plan and scope statement and often updates the plan as the project progresses. In addition, the process groups are seldom either discrete or onetime events; they are overlapping activities that occur at varying levels of intensity throughout the project life cycle (PMBOK, 2008).

**Table 1.1    Mapping project management processes to process groups and knowledge areas**

Project management areas and process groups

| Knowledge area processes | Initiating process groups | Planning process groups | Executing process groups | Monitoring and controlling groups | Closing process groups |
|---|---|---|---|---|---|
| 1. Project integration management | 1. Develop project charter;<br>2. Develop preliminary project scope statement | 1. Develop project management plan | 1. Direct and manage execution | 1. Monitor and control project work;<br>2. Integrated change control | 1. Close project |
| 2. Project scope management | | 2. Scope planning;<br>3. Scope definition;<br>4. Create work breakdown structure (WBS) | | 3. Scope verification;<br>4. Scope control | |
| 3. Project time management | | 5. Activity definition;<br>6. Activity sequencing;<br>7. Activity resource estimating;<br>8. Activity duration estimating;<br>9. Schedule development | | 5. Schedule control | |
| 4. Project cost management | | 10. Cost estimating;<br>11. Cost budgeting | | 6. Cost control | |
| 5. Project quality management | | 12. Quality planning | 2. Perform quality assessment | 7. Perform quality control | |
| 6. Project human resource management | | 13. Human resource planning | 3. Acquire project team;<br>4. Develop project team | 8. Manage project team | |
| 7. Project communications management | | 14. Communication planning | 5. Information distribution | 9. Performance reporting;<br>10. Manage stakeholders | |
| 8. Project risk management | | 15. Risk management planning;<br>16. Risk identification;<br>17. Qualitative risk analysis;<br>18. Quantitative risk analysis;<br>19. Risk response planning | | 11. Risk monitoring and control | |
| 9. Project procurement management | | 20. Plan purchase and acquisitions;<br>21. Plan contracting | 6. Request seller reply;<br>7. Pick sellers | 12. Contract administration | 2. Contract closure |

*Source:* Adapted from PMBOK (2008).

The knowledge areas in PMBOK (2008) are defined by their specific knowledge requirements that a project manager should be trained in order to do a professional job. One such knowledge area is project quality management which, in PMBOK terms, supports the project in achieving its quality objectives. The PMBOK guidelines on project quality will be discussed further in Chapter 4.

In PRINCE2 (2002) there are eight processes, Each process consist of a set of activities that are required to start, plan, direct, deliver and close a project. These eight processes are:

1. Starting up a project (SU); this process covers pre-project activities required to commission the project
2. Initiating A project (IP); this sets out the activities the project manager must carry out in order to establish the project on a sound footing. The key deliverable from this process is Project Initiation Document (PID).
3. Directing a project (DP); this process describes the project board's activities in exercising overall project control.
4. Managing stage boundaries (SB); this process enables the project manager and project board to review the performance of the current stage.
5. Controlling a stage (CS); this process describes how the project manger reports progress and exceptions to the project board.
6. Managing product delivery (MP); this process addresses the team manager's role in supervising the detail work of the specific work package or product.
7. Closing a project (CP); this process describes the closure activities towards the end of the final stage of the project.
8. Planning (PL); this process is used by all other processes featuring the design and creation of plans.

It is worthwhile to note that in the newer version of PRINCE2 (2009), the planning process (PL) has been excluded.

Similar to the 'knowledge areas' of PMBOK (2008), PRINCE2 (2002) included five 'components:

1. business case
2. management of risk
3. quality in a project environment
4. configuration management and
5. change control;

and three techniques

1. project-based planning
2. quality review technique and
3. change control approach.

In PRINCE2 (2009) these components and techniques are replaced by 'themes'. The themes are described as those aspects of project management that need to addressed continually throughout the life cycle of the project. There are seven PRINCE2 (2009) themes, as outlined in Table 1.2.

In PRINCE2 (2009) Quality is a theme to ensure the project products meet business expectations and also to track the required quality methods. Therefore the focus of project quality is on 'product quality' and 'process quality'. The PRINCE2 guidelines on project quality will be discussed further in Chapter 3.

As PMBOK (2008) and PRINCE2 (2009) are regarded as recognised sources and bodies of knowledge in project management their major aspects, especially related to project quality, are reviewed in this book. However, in spite of their specific strengths and detailed guidelines project managers can be forgiven when they prefer to pass these documents to functional specialists such as quality managers or regulatory managers. As a result the application of these guidelines often ends up as ticking boxes in papers.

**Table 1.2    The PRINCE2 themes**

| Theme | Answers | Purpose |
|-------|---------|---------|
| Business case | Why? | Establish mechanisms to assess whether the project is viable |
| Organisation | Who? | Define the project structure of accountability and responsibility |
| Quality | What? | Defines the means to verify that products are fit for purpose |
| Plans | How? How much? When? | Facilitate communication, control and progress |
| Risk | What if? | Identify, assess and manage uncertainties |
| Change | What's the impact? | Identify, assess and control changes to baselines |
| Progress | Where are we now? | Establish mechanisms to monitor actual against planned achievements |

*Source*: Adapted from PRINCE2 (2009).

## PROJECT, PROGRAMME AND PORTFOLIO

'In practice the terms are quite often mixed up or applied rather loosely creating a lot of misunderstanding and miscommunication' (PMBOK, 2008). It is sometimes useful to make distinction between a project, a programme and a portfolio. Although they share the same rigour of structured approach and basic processes, they also vary in managing the scope and measuring outcomes.

To reiterate, in PMBOK (2008), Project is defined *as a temporary endeavour undertaken to create a unique product, service or result.* The definitions of programme and portfolio in PMBOK (2008) are as follows:

> *A Programme is a group of related projects managed in a co-ordinated way to obtain benefits and control not available from managing them individually. (PMBOK, 2008)*

> *A Portfolio is a collection of projects and programmes and other work that are grouped together to facilitate effective management of that work to meet strategic business objectives. (PMBOK, 2008)*

The PMBOK (2008) definition of a programme is broadly in congruence with other definitions in literature (Turner, 1999; Murray-Webster and Thiry, 2000; MSP, 2007). Turner (1999) defines a programme as 'a group of projects managed together for added benefits'. A programme is defined in MSP (2007) as 'a specific set of projects identified by an organisation that together will deliver some defined objectives, or a set of objectives, for the organisation'. Murray-Webster and Thiry (2000) emphasise the importance of *strategic and tactical benefits* of programme management and thus are in conflict with the 'strategic business objectives' aspect of the PMBOK (2008) definition of a portfolio. Increasingly there is a recognition (Artto, Martinsuo, Gemundsen and Murtoaro, 2009) that programmes should be the means of achieving the strategic and corporate objectives of an organisation.

The key question is what are the additional benefits, if any, of programme management over project management? The additional benefits might include the elimination of risk arising from interfaces between the projects, the coherent prioritisation of resources and reduction in management effort. Another question is, is there a significant difference in approaches? The heart of the matter is that the programme management will focus on the issues relating to the changes in the organisation and the outcome of the programme. A programme may include elements of related work outside of the scope of the discrete projects in the programme to meet the strategic objective of the business. Table 1.3 compares the key distinctive features of project and programme management.

**Table 1.3    Project and Programme management**

| Project features | Programme features |
|---|---|
| • Outputs<br>• Closely bounded and scoped deliverables<br>• Benefits after closure<br>• Efficient approach | • Outcomes<br>• Wider strategic benefits and scope<br>• Benefits during and after<br>• Effective approach |

The definition of a Portfolio in PRINCE2 (2009) is in a broader context as 'all the programmes and stand-alone projects being undertaken by an organisation, a group of organisations, or an organisational unit' and there is a visible omission of the 'strategic business objectives' of PMBOK (2008). Another interpretation, arguably a more popular, of a project portfolio is similar to managing a financial portfolio (www.michaelgreer.com). In this type of Project Portfolio Management (PPM), it begins with the organisation developing a comprehensive list of all its projects and enough descriptive information about each to allow them to be analysed and compared. After the project inventory is created, the PPM process requires department heads or other unit leaders to examine each project and prioritise it according to established criteria. Finally, the project portfolio is reevaluated by the portfolio management team on a regular basis (monthly, quarterly, etc.) to determine which projects are meeting their goals, which may need more support, or which may need to be downsized or dropped entirely. Effective PPM can help make a project manager's life much easier and more professionally rewarding. More importantly, it can help an organisation align its project workload to meet its strategic goals, while making the best use of limited resources.

Although the fundamentals of project quality are applicable to the management of a project, a programme or a portfolio there are some differences in emphasis with the application of three dimensions. In project management the emphasis is more on the product quality and the process quality while in programme management the emphasis is more on the organisation quality. The focus of programme management is to accelerate the change triggered by stakeholders and by the changing needs of systems, scope and organisation culture. Projects in turn may have the product development and delivery on time and within budget as the dominant basis. In the management of project portfolios, similar to financial portfolios, the product quality is likely to be in the driving seat.

## PROJECT SUPPLY CHAINS

The essential success criterion of a project is the timely, accurate to quality and cost-effective delivery of materials, systems and facilities. There are many stakeholders, contractors and suppliers involved in a project. In a major infrastructure scheme such as Heathrow Terminal 5 there are likely to be more than 100 key contractors and consulting firms. Thus, supply chain management methodologies and processes are crucial to ensuring that project resources are delivered as required.

Although supply chain management should be an essential process within the project manager's toolkit its importance in project management is not properly recognised. As discussed earlier, due to the perception of the one-off and unique nature of a project versus the repetitive nature of operations, the traditional approach of project management has been consciously different to that of operations management. In the context of a major project, supply chain management can be linear or non-linear. A supply chain is considered linear when a material, product or service is sourced from a single supplier. This single-source linear procurement is more common in operations management. However, in a project supply chain a major contractor is served by several subcontractors, each subcontractor may be served by several subcontractor, and the process becomes non-linear. Hence the perspective of the linear supply chain includes the procurements that are well defined from a single supplier and perform as specified. On the other hand, non-linear supply chains occur when risks appear from a multiple tiers of suppliers and the intended linear process becomes unreliable. Some supply chain risks in projects include lack of supplier commitment, poor order control, unexpected variations in lead time, critical material damaged in shipment and changes induced by suppliers and project members. These non-linear project risks have the potential to generate cumulative negative influences across the project. In order to minimise such non-linear project risks related to the supply chain the basic concepts, skills and tools of supply chain management form essential support elements of project management. These basic concepts and tools are equally applicable to the success of operation management, whether in manufacturing or services. Some examples of these concepts in supply chain management follow.

It is important that a 'total supply chain management approach' is applied and all the building blocks of the supply chain are examined. The synergy that results from the benefits contributed by all elements as a whole far exceeds the aggregate of gains achieved for an individual element. The integrated approach is truly more than the sum of its parts. If one concentrates exclusively on isolated areas, a false impression may be inevitable and inappropriate action taken.

A model for total supply chain management (Basu, 2011b) comprises six building block configurations:

- customer focus and stakeholders
- resources and time management
- procurement and supplier focus

- supply and stock management
- building and installation
- handover and closure.

In addition there are three cross-functional integrating processes:

- systems and procedures
- regular reviews
- quality and performance management.

This model (Basu, 2011b) is illustrated in Figure 1.2. Each of the building blocks is briefly described below.

It is also important to point out that there are three streams or categories in Figure 1.2 depending on the affinity of the building blocks. These are:

- *Project planning chain*: in this stream the building blocks are dealing with project planning activities and the information flow. The building blocks in this stream are:
  - customer focus and stakeholders
  - resources and time management
  - procurement and supplier focus.
- *Project delivery chain*: here, the building blocks relate to the project implementation and closure activities and physical flow of materials on site. The building blocks in this stream are:
  - supply management
  - building and installation
  - handover and closure.
- *Project integration*: at this stage the building components of project supply chain are acting as the integrators of other building blocks as various stages of the project life cycle. The building components in this stream are:
  - systems and procedures
  - regular reviews
  - quality and performance management.

Quality and performance management in a project supply chain acts both as a driving force of improvement and a fact-based integrating agent to support the planning, operations and review processes. The foundation of performance management is rooted to quality management principles supported by key performance indicators.

There are many different definitions and dimensions of quality to be found in books and academic literature. Basu (2004) defines quality with three dimensions: design quality (specification), process quality (conformance) and organisation quality (sustainability). When an organisation develops and defines its quality strategy,

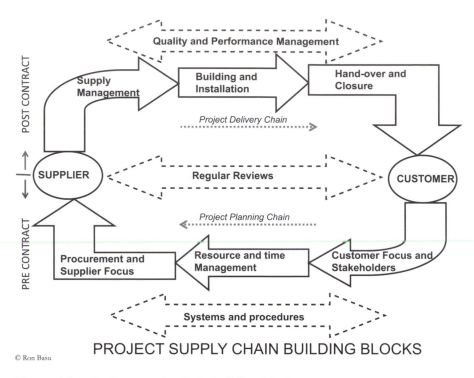

Figure 1.2    Project supply chain building blocks

it is important to share a common definition of quality and each department within a company can work towards a common objective. The product quality should contain defined attributes of both numeric specifications and perceived dimensions. The process quality, whether it relates to manufacturing or service operations, should also comprise some defined criteria of acceptable service levels so that the conformity of the output can be validated against these criteria. Perhaps the most important determinant of how we perceive sustainable quality is the functional and holistic role we fulfil within the establishment. It is only when an organisation begins to change its approach to a holistic culture, emphasising a single set of numbers based on transparent measurement with senior management commitment, that the 'organisation quality' germinates. The dimensions and definitions of project quality are discussed further in Chapter 3.

A good reference line of key performance indicators of a supply chain is the balanced scorecard of Kaplan and Norton (1996). Kaplan and Norton argue that 'a valuation of intangible assets and company capabilities would be especially helpful since, for information age companies, these assets are more critical to success than traditional physical and tangible assets'. The balanced scorecard retains traditional financial measures, customer services and resource utilisation (internal business process) and includes additional measures for learning (people) and growth (innovation). This approach complements measures of past performance with drivers for future development.

## STAKEHOLDERS MANAGEMENT

To manage the potential conflicts within project management, the project manager makes use of numerous project management processes and tools. In addition to the guidelines in PMBOK (2008) and PRINCE2 (2009) there are many project management tools to assist the project managers and team members such as the Gantt chart, critical path analysis and earned value management (Burke, 2003; Meredith and Mantel, 2003) . The application of processes and tools of project management also has an impact on the consistent management of the project stakeholders. 'Stakeholders are persons or organisations who are actively involved in the project or whose interests may be positively or negatively affected by the performance or the completion of the project' (PMBOK, 2008). Identifying and understanding the stakeholders is vital in enabling a project manager and the team members to communicate appropriately and manage the expectations of stakeholders.

The internal stakeholders include: top management, functional managers, project manager and team managers. The external stakeholders include: clients, competitors, suppliers, regulators and environmental groups. Moreover, the major infrastructure projects exhibit a number of idiosyncratic functions; in each project the workforce is transient, multiple crafts are involved, projects are planned and the work is in short time frames. Furthermore, there is a large variety of material, equipment and services that must be planned and installed with flexibility.

Stakeholder management is the continuing development of a relationship with stakeholders for the purpose of achieving a successful project outcome (McElroy and Mills, 2000). A stakeholder can affect either the *project* scope or *product* scope. A stakeholder analysis should therefore be carried out at the very beginning of the project and must feed directly into the initial vision and scope document. A stakeholder analysis can uncover many useful aspects regarding the extent of the assignment, for example who has overlapping responsibilities and whose goals do not align with the responsibilities assigned to them or which business processes are common and which are redundant.

There are many ways of preparing this analysis. Some simple steps could be followed:

1. Determine who all the stakeholders are and categorise them according to their interest and influence in the project (see Figure 1.3).

2. Build awareness, influence, descriptions, goals and responsibilities for each.
3. Categorise each group of stakeholders, after preliminary interviews, according to their level of support for respective project goals. These categories could be 'strong support', 'passive support', 'neutral', 'passive opposition' and 'strong opposition'.
4. Identify both the current position and the required position.
5. Identify the reasons for opposition.
6. Develop an action plan (e.g. training, mentoring, change of responsibility, concession etc.) to bring each group of stakeholders to the required position.

You may use this matrix in Figure 1.3 as part of a group exercise not only to prioritise which stakeholders are the most important to consider but also to involve them in project design. A list of questions may be addressed to stakeholders:

- Who stands to lose or gain significantly from the project?
- Whose actions could potentially affect the project's success?
- Who has doubts about the goals and outcome of the project?
- Who is aware of the goals and confident of success?

Although it is vital to ensure stakeholder analysis at the earliest stage of the project, it is a dynamic process. The position and level of commitment of each group of stakeholders will change as their knowledge and engagement with the project will vary. Furthermore, new stakeholders may appear at subsequent phases of the undertaking. It is sensible to accept that you may not 'win them all' and it is often innovative to form a coalition of heterogeneous ideas. The primary focus should be on gaining the support of the key players who control major resources and who have the highest influence on project outcomes.

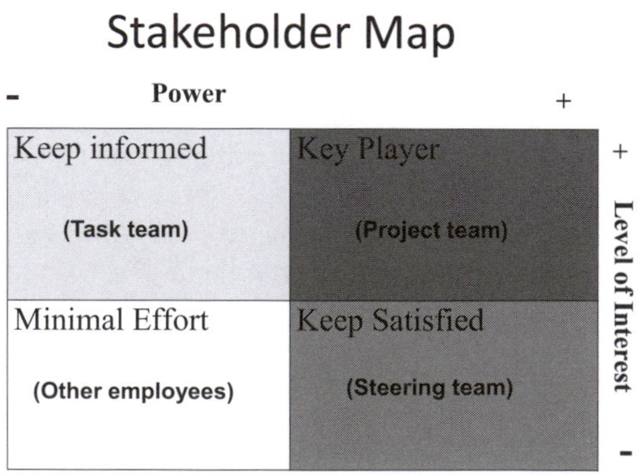

## Stakeholder Map

| | Power | | |
|---|---|---|---|
| **–** | | **+** | |
| Keep informed (Task team) | Key Player (Project team) | **+** | Level of Interest |
| Minimal Effort (Other employees) | Keep Satisfied (Steering team) | **–** | |

**Figure 1.3    Stakeholder matrix**

## PROJECT MANAGEMENT AND CHANGES

Project management is derived from changes in organisational strategies, national and global economies and environments (Grude and Turner, 1996). The role of project managers on change projects is that they should manage the change in a structured way and create a project organisation to implement the change. In many change management projects (e.g. product development, systems development and total quality initiatives) the goals of the change and methods for implementing the change are not well-defined at the beginning. Management by projects should be appropriate for change projects when the customer requirements are varying and/or the methods of achieving them are varying.

The planning, execution and delivery of well-structured projects are also characterised by rapid changes, resulting in new needs arising for stakeholders and at the same time non-availability of sufficient information for practitioners to adjust planning to respond to the changes. It is known that in the changing environment, project scope also often grows. Furthermore, as project management matures, the field goes beyond the generic description of practice to evoke differences among different project types and contexts. Even within the same project, the maturity can vary among practitioners as well as in different phases and processes. Within the decision-making process, tools and information technology (IT) are often required, particularly in larger organisations, for processing information which may vary between organisations (Taveira, 2008). All of these have implications on the dimensions of project quality.

Project management parameters such as cost, time and scope form a system, and a change in one of these is interlinked with others. For instance, any major change in the scope that is not in the original plan can significantly affect other parameters, including the critical cost and time factors. However, avoiding scope creep totally is not possible (Atkinson, Crawford and Ward 2006). Similarly, risk or uncertainty is seen as a usual condition to be taken into consideration for managing change. The dimension of organisation quality (see Chapter 3) relates to people-related attributes which are essential in managing changes and sustaining changes with key stakeholders. Some researchers (Fong, 2003; Kadefors, 2004) have specifically highlighted the importance of 'team relationship management'. The emergence of these factors in change management as well as the issues related to the fundamentals of project management are valuable in investigating the role of project quality for effective outcomes.

With the key fundamentals of project management in perspective, the review now narrows down to the specific processes and stages of 'project life cycle' in the following section.

## PROJECT LIFE CYCLE

Similar to living beings, projects have life cycles and from the beginning they grow in size, then peak, start to decline and finally close. The life cycle of a project (Figure 1.4) typically goes through four stages: initiation, design, execution and closure (Turner, 1999). This is comparable to the phases of a product life cycle: launch, growth, maturity and decline. It is important to note, as shown in Figure 1.5, that these four aspects of project life cycle are also in congruence with the eight processes of PRINCE2 (2002). The nomenclature of each phase of the project life cycle often varies from Turner's given names in many project applications (e.g. definition, design, implementation and handover) or it may have more stages (e.g. concept, feasibility, implementation, operation and termination in BS 6079). However, alternative periods of project life cycle can be easily aligned to Turner's given names.

In PMBOK (2008) project life cycle is defined as a collection of generally sequential project phases whose names and numbers are determined by the control needs of the organisation or organisations involved in the project. Project phases are divisions within a project or project life cycle where extra control is needed. Therefore there are significant variations of the names and numbers of the phases in a project life cycle which are described in PMBOK (2008), PRINCE (2009) or BS 6079. The terminology and phasing of the project life cycle also vary according to the type of a project and its area of application. Some application areas like the IT sector have project life cycle structures with common phase names which are well-documented and applied throughout the respective sector.

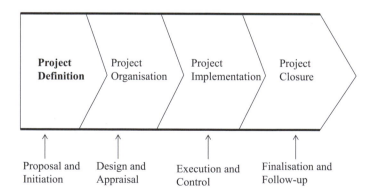

**Figure 1.4    Project life cycle (based on Turner 1999)**

## Project Life Cycle
PRINCE2

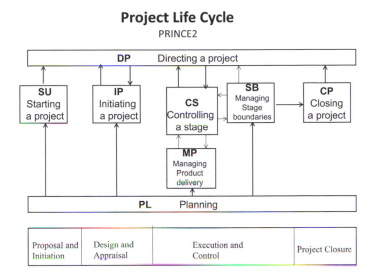

**Figure 1.5    PRINCE2 and project life cycle (based on PRINCE2)**

There are many reasons for dividing a project into life cycle stages, including:

- Provides manageable chunks
- Enables project control and associated risks in each stages
- Allocates appropriate skills and management roles at each stage
- Aids communication with a common theme in each stage
- Enables progressive development.

It the important to note that these advantages of the project life cycle are best achieved by making certain that the people working in two successive stages work closely to ensure that the product that is handed over meets the needs of the next stage. There should also be the signing of the relevant documents and due emphasis on the integration of project management processes and product design-oriented processes in a project life cycle. The methodology of DMAIC (Define, Measure, Analyse, Improve, Control) has added the rigour of project life cycle to the implementation and closure of Six Sigma projects (Basu, 2009).

## SUMMARY

This chapter provides an overview the fundamentals of project management, beginning with project management definitions and processes, followed by project supply chains and project life cycle to position the role of project quality in managing projects. The contents include a review of relevant literature and the bodies of knowledge, e.g., PMBOK (2008) and PRINCE2 (2009). The importance of quality management is visibly embedded in the domains of operations management and supply chain management. However, in project management the role of quality appears to be treated as a regulatory requirement influenced by PMBOK and PRINCE2 guidelines: thus quality is mostly managed in isolation by a specialist team. Quality management should be a mainstream process in managing projects to enable successful projects with longer-lasting outcomes.

The characteristics of a project, a programme and a portfolio have been addressed to identify the differences, if any, in approaches in managing them with particular reference to the dimensions of quality. It is apparent that the role of quality in managing a project or a programme has been recognised but the method of application regarding quality management is not clearly established. It is also indicative that the dimension of organisation quality is more dominant in a programme management compared to project management or portfolio management.

# CHAPTER 2

# THE DEFINITION AND DIMENSIONS OF PROJECT QUALITY

## INTRODUCTION

In the preceding chapters the importance of quality in the success of a project and the role of quality in project management processes were addressed. It is generally accepted that the minimum success criteria of projects are that they should be completed to time, to budget and to quality. However, when one explores what is meant by quality the answers are often vague and variable. If someone talks about 'working on project quality', they may simply mean activities related to quality management systems recommended in bodies of knowledge (e.g. PMBOK, 2008; PRINCE2, 2009) and they ensure the compliance to procedures by 'ticking boxes'. Quality in a broader context has many meanings depending on customers, ranging from luxury and merit to excellence, good value for money or convenience and even practicality. A generic definition of quality is simply 'meeting the customer requirements', but this has been expressed in many ways, e.g.;

- 'conformance to requirements' – Crosby (1992)
- 'fitness for use' – Juran (1989)
- 'quality should be aimed the needs of the consumer' – Deming (1986)
- 'the total composite product and service characteristics of the organisation to meet the expectation by the customer' – Feigenbaum (1983)
- 'the totality of characteristics of an entity that bear on its ability to satisfy stated and implied need' – ISO 9000:2000.

If we can't find a comprehensive definition of project quality we can't assess its efficacy and therefore we can't apply it effectively to deliver successful projects. Only Feigenbaum's definition seems to cover the 'total' concept of quality covering product, service (conformance) and organisation. However, the consistency of conformance is not explicit here. Therefore the definition of quality should be rephrased as:

Quality is the consistent conformance to customer expectations

## DEFINITION OF PROJECT QUALITY

Basu (2004) proposes a three-dimensional model of quality is shown in diagrammatic form in Figure 2.1.

When an organisation develops and defines its quality strategy, it is important to share a common definition of quality so that each department within a company can work towards a common objective. The product quality should contain defined attributes of both numeric specifications and perceived dimensions. The process quality, whether it relates to manufacturing or service operations, should also contain some defined criteria of acceptable service level so that the conformity of the output can be validated against these criteria. Perhaps the most important determinant of how we perceive sustainable quality is the functional and holistic role we fulfil within the organisation. It is only when an organisation begins to change its approach to a holistic culture, emphasising a single set of numbers based on transparent measurement with senior management commitment, that the 'organisation quality' germinates. We have compiled a set of key organisation quality dimensions (see Table 2.1).

**Figure 2.1    Three dimensions of quality**

**Table 2.1     Basu's organisation quality dimensions**

- Top management commitment
- Sales and operations planning
- A single set of numbers
- Skills of using tools and techniques
- Performance management
- Knowledge management and continuous learning
- Communication and a teamwork culture
- Self-assessment

*Top management commitment* means that organisational quality cannot exist without the total commitment of the top executive team.

*Sales and operations planning* is a monthly senior management review process to align strategic objectives with operation tasks.

*A single set of numbers* provides the common business data for all functions in the company.

*Using tools and techniques* relates to the fact that without the effective application of tools and techniques, the speed of improvement will not be assured.

*Performance management* includes the selection, measurement, monitoring and application of key performance indicators.

*Knowledge management* includes education, training and development of employees, sharing of best practice and communication media.

*Teamwork culture* requires that communications and teamwork should be practised in cross-functional teams to encourage a borderless organisation.

*Self-assessment* enables a regular health check of all aspects of the organisation against a checklist or accepted assessment process such as that of the European Foundation of Quality Management (EFQM).

We are more familiar with the expectations and perceptions of quality related to product and services that we experience in our day-to-day life, for example when we buy a motor car or an airline ticket. Table 2.2 shows a comparison of quality characteristics of a project with those generally applied to a consumer product (car) or a service (flight):

**Table 2.2    Quality characteristics for a project, a car and a flight**

| Dimension of quality | Car | Flight | Project |
|---|---|---|---|
| Design quality | Shape, speed, acceleration, fuel consumption, controls | Price, leg room, on-board meals and drinks, entertainment | Specifications of project deliverables, quality management system, business case, project management plan |
| Process quality | Time between service, actual performance on speed and fuel | Keeping the published flight times, actual on-board service | Performance of time, cost, quality, safety and risks, quality audits |
| Organisation quality | Knowledge and courtesy of sales and service staff | Skills, response and courtesy of airline staff, after-sales service | Stakeholder management, skills and training, supplier partnership, teamwork and communications |

We now need to substantiate the above statements. In the following sections of this chapter the rationale of these three dimensions to define project quality is supported by the published data and reflective analysis. The analysis also identifies the gaps in current thinking related to project quality.

## DIMENSIONS OF QUALITY

According to *The Oxford English Dictionary* (OED), 'dimension' is an attribute of measurable form that may be seen as characterising an abstract thing. 'Quality' is a special feature, entity or characteristic by which a thing is considered in thinking or speaking of its nature, condition or properties. In the context of this research a definition of quality as an entity is supported by 'dimensions', while 'attributes' are indicators or components of dimensions. This approach is agreement with the publications on dimensions of quality (Parasuraman, Zeithamel and Berry, 1984; Cronin and Taylor, 1992; Arunasalam, Paulson and Wallace, 2003). There are many different dimensions and definitions of quality that have been well expressed in literature related to operations and to a limited extent in literature related to project management. This section will present these selected classifications and support a three-dimensional definition of quality (see Figure 2.1) to reflect its appropriate application in project management.

Two of the most quoted dimensions of quality in operations management are given by the quality dimensions developed by Garvin (1984) and Parasuraman, Zeithamel and Berry (1984) (see Table 2.3).

**Table 2.3    Dimensions of quality**

| Garvin's (1984) product quality dimensions | Parasuraman et al.'s (1984) service quality dimensions |
|---|---|
| *Performance* refers to the efficiency (e.g. return on investment) with which the product achieves its intended purpose. *Features* are attributes that supplement the product's basic performance, e.g. tinted glass windows in a car. *Reliability* refers to the capability of the product to perform consistently over its life cycle. *Conformance* refers to meeting the specifications of the product, usually defined by numeric values. *Durability* is the degree to which a product withstands stress without failure. *Serviceability* is used to denote the ease of repair. *Aesthetics* are sensory characteristics such as a look, sound, taste and smell. *Perceived quality* is based upon customer opinion. | *Tangibles* are the physical appearance of the service facility and people. *Service reliability* deals with the ability of the service provider to perform dependably. *Responsiveness* is the willingness of the service provider to be prompt in delivering the service. *Assurance* relates to the ability of the service provider to inspire trust and confidence. *Empathy* refers to the ability of the service provider to demonstrate care and individual attention to the customer. *Availability* is the ability to provide service at the right time and place. *Professionalism* encompasses the impartial and ethical characteristics of the service provider. *Timeliness* refers to the delivery of service within the agreed lead time. *Completeness* addresses the delivery of the order in full. *Pleasantness* simply means the good manners and politeness of the service provider. |

The dimensions of quality expounded by Garvin (1984) appear to relate primarily to the quality of the product. Service quality as explained by Parasuraman, Zeithamel and Berry (1984) is perhaps even more difficult to define or measure as compared to the definition of product quality, because it also contains abstract dimensions such as empathy, pleasantness and assurance. This was later enhanced and developed by Zeithmal, Parasuraman and Berry (1990) as the SERVQUAL methodology, which identified gaps between the perceptions and expectations for the dimensions of service quality. Cronin and Taylor (1992) further extended the measurement of the dimensions of service quality in SERVQUAL, proposed a performance-based scale of measuring service quality and named the instrument as SERVPERF. There is evidence of academic research to assess service quality in various service industries (Arunasalam, Paulson and Wallace, 2003; Parkdil and Harwood, 2005; Gaur and Agarwal, 2006). An empirical study by Jain and Gupta

(2004) concluded that because of its psychometric soundness, SERVPERF should be the preferred choice to compare service quality across industries.

## DEFINITIONS OF PROJECT QUALITY

The definition of quality is underpinned by dimensions of quality. A definition of quality in operations management containing two dimensions (design quality and process quality) is taken from Ray Wild's *Operations management* (2002, p. 644) as shown below:

> *Wild's definition of quality*
> *The quality of a product or service is the degree to which it satisfies customer requirements.*
>
> *It is influenced by:*
> *Design quality: the degree to which the specification of the product or service satisfies customers' requirements.*
>
> *Process quality: The degree to which the product or service, which is made available to the customer, conforms to specification.*

The list of quality dimensions by both Garvin (1984) and Parasuraman, Zeithamel and Berry (1984) are widely cited (Cronin and Taylor, 1992; Arunasalam, Paulson and Wallace, 2003). However, one problem with a large number of dimensions is that of communication. It is not easy to devise a strategic plan on quality based on many dimensions, as proposed by Garvin (1984) and Parasuraman, Zeithamel and Berry (1984), as these could be interpreted differently by varying departments. Wild's definition with two dimensions of design and process quality, however, provides a broad framework to develop a company-specific quality strategy. Turner (2002) also agrees with Wild's (2002) dimensions of product quality and process quality.

Nonetheless, one important dimension of quality is not clearly visible in the above models: the quality of the organisation and people-related issues. This is a fundamental cornerstone of the quality of a holistic process and an essential requirement of an approved quality assessment scheme such as EFQM (European Foundation of Quality Management). It is the people that make things happen.

In the Kano Model of customer satisfaction in operations management, Noriaki Kano (1996) defines three attributes to quality: basic needs, performance needs and excitement needs. Kano explains that to be competitive, products and services must flawlessly execute all three attributes of quality.

In the initial success model of DeLone and McLean (1992) related to information systems, 'organisational impact' was recognised as the measure of effectiveness success, while 'systems quality' measures technical success and 'information quality' measures semantic success and user satisfaction. Although the authors appear to focus on success criteria in information management rather than the dimensions of quality enabling the achievement of those criteria, it could be argued that in this model systems quality relates to design quality, information quality to process quality and organisational impacts to organisation quality.

In their updated model, DeLone and McLean (2003) (see Figure 2.2) include 'service quality' to combine 'individual' and 'organisational impact' into a single variable, 'net benefits'. It appears that the authors, perhaps inadvertently, have introduced the difficulties of interpreting multidimensional aspects of 'use' and 'user specification'. These features may arguably be more specific to information systems. However, in a broader context, service quality appears to contain the ingredients of organisational impact or organisation quality. In turn it is easier to interpret the sustainability of service through user satisfaction to incorporate user specification, thus leading to net benefits.

Grover, Jeong and Segars (1996) extended the initial model of DeLone and McLean (1992) and used an alternative theoretically based perspective (the theory

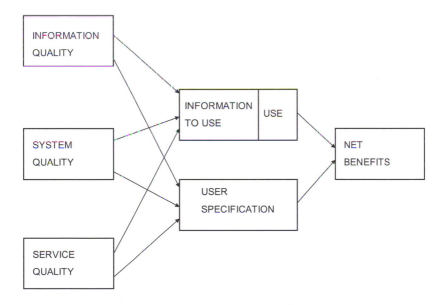

**Figure 2.2    The updated DeLone and McLean Model (2003)**

of organisational effectiveness) to build a construct for information systems (IS) effectiveness. This IS effectiveness framework of Grover, Jeong and Segars (1996) complements the IS success model of DeLone and McLean (1992) and at the same time suggests an area of further extension, namely organisational impacts and market impacts.

Deming (1986) believes that quality in operations management is everyone's business and says that to find the best way means getting the facts, collecting data, setting standard procedures, measuring results and getting prompt and accurate feedback of results so as to eliminate variations to the standard. He sees this as a continuous cycle. Deming emphasises that people can only be 'won over' if there is trust at all levels. This means that management is prepared to allow and encourage employees to take responsibility, and that employees are prepared to accept that responsibility. Employee participation, through understanding objectives, processes and contributing through improvement suggestions, is an important part of the Deming philosophy required to sustain results.

Arguably Juran was the first 'guru' to emphasise that quality in operations management was achieved by communication. The trilogy Juran suggests for quality comprises planning, control and improvement (Juran, 1989). His approach includes an annual plan for quality improvement and cost-effectiveness, and continuous education on quality. Juran's foundations are still valid and are embedded within Six Sigma, Lean Sigma and Fit Sigma (Basu and Wright, 2003) philosophies. He argues, and few would disagree, that inspection at the end of the line, post-production, is too late to prevent errors. Juran says that quality monitoring needs to be performed during the production process to ensure that mistakes do not occur, and that the system is operating effectively. Juran adds that the role of upper management is more than making policies; they have to show leadership through action – in other words, they have to 'walk the talk' and not just give orders and set targets. Juran propagates that quality is not free and that investment is needed in training, often including statistical analysis, at all levels of the organisation.

Feigenbaum (1983) is recognised for his work in raising quality awareness in operations management in the USA. The term total quality management originated from his book *Total quality control*. Feigenbaum states that total quality control has an organisation-wide impact. It involves three aspects: first, managerial and technical implementation of customer-oriented quality activities as a prime responsibility of general management. Secondly, it comprises the mainline operations of marketing, engineering, production, industrial relations, finance and service. Finally, there is the quality-control function itself. He adds that a quality system is the agreed, company-wide operating work structure, documented in integrated technical and managerial procedures, for guiding the coordinated actions of the people, the machines and company-wide communications. This should be executed in the most practical ways with the focus on customer quality satisfaction. According to Dale (2007), Feigenbaum's most important contribution to quality was to recognise that the three major categories of the cost of quality are appraisal, prevention and cost of failure. Arguably another important contribution was in the definition of 'total' quality covering product, service (conformance) and organisation.

Crosby (1992) is noted for saying – in an apparent contradiction of Juran (1989) – that quality in operations management is free. Indeed Crosby even produced a book with this very title in 1979. He emphasises cultural and behavioural issues ahead of the statistical approach of Deming and Feigenbaum. According to Crosby, if staff have the right attitude, know what the standards are and do things right first time, every time, the cost of conformance will be free. The cumulative effect is that motivated workers will go further than just 'doing things right'. Instead, they will detect problems in advance, be proactive in correcting situations and ultimately will even be quick to suggest improvements. Crosby concludes that workers should not be blamed for errors, but rather that management should take the lead and the workers will follow. Crosby's definition of quality ('conformance to requirements') is easily refuted: if requirements are wrong, then failure is certain.

There is one important dimension of quality that is clearly visible in the quality concepts of Deming, Juran, Feigenbaum and Crosby, and that is the quality dimension of the organisation. This in turn is the dimension of sustainable or ongoing quality which is expected to be delivered continuously to customers, and is supported by the whole organisation. It is also a fundamental cornerstone of the quality of a holistic process, and an essential requirement of an approved quality assessment scheme such as the European Foundation of Quality Management (2003).

In the environment of project management, the definitions and dimensions of quality appear to be less pointed. The guidelines in the public domain comprise the Body of Knowledge (Association of Project Management, 2006), a *Guide to Project Management Body of Knowledge* (Project Management Institute, 2004, 2008), ISO 10006 (2003), PRINCE2 (2002, 2009), and BS 6079 (British Standards Institution, 2002). *The Body of Knowledge* (BOK) (Association of Project Management, 2006) states that 'quality applies to everything in project management: commercial, organisation, people, control, technical, etc.'. That's fine, but it begs the question: what is quality? The BOK however recognises the definition of TQM as 'what the client really wants, defining the organisation's mission, measuring throughout the whole process how well performance meets the required standards'. The definition of TQM involving the total organisation in the implementation of continuous improvement in a project environment was first described in Levitt and Nann (1994), and the BOK seems to have a passing reference to TQM.

In the PMBOK (2004, 2008) the definition of project quality is also unclear. Here quality is defined as ' the level to which product or service meets its specification or meets the expectations of the users'. However, Section 8 of the document is dedicated to project quality management comprising quality planning, quality assurance and quality control. Furthermore, in Section 8.1, the document identifies which quality standards are relevant to the project and determines how best to satisfy them. It describes how the project management team will implement its quality policy with the aid of a formal quality plan. Here, quality seems to relate to 'standards'. These benchmarks are then inserted into the quality plan with a process that can identify whether or not the team is managing the project in accordance with the quality policy that has been established.

*ISO 10006, Quality management – guidelines to quality in project management* (International Standards Organisation, 2003), claims to provide 'guidance on quality system elements, concepts and practices for which the implementation is important to, and has an impact on, the achievement of quality in project management'. However, the application of this document is more likely to have the opposite effect. In fact, it identifies virtually the same set of project management processes and knowledge areas as PMBOK (2004, 2008). There is no definition of quality and moreover, no quality management process. Pharro (2002) comments, 'The guide (ISO 10006) focuses on the standard of project management and does not cover the *doing* of the activities necessary to complete the project.'

PRINCE2 (2002, 2009) is a project management methodology owned and maintained by the UK Government. It has grown organically to be adopted by both private and public organisations. The document (PRINCE2, 2002) identifies 'quality in a project environment' as a PRINCE2 component and 'quality review technique' as a PRINCE2 technique. The definition of quality, though not plain, is stated as 'its ability to show that it meets expectations or satisfies stated needs, requirements or specifications'. This methodology presumes that the project will be managed under the umbrella of a published Quality Management System (QMS) conforming to ISO 9001. QMS in PRINCE2 appears to be similar to a quality plan indicated in ISO 10006 and PMBOK. There is no unmistakable definition of quality in the document and the link between 'quality in a project environment' and the 'quality review technique' is also opaque. However, the guidelines for the formal quality review in a project are useful and comprise three steps:

1. *Preparation*: where the project deliverable or product is measured against quality criteria contained in the product description and question lists are created.
2. *Review*: where the product is 'walked through' against question lists and follow-up actions are agreed.
3. *Follow-up*: where the identified errors in the product are fixed, agreed and signed off.

In the new edition of PRINCE2 (2009) quality is described as a theme to define and implement the means by which the project will create and verify products that are fit for purpose. Quality is defined as 'the totality of features and inherent or assigned characteristics of a product, person, process, service and/or system that bear on its ability to show that it meets expectations or satisfies stated needs, requirements or specification'. The application of these guidelines is discussed in Chapter 4.

BS6079 (British Standards Institution, 2002) is a *Guide to project management*. The document identifies key stages of the project life cycle, thus the project management processes are divided into two parts: project planning and project control. It appears to be most suitable for large engineering projects with the project manager in full command. It is not prescriptive regarding project management techniques and there is no direct definition of quality in BS 6079. A definition of quality is also missing in *BS 6079 Part 2: Vocabulary* (British Standards Institution, 2000). As regards the quality plan, the document refers to ISO 10006 and thus suffers from similar weaknesses in the area of quality management (Pharro, 2002).

Turner (2002) defines quality in the context of project management and this in turn appears to agree with Wild's (2002) dimensions of product quality and process quality. Turner (2002) also indicates that the right 'attitude' is an important element of achieving the project success. It could be argued that attitude is people-related and falls within the domain of organisation quality. However, a passing reference to attitude does require further clarification and enhancement. The published papers in academic journals are also unsatisfactory regarding the definition and dimension of project quality. Grude, Turner and Wateridge (1996) reported that 'quality management received no mention until the 1990s'.

Bubshait (1994) appears to be one of the early authors to publish a definition of project quality and emphasise owner involvement in project quality. 'Owner' is not defined by the author, but it is likely to relate to the sponsor or clients funding the project. It is to be noted that quality characteristics expounded by Bubshait (1994) also include factors for the ongoing outcome or sustainability of the project. Although it is not clear from the results of the survey, the author concludes that 'owner involvement is essential to project quality'.

Rounce (1998) attempts to define the 'plethora of reasons' contributing to architectural design management problems and the adverse effects arising from lack of quality in the design management process. Quality in the design process has been defined as 'meeting agreed requirements or conformance to requirements'. The author also puts forward indicators of quality in design management. It is indicative that in the context of project quality, Rounce (1998) also emphasises conformance to requirements (process quality) and appears to recognise 'quality to all members' (organisation quality).

Tennant and Roberts (2001) have recognised the role of quality management in the speed and effectiveness of product development projects in the Rover Group in the UK. The authors seem to indicate the definition of project quality as given with a passing reference to Feigenbaum's concept of new design control as the establishment of performance quality and reliability quality of the product. The robustness of the concept quality in this paper is difficult to assess, although the demise of the Rover Group in the UK may not be a good testament to the recommendations therein.

## SUMMARY ANALYSIS

A closer examination of the relevant literature reveals that the focus of quality is more visible in the domain of operations management compared to project management. Table 2.4 summarises the key findings of the literature on the dimensions and definition of quality.

It is indicative from the above analysis that quality experts support the concept of three dimensions of quality in the environment of operations management. These comprise standards (product quality), conformance (process quality) and sustainability (organisation quality). In broad terms, Garvin (1984), Parasuraman, Zeithamel and Berry (1984) and Wild (2002) focus more on product quality and process quality. It could be argued that intangible attributes of SERVQUAL and SERVPERF (such as responsiveness, empathy and professionalism) as identified by Parasuraman, Zeithamel and Berry (1984) and Cronin and Taylor (1992) are people-related and could be linked to organisation quality.

In the environment of project management there is a strong emphasis on design specifications (product quality) and project methodology (process quality) and some recognition (e.g. Rounce, 1998) of 'quality to all members' (organisation quality). Turner (2002) identified design quality and process quality as two dimensions of project quality (similar to Wild, 2002) as in operations management. However, the published project management standards and guidelines (e.g. PMBOK, ISO 10006, BS6079 and also PRINCE2) all lack a clear definition of the dimensions of quality. As discussed in Chapter 2, although stakeholder management, which is a key component of organisation quality, has been recognised and practiced as a fundamental process of project management it is not yet embedded within the culture of managing project quality (McElroy and Mills, 2000).

**Table 2.4      Key findings of literature on the dimensions and definition of project quality**

| Source | Key findings | Domain |
|---|---|---|
| Garvin (1984) | Dimensions of 'product quality' – performance, features, reliability, conformance, durability, serviceability and perceived quality | Operations |
| Parasuraman, Zeithamel and Berry (1984)

Parasuraman, Zeithamel and Berry (1984)

Cronin and Taylor (1992) | Dimensions of 'service quality' – tangibles, service reliability, responsiveness, assurance, empathy, availability, professionalism, timeliness, completeness
SERVQUAL methodology – assessment of service quality
SERVPERF methodology – assessment of service quality | Operations

Operations

Operations |
| Wild (2002) | Design quality – specifications
Process quality – conformance | Operations |
| Kano (1996) | Three attributes of quality (customer satisfaction) – basic needs, performance needs and excitement needs | Operations |
| DeLone and McLean (1992)
Grover, Jeong and Segars (1996) | Information quality – process quality
System quality – design quality
Service quality – organisational impact
Extended DeLone and McLean model to organisation effectiveness | Information systems
Information systems |
| Deming (1986) | Continuing quality improvement cycle
Employee participation to sustain improvement | Operations |
| Juran (1989) | Annual quality improvement plan, cost effectiveness, communication and continuous education | Operations |
| Feigenbaum (1983) | Coined the phrase 'Total Quality Control'
Total quality involves organisation wide impact | Operations |
| Crosby (1979) | Cost conformance would be free achieved by quality assurance by staff attitudes and skills training | Operations |
| Project Management Institute (2004)
Association of Project Management (2006) | 'Quality applies to everything in project management: commercial, organisation, people, control, technical etc.'.
No clear definition of project quality | Projects |
| ISO 10006 (International Standards Organisation, 2003) | Identifies quality plan as a document specifying general procedures and associated resources but not related to project phases.
No clear definition of project quality | Projects |
| BS6079 (British Standards Institution, 2002) | Identifies key stages of project life cycle and refers to ISO 10006 for quality plan.
No clear definition of project quality | Projects |
| PRINCE2 (2009) | Identifies quality in a project environment and assumes quality management system to conform to ISO 9001.
No clear definition of project quality | Projects |
| Bubshait (1994) | Owner involvement in project quality characterised by conformance and longer-lasting organisation criteria | Projects |
| Rounce (1998) | Suggests quality in design management and identifies conformance to requirements and 'quality to all members' | Projects |
| Turner (2002) | Design quality and process quality in projects and right 'attitude' for success | Projects |
| Tennant and Roberts (2001) | Quality management as conformance to project management policy (PMP) document | Projects
Product development |

## CONCLUSIONS

It is evident from the above analysis that in the environment of project management, the definitions and dimensions of quality appear to be less clear-cut. In the *Body of Knowledge* by the APM (2000), the definition of quality is rather broad ('quality applies to everything in project management') but it recognises the dimension of TQM as 'what the client really wants, defining the organisation's mission, measuring throughout the whole process how well performance meets the required standards'. This is indicative of organisation quality. In the PMBOK (2004), the definition of project quality is also not clear, although Section 8 of the document is dedicated to project quality management comprising quality planning, quality assurance and quality control. Also in PRINCE2, there is no clear definition of quality in the document. Additionally, the link between 'quality in a project environment' and 'quality review technique' is not clear. The guidelines in ISO 10006 are disappointing, although the document is closer to PMBOK. The emphasis of quality in official standards appears to be on design quality (guidelines to quality systems) and process quality (conforming to standards).

The papers by Bubshait (1994) and Rounce (1998) are not pointed regarding the definitions and dimensions of quality, but they indicate recognition of organisation quality. For example, Bubshait's quality requirements from an owners' viewpoint include operability and maintainability, and Rounce suggested 'meaning of quality known to all members' as an indicator of project quality, even at the design stage of the life cycle. The findings on organisation effectiveness (Crawford and Turner, 2008; Jamieson and Morris, 2008) also underline the role of organisation culture in the governance of successful projects. It is also evident that, albeit primarily in the domain of operations management, Deming (1986), Juran (1989) and Feigenbaum (1983) are proponents of organisation quality.

On the basis of the above analysis, the first proposition has been derived as follows:

> *PROPOSITION 1: There exists a new dimension of quality in projects beyond the product and process quality and that is organisation quality.*

The detailed analysis of the gaps in the current thinking has clearly identified organisation quality as an essential component of project quality to supplement the other two dimensions in practice, viz, design quality and process quality (Turner, 2002). Therefore the dimensions of project quality as illustrated in Figure 2.1 are supported by the analysis in this chapter.

On the basis of the above conclusions the following definitions of project quality is recommended:

*Project quality is the philosophy of the adherence of standards to fulfil acceptable delivery objectives throughout the life cycle of a project and there are three clear dimensions of project quality given by design quality, process quality and organisation quality.*

# CHAPTER 3

# THE APPLICATION OF THE GUIDELINES OF PROJECT QUALITY IN BODIES OF KNOWLEDGE

## INTRODUCTION

In Chapter 2 we reviewed published standards and guidelines of project management (e.g. PMBOK, PRINCE2, ISO 10006 and BS6079) to explore as widely as possible the dimensions and definitions of quality in project management. In this chapter, these standards and guidelines are reviewed to examine how quality is applied and practiced in project management. As the scope of this book is focused on project quality, we examine the guidelines in the bodies of knowledge that are most relevant to project quality. As discussed in Chapter 2, ISO 10006 is an ineffective follower of PMBOK and BS6979 is more aligned with PRINCE2. Hence the relevant guidelines in PRINCE2 (2002, 2009) and PMBOK (2004, 2008) are analysed in this chapter with particular reference to the three dimensions of quality – product, process and organisation.

## GUIDELINES OF MANAGING PROJECT QUALITY IN BODIES OF KNOWLEDGE

In both versions of PRINCE2 (2002 and 2009) quality review as a technique is retained, although in PRINCE2 (2009) quality is shown as a 'theme' rather than as a 'component', as it is in PRINCE2 (2002). The changes related to the topic of quality in the new version of PRINCE 2 (2009) are not significant. However, the recognition of the three dimensions of quality – product, process and organisation – is more visible in PRINCE2 (2009).

The principle of 'focus on products' is claimed to be central to the PRINCE2 approach to quality. It aims to provide a common understanding of 'product breakdown structure' in a project and the criteria against which the products will be assessed: all evidence of the importance of product quality. It is only after establishing the quality criteria for the products that the detailed project costs and timescales can be estimated. The quality theme addresses the quality methods and responsibilities for the management of the project. It also covers the implementation of continual improvement during the project. This implies the importance of process quality and also organisation quality. PRINCE2 (2009) also indicates that capturing and acting on lessons contributes to the quality approach as a means of continuous improvement.

The quality audit trail in PRINCE2 (2009) (see Figure 3.1) indicates the focus on products from the outset and provides a framework for both quality planning and control. However, it is weak in details.

The quality audit trail in Figure 3.1 aims to identify the project's products from customers' requirements, including the quality criteria by which they will be measured. It also indicates quality methods and responsibilities in developing and accepting these criteria. The framework includes the technique of quality review to provide the means of assessing a product against its stated quality criteria, but leaves the selection of most appropriate means to control quality to the project manager.

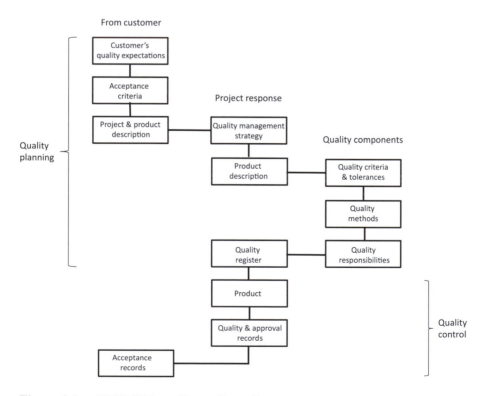

**Figure 3.1    PRINCE2 quality audit trail**

Adapted from PRINCE2 (2009).

The content of the quality theme in PRINCE2 (2009) is good in concept and intent, recognising product quality and process quality explicitly and organisation quality tacitly. However, a major gap in the PRINCE (2009) guidelines is that it is unclear how these guidelines can be successfully implemented across all levels of the stakeholders of the project. This is where the importance of organisation quality prevails.

Chapter 8 of PMBOK (2008) is dedicated to project quality management and recognises three processes related to quality (see Figure 3.2).

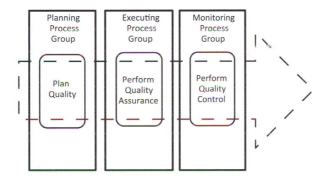

**Figure 3.2    Overview of three project quality management processes**
Adapted from PMBOK (2008).

1. Plan quality: plan quality is designed to gather the project quality requirements and to capture them in the quality management plan. 'The higher the quality requirements, the more time and money you may need to achieve the project result' according to PMBOK (2008). Higher quality may include less rework and higher stakeholder satisfaction-related costs might also rise. Capturing the quality requirements starts with using the scope baseline to identify the quality requirements for the deliverables. This is a recognition of product quality which also acknowledges the importance of customer satisfaction. The quality management plan in PMBOK (2008) also identifies the tools and techniques to be used for quality management, such as control charts, benchmarking, statistical sampling and Six Sigma. This is a part recognition of process quality.
2. Perform quality assurance: it covers the audit process to ensure that that the agreed quality metrics are used by the quality control process. If gaps are found then the assurance process will provide change requests to improve the effectiveness of quality policy and procedures. This might lead to updates in the quality management plan, in the schedule and cost baseline due to the impact of changes.

3. Perform quality control: it is defined as 'the process of monitoring and recording results of executing the quality activities to assess performance and recommend necessary changes'..Perform quality control is based on the quality management plan and quality metrics and reveals the poor quality of the project deliverable. Recommendations are made to rectify the poor quality. This is a recognition of process quality. Executing the perform quality control process is based upon the quality management plan and quality management metrics leading to 'quality control measurements'. The outcomes of these measurements will result in either acceptable deliverables or in change requests. Once the defects identified in change requests are repaired the related deliverable will be checked again and the cycle is repeated until the deliverable reaches an acceptable standard.

The guidelines for project quality management in PMBOK (2008) appear to follow Deming's (1986) PDCA (Plan-Do-Control-Act) cycle and recognised primarily product quality and process quality. The anticipated training requirement in quality assurance is missing in perform quality assurance which focuses on quality processes. However, PMBOK (2008) recommends that the project management team should have working knowledge of some basic tools, such as cause and effect diagrams, control charts and Pareto charts. This indicates a tacit recognition of organisation quality.

## APPLICATION OF BODIES OF KNOWLEDGE TO IMPROVE PROJECT QUALITY

There are reported examples of the successful application of PRINCE2 (2004, 2009) in project management in the UK. In the new edition of PRINCE2 (2009) the quality theme 'also covers the implementation of continuous improvement during the project'. A case study of Ericsson Services Ireland (ESI) by APMG (www.apmgroup.co.uk, accessed 22/10/07) concluded that PRINCE2 was designed to be tailored to local requirements. In particular, it helped the staff of ESI to be more goal-oriented, controlled risk and cost reduction, and the methodology fitted well with the software development quality process. However, as the case study appeared to be produced by PRINCE2 training as a promotional document, the potential pitfalls were missing and it cannot be viewed as a wholly unbiased document. The case study was also a report on the methodology in general, rather than the role of PRINCE2 in project quality.

If the success of PRINCE2 is measured by the number of consultants, user groups, practitioners etc., then its presence, particularly in the UK, cannot be doubted. Indeed, PRINCE2 has become a veritable training industry. According to the Office of Government Commerce in the UK (www. ogc.gov.uk, accessed 23/10/07), it was estimated in 2004 that the people and organisations engaged in PRINCE2 included:

- 250,000 trained practitioners
- 20 user groups
- 120 accredited training and consultancy organisations
- 50+ software tools supporting PRINCE2
- More than 1.6 million pages on the World Wide Web.

However, these figures do not indicate the role or effectiveness of PRINCE2 in managing project quality in practice.

In partnership with the Office of Government Commerce (OGC) there are many case studies published by the APM Group (http://www.csid.com.cn/UpFile) to promote the application of PRINCE2. Here is an example of its early application in 2001:

---

**CASE EXAMPLE PRINCE2 IN CHESHIRE CONSTABULARY**

The Cheshire Constabulary applied PRINCE2 on a £100 million flagship project to relocate police headquarters in 2001. The overriding message that emerges from this case example, according to OGC, is that the Cheshire Constabulary was able to achieve senior-level commitment to the adoption of PRINCE2. This appeared to give credibility and visibility to the way the major change programmes were to apply PRINCE2. The project also indicated that the PRINCE2 concepts were used with due consideration of the business environment in which they are applied. Furthermore, project managers came from the business side, which ensured the continual alignment of project objectives with business objectives. Appointing professional project managers to work alongside the business managers brought greater (project) experience to the Constabulary. OGC also expected that the experiences of the Cheshire Constabulary should provide valuable input to other organisations who are implementing PRINCE2 to provide a framework for delivering major business change.

---

The shortcomings of ISO 10006 (International Standards Organisation, 2003) in its application to manage project quality are unequivocal. Pither and Duncan (1998) were highly critical of the ability of ISO 10006 to guide project quality and identified four major gaps in the document. First, 'there are no quality management processes'. Secondly, the document says that it is 'not a guide to project management itself', yet the level of detail provided and the phraseology used in most clauses and sub-clauses run counter to this stated intent. Thirdly, the standard recognises that project phases and project life cycles exist, but it provides no guidance on how the identified project processes relate to project phases. Finally, the document is inconsistent in that much of the guidance it gives and encourages simply 'ticking boxes'. The limitations of ISO 10006 are to a great extent compensated by guidelines to project quality plans in ISO 10005 (International Standards Organisation, 2005). General guidelines for the development, revision, acceptance, application and revision of project quality plans are included in ISO 10005 and these could be customised to the specific requirements of a major project. The general guidelines of the more established ISO 9001 (International Standards Organisation, 2000) also offer a stable benchmark of developing a project quality plan. The 2000 version of ISO 9001 requires involvement by upper executives, in order to integrate quality into the business system and avoid delegation of quality functions to junior administrators. As discussed later, even the older version of ISO 9000 offered a helpful framework in managing project quality when it was adapted to meet project objectives (Hiyassat, 1999; Serpell, 1999).

There are many success stories of the application PM BOK on the website of the Project Management Institute (http://www.pmi.org/Business-Solutions). For example:

---

### CASE EXAMPLE PMBOK SUCCESS IN NEW ZEALAND

Te Apiti Wind Farm Project was completed by Meridian Energy Ltd, New Zealand's largest state-owned renewable energy generator. Over 20 km of roadways had to be constructed with 40 km of underground cabling in a terrain of the 1150-hectare site. The project presented many additional challenges: it experienced 'the 100-year storm' on 16 February 2006 and there were numerous gullies, streams, steep drop-offs and unstable soil, and a major Natural Gas Corporation pipeline ran through the site.

The project team applied project management skills to risk management using A Guide to the Project Management Body of Knowledge (PMBOK® Guide), third edition, which outlines methods to determine potential project risks and provides techniques for incorporating those risks into the project plan. The project was completed five days ahead of schedule, with an 'exemplary safety record' and within its NZ$200 million budget.

---

However there are critiques of the third edition of PMBOK (2004). Whitty and Schulz (2005) comment, 'PMBOK (2004) has more to do with the appearance of a capability for [project] productivity than it does with productivity' and recommend a reformation of PMBOK. The authors also observe that project management literature supported by PMBOK rarely attempts to make any causal connection with project quality. These criticisms are broadly valid in the new edition of PMBOK (2008). The concern of a higher cost to achieve a higher quality level in project is also, perhaps incorrectly, emphasised in PMBOK (2008). This is in contradiction with the fundamentals of the 'cost of quality model' (Crosby, 1992; Basu, 2004) where there is trade-off between the cost of control and the cost of failure.

PMBOK is a collection of processes and knowledge areas generally accepted as constituting best practice within the project management discipline in the USA and worldwide, just as PRINCE2 is a widely acknowledged standard in the UK. There are published comparisons between PMBOK and PRINCE2 showing how these two project management standards may complement each other. For example, Siegelaub (2004) commented on the prescriptive theme on PRINCE as compared to PMBOK, and also presented a summary of both the contrasts and similarities between PMBOK (2004) and PRINCE2 (2002) as shown in Tables 3.1 and 3.2.

**Table 3.1    Contrasts between PMBOK (2004) and PRINCE2 (2002) (Siegelaub 2004)**

| PMBOK (2004) | PRINCE2 (2002) |
|---|---|
| Comprehensive | Focuses on key risk areas only; does not claim to be complete |
| Largely descriptive, prescriptive on a high level | Highly prescriptive, especially on process structure, but adaptable on any size of project |
| Core and facilitating processes; need to be scaled to needs of project | All processes should be considered; also need to be scaled |
| Customer requirements-driven | Business case driven |
| Sponsor and stakeholders | Clear project ownership and direction by project board |
| US and international standard | UK standard |

**Table 3.2    Similarities between PMBOK and PRINCE2 components (Siegelaub, 2004)**

| PMBOK (2004) knowledge areas | PRINCE2 (2002) components |
|---|---|
| Integration | Combined processes and components |
| Scope, time, cost | Plans, business case, configuration management |
| Quality | Quality review technique |
| Risk | Risk |
| Communications | Change control |
| Human resources | Organisation |
| Procurement | Not covered |

A review of BS6079, PRINCE2 and ISO 10006 by Pharro (2002) questions whether any of these publications are meant to be a methodology, a method, or a standard. The analyses of Pharro are also at a high level and do not attempt to compare or recommend any one methodology over the other.

In spite of the visible weakness of ISO 10006 (Stanleigh, 2007), laudable attempts were made in the 1990s to apply ISO 9000 in managing project quality, especially in construction projects in developing economies. Chew and Chai (1996) identified some of the advantages of implementing ISO 9000 to a construction company including the documented reference and tractability of quality problems. However, they also indicated obstacles in introducing ISO 9000. A survey of the problems in Malaysia conducted by the authors showed a lack of management commitment in 38 per cent of the surveyed organisations.

Another study by Hiyassat (1999) in a construction company in Jordan showed that a significant number of employees of the firm were not aware of what ISO 9000 standards were all about. The percentage of employees who were not apprised of the implementation of the standards increased as they moved further away from the top-level management. The author commented that the success of an ISO 9000 system would depend on a carefully planned and well-structured change management programme.

Serpell (1999) presented the characteristics, problems and benefits of the integration of a quality system based on ISO 9000 in construction projects in Chile. The limitations or barriers to the implementations process were mostly faced by contractors, primarily due to the lack of knowledge of the concepts and tools of quality systems. There was also visible difficulty in generating the commitment of site personnel. However, there were also benefits of the quality system perceived by contractors, project teams and owners. The common features of benefits were the mutual trust between contractor/owner and the reduction of rework.

Managing Successful Programmes (MSP, 2007) is another manual that contains the latest OGC best practice in programme management, and appears to follow the path of PRINCE2 in project management. A programme is defined in MSP as 'a specific set of projects identified by an organisation that together will deliver some defined objective, or set of objectives, for the organisation'. The objectives, or goals, of the programme are typically at a strategic level so that the organisation can achieve benefits and improvements in its business operation. A recent article stresses the difference between project and programme management but does not show a consensus on quality management (Artto, Martinsuo, Gemundsen and Murtoaro, 2009). According to Artto and colleagues, programmes take an open system view and seek change in permanent organisations and projects and, in turn, have product development as the dominant basis.

The revised version of MSP (2007) presents a structure which is based on three levels of core concepts. There is no published evidence of the effectiveness of MSP guidelines. However, in the revised version of MSP, it is visible that the focus of critical success factors (CSFs) has been recognised as part of quality management. It could also be argued that a greater emphasis on 'the people and leadership dependent aspects of ensuring quality' is a recognition that everyone understands the area of critical importance to ensure success.

In 2005 as part of PRINCE2 best practices the OGC identified eight common mechanisms which lead to project failure. Table 3.3 shows how these causes relate to the three dimensions of project quality.

The analysis in Table 3.3 indicates that PRINCE2, at least in intent, has been designed to identify and remove the common causes of project failure. The removal of the causes of common failure mechanisms is enabled mainly by the people related issues of the organisation quality. This is expected to create a more stable and controlled environment in which to deliver projects.

**Table 3.3    Causes of project failure**

| Causes of project failure | Related dimensions of project quality |
|---|---|
| Lack of clear links between the project and the organisation's key strategic priorities (including agreed measures of success) | Organisation quality |
| Lack of clear senior management and ministerial ownership and leadership | Organisation quality |
| Lack of effective engagement with stakeholders | Organisation quality |
| Lack of skills and a proven approach to project management and risk management | Organisation quality |
| Too little attention to breaking development and implementation into manageable steps | Process quality |
| Evaluation of proposals driven by initial price rather than long-term value for money (especially securing delivery of business benefits) | Process quality Product quality |
| Lack of understanding of, and contact with, the supply industry at senior levels in the organisation | Organisation quality |
| Lack of effective project team integration between clients, the supplier team and the supply chain | Organisation quality |

*Source*: OGC (2010).

## SUMMARY ANALYSIS

Table 3.4 summarises the key findings of the literature on the application of quality in project management.

**Table 3.4    Key findings of the literature on the application of quality in project management**

| Source | Key findings | Domain |
|---|---|---|
| ESI (www.apmgroup.co.uk) | PRINCE2 was designed to be tailored to a local project quality process in Ireland | PRINCE2 Project management |
| OGC (www.ogc.gov.uk) | Application of PRINCE2 in 20 user groups and 120 training organisations | PRINCE2 Project management |
| Pither and Duncan (1998) | Critical of ISO 10006: the standard recognises project life cycle but provides no guidance to quality related to project phases. | ISO 10006 Project management |
| Whitty and Schulz (2005) | PMBOK rarely attempts to make connections with project quality | PMBOK Project management |
| Siegelaub (2004) | PRINCE2 is highly prescriptive as compared to PMBOK despite many similar features | PMBOK and PRINCE2 Project management |
| Chew and Chai (1996) | Limited success of ISO 9000 in the quality of construction projects in Malaysia | ISO 9000 Project management |
| Hiyassat (1999) | Limited success of ISO 9000 in construction project quality in Jordan | ISO 9000 Project management |
| Serpell (1999) | Training of contractors in ISO 9000 to attain some success in construction quality in Chile | ISO 9000 Project management |
| MSP (2007) | Guidelines for programme management but no published data to support their effectiveness | MSP Programme management |
| Artto, Martinsuo, Gemundsen and Murtoaro (2009) | Absence of a consensus in the application of quality in project and programme management | Programme management Project management |

There is evidence of proactive support from professional bodies and organisations (e.g. APM, PMI and OGC) to promote the application of project quality methodology by published guidelines, such as PMBOK, PRINCE2 and MSP, for project organisations. Some project organisations appear to customise their quality management systems as company standards following the guidelines such as PRINCE2 (www.apmgroup.co.uk, accessed 18/10/07).

There appears to be a sector of the training industry to buttress PRINCE2 (www. ogc.gov.uk, accessed 23/10/07). The UK Government-supported projects appear to be guided by PRINCE2 and MSP as a condition for contract, but there seems to remain a lack of evidence in the public domain as to whether the applications of these guidelines have helped or hindered the effectiveness of project management. Furthermore, it is not clear from published literature how effective the applications of these guidelines is in all projects other than merely 'ticking boxes' (Pither and Duncan, 1998). Some overseas project organisations also attemped to apply ISO 9000 guidelines to some degree of success in project management (Chew and Chai, 1996; Serpell, 1999). The weakness of ISO 10006 as a global standard has been clearly identified (Stanleigh, 2007).

## CONCLUSIONS

The guidelines provided by PMBOK (2008) have the recognition of International Standards Organisation although their application is more prevalent in the USA. With the proactive encouragement of the UK Government through the Office of Government Commerce PRINCE2 (2009) is an accepted body of knowledge in major projects in the UK. PRINCE2 (2009) is also gaining influence in Europe, South Africa and Australasia. It is important to recognise that both PMBOK (2008) and PRINCE2 (2009) are intended as guidelines for project management good practices and as prescriptive standards.

Both PMBOK (2008) and PRINCE 2 (2009) heavily emphasise process quality, although in PRINCE2 (2009) there is also a strong emphasis on product-based quality metrics and some tacit recognition of organisation quality. However, in practice (Pither and Duncan,1998; Whitty and Schulz, 2005; Artto, Martinsuo, Gemundsen and Murtoaro, 2009) the application of the guidelines is mostly manifested as quality documents in the project office and ticking boxes. The onus is now on the project managers and practitioners to enhance the understanding of these guidelines by the key stakeholders so that there is more emphasis on total quality assurance and prevention of failures.

There are many good aspects of general guidelines and best practices in both PMBOK (2008) and PRINCE2 (2009). Generic guidelines of a project quality plan in ISO 10005 (International Standards Organisation, 2005) are also useful.

These are not prescriptive and should be adopted and adapted to the specific requirements of organisations and projects. There is a PDCA-based structure in PMBOK (2008) and a framework of quality audit trail in PRINCE2 (2009). These appear to complement each other. Based upon the analysis of PMBOK (2008) and PRINCE2 (2009) a project organisation should consider the following interdependent components in a developing and applying a quality management strategy:

1. *Develop a quality management organisation and plan* to include the organisation, budget, and quality processes to manage designing products, processes for tenders and procurement and construction and the project organisation.
2. *Establish project success criteria and key performance indicators* to monitor and improve the quality of each deliverable.
3. *Ensure the induction of the quality management plan* by appropriate communication means to key stakeholders, especially the project team members and the first-tier contractors.
4. *Manage regular quality forums* facilitated by quality leaders with project team leaders and quality Representatives of first-tier contractors to review quality-related issues and ensure stakeholder management.
5. *Consider operational excellence concepts* such as supply chain management principles, Lean and Six Sigma for longer-running major projects.
6. *Perform quality audits* in cooperation with the delivery teams and major contractors and suppliers to ensure the conformance of the quality plan and quality metrics.
7. *Establish regular self-assessment* by introducing an EFQM-based holistic process and ensure continuous learning.

# CHAPTER 4

# PROJECT SUCCESS CRITERIA AND SUCCESS FACTORS

## INTRODUCTION

The purpose of this chapter is mainly to investigate the criteria for measuring the success of a project and the key factors of project successes, which practitioners can make use of to minimise or eliminate failures and thus improve project success.

Project success criteria are 'a definition in measurable terms of what must be done for the project to be acceptable to the client, stakeholders and end-users who will be affected by the project' (OGC, www.ogc.gov.uk, accessed 11/10/08). The success factors of a project are the elements or activities required for ensuring the success criteria of the project (Wateridge, 2002). Grude, Turner and Wateridge (1996) emphasise that project success criteria and success factors are inextricably linked to the definition and application of project quality and performance. In agreement with Grude, Turner and Wateridge (1996), it could be argued that the use of Key Performance Indicators (KPIs), for example, would provide the project with objective criteria against which it could be measured, and indeed KPIs are in the domain of quality management. Likewise success factors, as reviewed later, could be considered as components of quality assurance to guarantee success criteria. The literature on project success factors, surprisingly, outweighs that on project success criteria. Turner and Muller (2005) identify four periods for the variations in the definition of project success. The authors argue that in the 1970s, project success focused on implementation, time, cost and functionality improvements. During the 1980s and 1990s, the quality of the planning and handover was considered more important. More recently the success criteria appear to be stakeholder-dependent and involve interaction between project supplier and project team.

As explained above, success criteria and success factors are two different entities. One is the cause (success factors) and the other is the effect (success criteria); one is the enabler (success factor) and the other is the result and outcome (success criteria). As will be discussed more in detail later, *success factors* relate to *project quality* and the impact of *success criteria* (longer-term outcome) relates to *project excellence*. Some examples of the components of success criteria and success factors are shown in Table 4.2.

## CAUSES OF PROJECT FAILURES

There is often a fine line between the success and failures of a project. As discussed earlier, the lack of clarity around quality is often the source of project disputes and project failures. There are also many examples of project failures (MPA, 2003). A cautious approach of a project manager, especially in the last decade, is to eliminate the causes of failures. This was illustrated by the OGC report (2010) which was commissioned by the Cabinet Office of the UK Government in 2005 to identify common mechanisms leading to project failures. The eight causes of failure identified in this report and their relevance to the three dimensions of project quality have been summarised previously in Table 3.3. With more focus on stakeholder management and communications there are signs of a paradigm shift from the elimination of the causes of failures to the installation of success factors. However, the causes of failures are also 'pillars of success'.

Studies in 1990s (Tullett, 1996; Tam, 1999) highlighted that projects were less likely to fail due to technical reasons. Rather, in the environment of increasing complexity and changes the causes of project failures, as illustrated in Chapter 1, are more due to management and people-related factors (Scott-Young and Samson, 2008). Bellis (2003) identified five key reasons of project failures. These reasons are also interlinked with the three dimensions of project quality, as shown in Table 4.1.

**Table 4.1    Causes of project failures and the dimensions of quality**

| Causes of project failures | Relevant dimension of quality |
|---|---|
| 1. Ineffective decision making in managing changes | Organisation quality |
| 2. Project schedules with unachievable delivery dates | Process quality |
| 3. Excessive 'scope creep' | Product quality |
| 4. Ineffective coordination with subcontractors and suppliers | Organisation quality |
| 5. Ineffective control and communication over progress, and concealment of project status until it is too late | Process quality |

The situation related to project failures can be significantly improved by the application of organisation quality attributed by project leadership, communications and people-related issues. This would change several issues and eliminate causes of failures, especially items 1 and 4 above, and will have positive impacts on the rest. Scheduling follows estimates of the time and resources necessary for each activity, followed by an assessment of the risks inherent in the plan (OGC, 2005). Resource availability on time is also critical, and failures often lead to serious scheduling problems. With the application of process quality attributed by the conformance of processes and control, including scheduling, should eliminate items 2 and 5 in Table 4.1

Common causes of project failure also include lack of clarity in project specifications, which leads to a mismatch of expectations between practitioners and stakeholders and change of project scope. This is indicative of the poor management of product quality. The application of product quality will clearly eliminate item 3 in Table 4.1.

These common causes of project failure reviewed here are consistent with the findings of prominent research bodies such as the UK Office of Government Commerce (OGC, 2005, 2010) and the Project Management Institute (2004). These bodies emphasised the need for greater attention to good product based planning and control and management of people issues. Therefore a balanced application of the three dimensions of quality (viz, Product, process and organisation) is vital to eliminate the causes of project failures.

## PROJECT SUCCESS CRITERIA AND SUCCESS FACTORS

Let us now turn our attention from project failures to project successes.

Grude, Turner and Wateridge (1996) pinpoint that quality was seldom considered as a condition for success in the 1980s and 1990s and cite the example of *Project management* by Lock (1992) (which had been a textbook in the UK for 25 years since 1968) where quality was mentioned only twice in the index, indicating its management as an important factor, but nothing more. Building on three prime criteria, functionality (quality), time and cost, the authors suggest eight success principles for assessing projects. These standards compare closely to ten factors linked to successful project management and identified by Pinto and Slevin (1988) as shown in Table 4.2.

**Table 4.2     Critical success criteria and factors for project management**

| Grude, Turner and Wateridge (1996) (success criteria) | Pinto and Slevin (1988) (success factors) |
|---|---|
| Commercial success | Project mission |
| Meets user requirements | Top management support |
| Meets budget | Schedule and plan |
| Happy users | Client consultation |
| Achieves purpose | Personnel |
| Meets timescale | Technical tasks |
| Meets quality | Monitoring and feedback |
| Happy team | Communication |
| Meets safety standards* | Troubleshooting |
| Client acceptance* | Stakeholder management* |
| Sustainable outcome* | Skills and governance* |
| | Continuous training* |

* Additional components included by the author are marked with asterisk.

Although the literature on project success criteria is thin, there is an abundance of publications where authors produce lists of project success factors. For example, Morris and Hough (1997) identified success factors from a study of seven major projects in the UK and then Morris (1997) developed this list into a project strategy model. This model was adapted by Turner (1999) as the 'Seven Forces Model' for project success: context, attitude, sponsorship, definition, people, systems and organisation. There are five success factors in each of the seven areas. The lists produced by other authors such as Grude, Turner and Wateridge (1996), Hartman and Ashrafi (2002) and Cooke-Davies (2001) are either adapted from, or closely linked to, the inventory by Pinto and Slevin (1988).

Jugdev and Muller (2005) identified four conditions for projects to be successful. However, the authors also acknowledged that these stipulations were no guarantee of success. The prerequisites were:

1. Success criteria should be agreed with stakeholders before the start of the project.
2. A collaborative working relationship should be maintained between the project owner (or sponsor) and the project manager.
3. The project manager should be empowered with flexibility to deal with unforeseen circumstances as they see best, with the owner giving guidance as to how they think the project should be best achieved.
4. The owner should take an interest in the performance of the project.

In their updated IS success model (see Figure 2.2) DeLone and McLean (2003) also explore the efficacy of the model in the success of e-commerce projects and also recommend how the six dimensions of the updated model can be used as a framework to organise success metrics identified in information and communication technology (ICT) literature, as shown in Table 4.3.

The metrics of Table 4.3 are not clearly defined by the authors and the list is not comprehensive for all e-commerce applications either. However, it provides a parsimonious framework to relate enabling success factors of IS projects and applications (e.g. system quality, information quality, service quality) with their respective success criteria or metrics.

There are suggestions, however, that project objectives vary depending on the project or sector, which in turn affects success factors (Andersen, 2006). Gilb and Johansen (2005) suggest the 'evolutionary development' (Evo) process for the success of software projects by focusing on the early delivery of high value to stakeholders A survey of project managers in the UK by White and Fortune (2002) indicated that in addition to the success criteria cited in project management literature – on time, on budget and to specification – there were two further criteria, that is, human and organisational aspects, concerned with the consequences of the project.

Turner and Cochrane (1993) described in their 'goals and methods' matrix (see Figure 4.1) four types of projects based upon whether the goals and methods of a project are well-defined or not. For example, projects with well-defined goals and methods are Type 1 projects, typified by engineering projects. Those with well-defined goals but not well-defined methods are Type 2 projects, typified by product development projects. Type 3 projects are typically information systems projects where methods are well-defined, but the goals are ill-defined. Type 4 projects have both poorly defined goals and methods and typically research and organisational change projects are in this category.

**Table 4.3    DeLone and McLean success metrics (2003)**

| Systems quality | Information quality | Service quality | Use | User satisfaction | Net benefits |
|---|---|---|---|---|---|
| Adaptability Availability Reliability Response time Usability | Completeness Ease of understanding Personalisation Relevance Security | Assurance Empathy Responsiveness | Nature of use Navigation Number of site visits Number of transactions executed | Repeat purchases Repeat visits User surveys | Cost savings Expanded markets Incremental additional sales Reduced search costs Time savings |

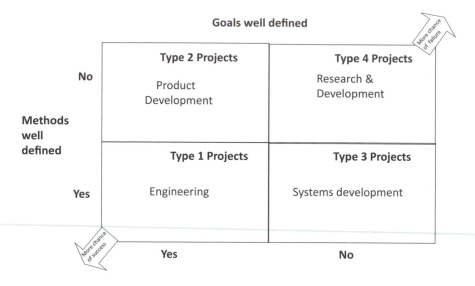

**Figure 4.1    The 'goals/methods' matrix**
*Source*: Turner and Cochrane (1993)

According to the model by Turner and Cochrane (1993) both Type 2 and Type 4, but especially Type 2, could relate to innovation and new product development initiatives where methods are not well-defined. In other words, these initiatives in general lack the rigour of project management methodology. Turner and Cochrane (1993) also argues that the success rate of a project will increase when both the goals and methods are well-defined. Thus arguably we have established well-defined goals and methods as two key success factors of a project, including an initiative on innovation and product development which should treated as a project. However, a third factor is missing, and that is the skills, leadership and communication of the people in the project organisation (Basu, 2004, 2010). The critically of 'goals well-defined' and 'methods well-defined' in achieving success in projects is not in dispute. Goals relate to the product quality and methods relate to the process quality. However, it is also critical to include 'organisation well-defined' or the organisation quality. You amy have the best product and the best process, but it is the people and organisation that make it happen.

The importance of the alignment of the three success factors is also reflected in the 'congruence' model of Tushman and O'Relly (1997). In this model (see Figure 4.2) the key building blocks of *people culture*, and *formal organisation* relate to 'organisation well-defined'. *Processes and methods* relate to 'methods well-defined' and *Strategy* aligns with 'goals well-defined'. The authors point out that a lack in alignment between the elements 'will lead to performance gaps' which can be interpreted as not meeting the success criteria.

For the above reasons it is important to recognise a third dimension ('organisation well defined') in Turner and Cochrane's (1993) model of project types and success requirements. If the third dimension is added then four types of project in Turner and Cochrane's (1993) model, as shown in Figure 4.1, becomes an enhanced model as shown in Figure 4.3.

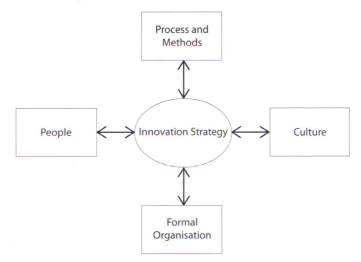

**Figure 4.2    The congruence model of innovation**

Adapted from O'Reilly and Tushman (1997).

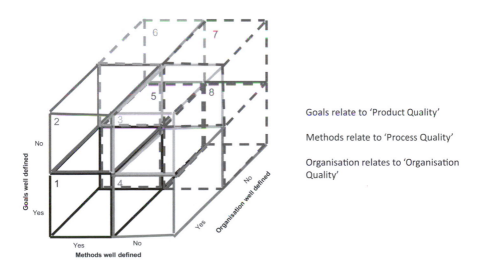

**Figure 4.3    Three dimensions of project success requirements (developed by the author)**

The examples of eight types of project are shown in Table 4.4.

**Table 4.4    Types of projects**

| Project type | Goals well-defined | Methods well-defined | Organisation well-defined | Examples |
|---|---|---|---|---|
| Type 1 | Yes | Yes | Yes | Major infrastructure |
| Type 2 | No | Yes | Yes | TQM/Six Sigma |
| Type 3 | No | No | Yes | Humanitarian |
| Type 4 | Yes | No | Yes | Change programme |
| Type 5 | Yes | Yes | No | Engineering |
| Type 6 | No | Yes | No | Information Systems |
| Type 7 | No | No | No | Blue-sky research |
| Type 8 | Yes | No | No | Product development |

## SUMMARY ANALYSIS

A summary of key findings of the literature on project success criteria and success factors is shown in Table 4.5.

On a closer examination, it is apparent that some of the success criteria and success factors are closely linked to the dimensions of project quality. Many of the success criteria of Grude, Turner and Wateridge (1996) (such as meets user requirements or achieves purpose) appear to relate closely to Turner's (2002) product quality. Some of the 'hard' success factors, especially of Pinto and Slevin (1988), (such as monitoring and feedback) also relate to Turner's (2002) process quality.

It is important to note that although different authors identified various lists of success factors, the common theme and most of the 'soft' or people-related factors of Pinto and Slevin (1988), (such as top management support, client consultation, communication and personnel) appear to be closely related to the aspects governing the 'organisation quality' as defined by Basu (2004). Shenhar, Dvir, Levy and Maltz (2001) also support the concept of benefits to the organisation, stating that project success is strongly linked to an organisation's effectiveness and to its success in the long run. The four conditions of project success as given by Jugdev and Muller (2005) also reflect the importance of people-related organisation quality.

**Table 4.5**    **Key findings of literature on project success criteria and success factors**

| Source | Key findings | Domain |
| --- | --- | --- |
| Pinto and Slevin (1988) | Introduced ten factors (both 'hard' and 'soft') contributing to the success of a project | Project management |
| Grude, Turner and Wateridge (1996) | Suggested eight critical success criteria for projects aligned with the list by Pinto and Slevin (1988) | Project management |
| Morris and Hough (1987) Morris (1997) | Identified success factors based on the study of seven projects leading to a project strategy | Project management |
| Turner (1999) | Adapted from Morris (1997) the 'seven forces model' (including people and organisation) for project success | Project management |
| Hartman and Ashrafi (2001) Cooke-Davies (2001) | Adapted success factors from the list of Pinto and Slevin (1988) | Project management |
| Jugdev and Muller (2005) | Identified four conditions, emphasising a collaborative working relationship, for using success criteria and success factors | Project management |
| DeLone and McLean (2003) | Suggested success metrics for the six dimensions of their updated model | Information systems |
| Andersen (2006) | Project objectives and success factors vary according to the sector | Project management |
| White and Fortune (2002) | Human and organisation aspects are concerned with the consequences of projects | Project management |
| Gilb and Johansen (2005) | Early delivery of high value to stakeholders | Information systems |
| Turner and Cochrane (1993) | Goals well-defined and methods well-defined leading to successful projects | Project management |

## CONCLUSIONS

Turner et al (1993) propose goals well-defined and methods well-defined as the two requirements of project success. The necessity of the third dimension, organisation well-defined, as a key project success factor is also supported in project management literature (Pinto and Slevin, 1998; Jugdev et al, 2005; Shenhar, Dvir, Levy and Maltz, 2001). Additionally within the field of innovation many publications (; Tushman et al, 1997; Kim et al, 2007) endorse the importance of the organisation of talents and culture as a key component of innovation and NPD. Hence the key success project success factors can be grouped in three dimensions of success requirements – goals well-defined, methods well-defined and organisation well-defined. The softer factors of organisation well-defined (e.g. skills, training, stakeholder management, communications, team work and top management commitment) relates very closely to organisation quality.

On the basis of the above analysis the second proposition has been derived as follows:

> PROPOSITION 2: The organisation quality in projects spans critical success factors and softer issues in project management lead to the sustainability of outcomes.

In the context of the dimensions of project quality, goals well-defined relates to product quality, methods well-defined relates to process quality and organisation well-defined. Therefore the three dimensions of project quality are incontrovertibly linked to the critical project success factors.

# CHAPTER 5

# PROJECT EXCELLENCE AND MATURITY MODELS

## INTRODUCTION

The purpose of this chapter is to review project excellence and maturity models and explore their links and efficacy with the variables of project quality and project excellence.

The use of the word 'maturity' implies capabilities which must be grown over time in order to produce repeatable success in project management (Westerveld, 2003) 'Excellence' connotes the achievement of a sustainable standard of success criteria (European Foundation of Quality Management, 2003). Maturity relates to the project organisation and excellence relates to the project outcome. The purpose of project excellence and maturity models is to enhance an organisation's ability to implement organisation strategy and project objectives through a successful and consistent delivery of projects. The underlying assumption is that the greater the maturity, the greater will be the effectiveness and efficiency in implementing projects. Consequently, the strategic organisational performance will also be elevated and is in turn expected to contribute to project excellence.

## EXCELLENCE AND MATURITY MODELS

There are many so-called project maturity and excellence models in the public domain of which, on the basis of published evidence, five models in particular are gaining international recognition (Association of Project Management, 2007). It is intended to examine these five models:

- OPM3: Organisational project management maturity model
- CMMI: Capability Maturity Model Integration
- OGC: Office of Government Commerce
- PEMM: Process and enterprise maturity model
- EFQM: European Foundation of Quality Management.

## OPM3: Organisational Project Management Maturity Model

This is owned by the Project Management Institute, provides requirements for assessing and developing capabilities in portfolio, programme and project management, and for helping organisations to advance organisational strategies through projects (www.opm3.com, accessed 10/02/08).

It contains three elements – knowledge foundation, assessment and improvement. According to PMI, the model benefits organisations irrespective of their size, geographic area or type of industry. It is sizeable and customisable. It categorises best practices and capabilities into two areas: project management domain (project, program, portfolio) and process improvement stages (standardise, measure, control, continuously improve). This categorisation helps in choosing high-priority improvement areas from the big list of improvement areas. An organisation assesses itself against all best practices and capabilities present in OPM3, and identifies improvement areas based on the above results. The benefits an industry can thus obtain are realising its current maturity on project management capabilities, identifying improvement areas and presenting project management awareness amongst senior management.

PMI offers two tools which can help an organisation implement OPM3. The first is OPM3 Online which allows one to conduct a self-assessment, and the second is a product called OPM3 ProductSuite in which a certified assessor carries out a much more granular assessment. Both tools contain all three elements (knowledge, assessment and improvement).

The OPM3 website claims the following benefits to an organisation using this model:

- OPM3 provides a way to advance an organisation's strategic goals through the application of project management principles and practices. In other words, it bridges the gap between organisational strategy and individual projects.
- OPM3 provides a comprehensive body of knowledge regarding what constitutes best practices in organisational project management.
- By using OPM3, an organisation can determine exactly which organisational project management best practices and capabilities it has and has not achieved – in other words, its organisational project management maturity.
- If the organisation decides to pursue improvements, OPM3 provides guidance on prioritising and planning.

## CMMI: Capability Maturity Model Integration

The United States Air Force funded a study at the Carnegie-Mellon Software Engineering Institute (www.sei.cmu.edu/cmmi, accessed 11/02/08) to create a model for the military to use as an objective evaluation of software subcontractors. The result was the Capability Maturity Model (CMM), which has been superseded by the more comprehensive Capability Maturity Model Integration (CMMI).

The CMM can be used, especially in large IT projects, to assess an organisation's competence against a scale of five process maturity levels. Each level ranks the organisation according to its standardisation of processes in the subject area being assessed. The five levels of maturity are initial, repeatable, defined, managed and optimising.

### Level 1 – Initial
At maturity level 1, processes are usually ad hoc and the organisation usually does not provide a stable environment. Success in these organisations depends on the competence of the people in the organisation and not on the use of proven processes. Level 1 software project success depends on having high-quality people.

### Level 2 – Repeatable
At maturity level 2, software development successes are repeatable. The processes may not repeat for all the projects in the organisation. The organisation may use some basic project management to track cost and schedule.

Basic project management processes are established to track cost, schedule and functionality. The minimum process discipline is in place to repeat earlier successes on projects with similar applications and scope. There is still a significant risk of exceeding cost and time estimates.

### Level 3 – Defined
The organisation's set of standard processes, which is the basis for level 3, is established and improved over time. These standard processes are used to establish consistency across the organisation. Projects establish their defined processes by the organisation's set of standard processes according to tailoring guidelines.

A critical distinction between level 2 and level 3 is the scope of standards, process descriptions and procedures. At level 2, the standards, process descriptions and procedures may be quite different in each specific instance of the process. At level 3, the standards, process descriptions and procedures for a project are tailored from the organisation's set of standard processes to suit a particular project or organisational unit.

*Level 4 – Managed*
Using precise measurements, management can effectively control the software development effort. In particular, management can identify ways to adjust and adapt the process to particular projects without measurable losses of quality or deviations from specifications. Organisations at this level set quantitative quality goals for both software process and software maintenance.

A critical distinction between maturity level 3 and maturity level 4 is the predictability of process performance. At maturity level 4, the performance of processes is controlled using statistical and other quantitative techniques, and is quantitatively predictable. At maturity level 3, processes are only qualitatively predictable.

*Level 5 – Optimising*
Maturity level 5 focuses on continually improving process performance through both incremental and innovative technological improvements. Quantitative process-improvement objectives for the organization are established, continually revised to reflect changing business objectives, and used as criteria in managing process improvement. The effects of deployed process improvements are measured and evaluated against the quantitative process-improvement objectives. Both the defined processes and the organization's set of standard processes are targets of measurable improvement activities.

A critical distinction between maturity level 4 and maturity level 5 is the type of process variation addressed. For example, at maturity level 4, processes are concerned with addressing special causes of process variation and providing statistical predictability of the results. However, at maturity level 5, processes are focused more on addressing common causes of process variation. They also involve changing the procedure to improve process performance in order to achieve the established quantitative process-improvement objectives.

Some consulting companies have adapted the CMMI model and developed software for assessing organisational and project maturity levels. For example, PM Solutions (www.pmsolutions.com, accessed 12/02/08) developed a formal tool called the Project Management Maturity Model (PMMM) following the Software Engineering Institute's (SEI) Capability Maturity Model's (CMM) five evolutionary maturity levels.

## OGC Maturity Models

Two maturity models are owned by the UK's Office of Government Commerce (OGC) (Association of Project Management, 2007) which are the PRINCE2 Maturity Model (P2MM) and the Portfolio, Programme and Project Management Maturity Model (P3M3).

P2MM is aimed to assist organisations to assess their maturity in application of PRINCE2 methodology in their projects. There is an external accreditation process conducted by an external consultant and the acccredation is verified and awarded by the APM (Association of Project Management). It evident that P2MM is suitable only to organisations using PRINCE2 as the standard project management method and it offers limited scope in total project management effectiveness.

P3M3 was developed in 2006 to build programme and portfolio maturity elements. It is designed to match 32 processes that span project, programme and portfolio management. It was also intended to be externally accredited, but is currently under review (http://www.ogc.gov.uk/documents/p3m3.pdf) to take into account recent changes in OGC guidelines.

Both these models contain the inherent weakness of the bygone ISO 9000 external acreditations, where an organisation focuses more on satisfying the consultants' checklists than identifying the real gaps in the processes.

## PEMM: Process and Enterprise Maturity Model

Hammer (2007) proposes a generic model to assess the maturity of process-based organisations. Although this model is specifically aimed at enterprises, it is useful to review its implication in project management processes. The model contains five process enablers and four enterprise capabilities as summarised in Table 5.1.

**Table 5.1    Process and maturity model**

| Five process enablers | Description |
|---|---|
| Design | The comprehensiveness of the specification of how the process is to be executed |
| Performers | The people who execute the process, particularly in terms of their skills and knowledge |
| Owner | A senior executive who has the responsibility for the process and its results |
| Infrastructure | Information and management systems that support the process |
| Metrics | The measures the company uses to track the process's performance |
| **Four enterprise capabilities** | **Description** |
| Leadership | Senior executives who support the creation of processes |
| Culture | The values of customer focus, teamwork, personal accountability and a willingness to change |
| Enterprise | Skills in, and methodology for, process redesign |
| Governance | Mechanisms for managing complex projects and change intitiatives |

*Source*: Adapted from Hammer (2007).

An early application of PEMM by Vodafone is summarised below:

---

**CASE EXAMPLE PEMM TRIAL IN VODAFONE**

In 2003 the Telecom Systems Department of Vodafone UK Technology (TS) took part in the trials of the Cabinet Office's Project Management Maturity Model (PMMM). The objectives of this 'improving capability' project were to:

- Improve Vodafone's project management capability to deliver the right business projects at the right time
- Ensure that the anticipated benefits of the projects can be identified, measured and realised

The project was initiated in April 2004 using PRINCE2 and was completed in December 2004. It was broken down into five main management stages:

- Initiation – baseline current capability
- Investigation – determine the solution and create standards
- Training – in the new standards for different stakeholder groups

- Roll out – convert all existing work to meet the new standards
- Assessment – formal assessment against PMMM and P2MM.

Vodafone was the first organisation to be awarded level 3 by the APM Group in both PMMM and P2MM. By the end of the project a £1.2M saving was already directly attributable to the project, with projected benefits £16M capex.

PEMM appears to be easy to administer while the last capability, governance, covers projects and change management intitiatives. Hammer (2007) claims that 'after a brief introduction even personnel who are new to processes can create and intrepret the two matrices (process and enterprise)'. This apparent simplicity is also the weakness of the model. As it is not regulated like CMMI or EFQM, poorly trained users may be 'marking their own exam papers'. There is also an apparent overlap between 'owner' in process capabilities and 'leadership' in enterprise capabilities. Although it claims to be comprehensive, some vital enablers (such as innovation, environment and safety and supplier partnership) are missing.

## P3M3: Portfolio Programme and Project Maturity Model

The public consultation draft version 2.0 (http://www.ogc.gov.uk/documents/p3m3. pdf) aims to produce a comprehensive maturity model for apparently distinctive requirements of portfolio, programme and project management. It originated as an enhancement of the maturity levels of CMMI and also comprises five maturity levels:

1. Level 1: Awareness of process
2. Level 2: Repeatable process
3. Level 2: Defined process
4. Level 2: Managed process
5. Level 2: Optimised process.

Although P3M3 contains three separate modules for portfolio (PfM3), programme (PgM3) and projects (PjM3) the distinctive requirements of maturity levels for three modules are not convincing. P3M3 focuses on seven process perspectives, as shown below, which exists in all three models in all five maturity levels:

1. Management control
2. Benefits management
3. Financial management
4. Stakeholder management
5. Risk management
6. Organisational governance
7. Resources management.

Each process perspective is provided with both generic attributes and specific attributes for each model and each level of maturity. The public consultation draft version 2.0 of P3M3 has very good ingredients for assessing the maturity level of a project. However, by aiming to differentiate the maturity levels of portfolio, programme and project management the selection of the appropriate model (e.g. PfM3, PgM3 or PjM3) is likely to be confusing. Furthermore, similar to CMMI, P3M3 fails to identify the enabling success factors and metrics based success criteria.

## EFQM: European Foundation of Quality Management

The EFQM Excellence Model (2003) is a framework for assessing business excellence. It serves to provide a stimulus to companies and individuals to develop quality improvement initiatives and to demonstrate sustainable superior performance in all aspects of the business.

The origin of the EFQM relates particularly to the Malcolm Baldridge Award and also to the Deming Prize. The Malcolm Baldridge National Quality Award (MBNQA) has been presented annually since 1988, to recognise companies in the USA who have excelled in quality management. The Deming Prize was awarded mainly in Japan during the 1950s and 1960s and was based upon ten examination criteria. The EFQM was founded in the late 1980s by 14 large European companies to match the assessment criteria in Europe, while the EFQM Excellence Model was launched in 1991. This model was regularly reviewed and an updated version was launched in 1999 which also included the RADAR (results, approaches, deploy, assess and review) logic.

The model is structured around 9 criteria and 32 sub-criteria with a fixed allocation of points or percentages. The criteria are grouped into two broad areas:

1. Enablers: how we do things – the first five criteria.
2. Results: what we measure, target and achieve – the second four criteria.

The scoring of each sub-criterion is guided by the RADAR logic, which consists of four elements:

- Results
- Approach
- Deployment
- Assessment and review.

The words on the RADAR scoring matrix reflect the grade of excellence for each attribute and what the assessor will be looking for in an organisation.

The EFQM excellence model is intended to assist European managers to better understand best practices and how to support them in quality management programmes. The EFQM currently has 19 national partner organisations in Europe, and the British Quality Foundation is such an organisation in the UK. Over 20,000 thousand companies, including 60 per cent of the top 25 companies in Europe, are members of the EFQM.

The model has been used for several purposes, of which the four main ones are given below:

1. **Self-assessment**: the holistic and structural framework of the model helps to identify the strengths and areas for improvement in any organisation and then to develop focused improvements.
2. **Benchmarking**: undertaking the assessment of defined criteria against the model, the performance of an organisation is compared with that of others.
3. **Excellence awards**: a company with a robust quality programme can apply for a European Quality Award to demonstrate excellence in all nine criteria of the model. Although only one EQA is made each year for company, public sector and small- and medium-sized enterprises (SMEs), several EQAs are awarded to companies who demonstrate superiority according to the EFQM excellence model.
4. **Strategy formulation**: the criteria and sub-criteria of the model have been used by many companies to formulate their business strategy.

The use of the model originated in larger business; however, the applications and interest have been growing amongst the public sector and smaller organisations. To satisfy these needs, special versions of the model are available for public-sector organisations and SMEs.

EFQM, or its adaptation to a self-assessment process, is an essential technique for achieving and sustaining operational excellence. However, an organisation has to be at an advanced stage of its quality programme to be able to use self-assessment in an effective manner.

A survey of EFQM members in 2000 (see Figure 5.1) showed a high proportion of the usage of the model in self-assessment and strategy formulation.

Although Figure 5.1 shows that 37 per cent of organisations used EFQM in project management, the purposes of these applications were not clear. Westerveld (2003) attempts to modify the key characteristics of EFQM (e.g. the 'Enablers' area and 'Results' area) to develop a project excellence model. The model has been based on the assumption that in order to manage a project successfully, the project organisation had to focus on:

- Result areas for project success criteria;
- Organisation areas for critical success factors.

The result areas of the model comprise six components: project results; appreciation by the client; appreciation by project personnel; appreciation by users; appreciation by contracting partners and appreciation by stakeholders. The organisational areas also include six components: leadership and team; policy and strategy; stakeholder management; resources; contracting and project management. Westerveld (2003) piloted the model in an enterprise resource planning (ERP) implementation project and the analysis showed that the functioning of project organisation could be improved on the areas of policy and strategy and partnership management.

The development of the project excellence model is also an initiative of a Special Interest Group (SIG) of the APM. This unit, with a particular interest in project and programme excellence models, appears to adopt the EFQM-based project excellence model of the IPMA (International Project Management Association, 2007) which has been used for assessing project management awards since 2002. The IPMA project excellence model is closer to the original EFQM model than that proposed by Westerveld (2003). The model assesses nine factors/criteria divided into two sections – project management and project results (similar to enablers and results in EFQM).

Another variation of the EFQM based Project Management Performance Assessment (PMPA) model was presented by Qureshi, Warraich and Hijaji (2009). The authors examined the level of impact of assessment criteria in major projects listed in Pakistan by conducting an empirical study and concluded that the PMPA model had a potential use to assess project management performance.

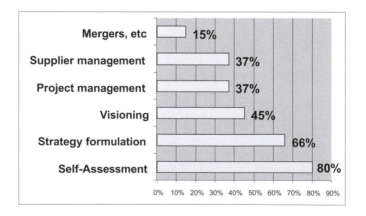

**Figure 5.1    Applications of the EFQM model**
Data from BQF (1999).

## SUMMARY ANALYSIS

A closer examination of the literature on excellence models reveals that although there are a few models in existence or under development, only EFQM-based models appear to have applications in operations management as well as project management. A summary of the key findings of the relevant literature on project excellence and the maturity model is shown in Table 5.2.

**Table 5.2    Key findings of literature on project excellence and maturity models**

| Source | Key findings | Domain |
|---|---|---|
| OPM3 (www.opm3.com) | Owned by the Project Management Institute and contains three elements – knowledge foundation, assessment and improvement. Aims to assess the capability of project organisations. | Project management |
| CMMI (www. www.sei.cmu.edu/cmmi/) | Can be used, especially in large IT projects, to assess an organisation's capability against a scale of five process maturity levels. | IT project management |
| OGC (www.ogc.gov.uk) | P2MM is intendd to assisst organisations to assess their maturity in application of PRINCE2 methodology in their projects. P3M3 is intended to build programme and portfolio maturity elements | Project management Programme management |
| PEMM (Hammer, 2007) | Process and enterprise model contains five process enablers and four enterprise capabilities to assess the maturity of process-based organisations | Project management Process management |
| EFQM (2003) | The model is a framework with five enablers and four results criteria for assessing business excellence. Also applied in projects | Operations management Project management |
| Westerveld (2003) | Suggested a model in Germany which was adopted as IPMA model: the model assesses nine criteria divided into two sections – project management and project results (similar to enablers and results in EFQM) | Project management |
| International Project Management Association (2007) | A model for project management based on EFQM | Project management |
| Association of Project Management (2007) | Reviewed OGC models and CMMI, OPM3 and IPMA | Project management Programme management |
| Qureshi, Warraich, A.H. and Hijaji (2009) | EFQM-based PMPA model has potential use in project management | Project management |

The guide by the APM (2007) should be useful to project managers in clarifying the purpose of the excellence models in the management of projects. However, it must be said with some justification, that it does not provide a 'recommended model' as standard. A standard complex model may be useful to external accreditation, but it can be argued that there are more benefits from identifying true gaps in systems and processes by using a simpler model which could be applied for a transparent process of self-assessment. It is evident that there is less value in attempting to invent another model, but there is greater benefit to be derived from the simplification of the application of models for self-assessment.

Due to the longer track record of EFQM, the IPMA project excellence model based on EFQM is likely to gain more acceptances in the project management community of Europe than OPM3 or CMMI. IT projects are, however, leaning towards the CMMI model. The IMPA model also appears to show gaps. For example, the model only shows the status quo of current quality management and performance. Furthermore, it is also weak on assessing some key factors of project success and organisation quality, such as communication and training, supplier partnership and supply chain management, and the application of operation excellence initiatives (such as Six Sigma and Lean Thinking). The allocation of points is also questionable depending on the nature of a project. However, conceptually the IPMA model appears to be robust as it is supported by learnings from the long track record of EFQM model in operations management. One could also argue that the enabling factors of project management can be aligned to three-dimensional project quality model as follows:

- Product quality relates to project objectives (14 per cent)
- Process quality relates to processes (14 per cent)
- Organisation quality relates to leadership, people and resources (22 per cent).

There is dearth of academic publications on excellence models (Westerveld, 2003; Qureshi, Warraich and Hijaji, 2009). It is important to note that the enabling factors relate to project quality and results or outcome criteria relate to project excellence (Westerveld, 2003; International Project Management Association, 2004). The above analysis is primarily based on publications from professional bodies and thus the discussion may appear to be descriptive. It is necessary to explore and validate these findings on the application of project excellence and maturity models by field research. It is also important to examine how these models can initiate processes towards longer-term project outcomes and project excellence.

# CONCLUSIONS

It is evident from the analyses in Chapter 5 and Chapter 6 that sustainable outcomes of a project leading to project excellence requires more constructs in addition to the dimensions of project quality. Self-assessment aided by excellence models contributes towards assessing and achieving project excellence

An appropriate project excellence model is a vital tool in managing project quality with a road map towards project excellence. There is no shortage of maturity and excellence models available to project managers and some are promoted proactively by consulting firms. For UK Government-sponsored projects there is also likely to be more encouragement to use P3M3 when it completes its consultation stage. However, it is important to emphasise the benefits of self-assessment and a holistic approach of assessing both the enablers and metrics of the assessment process. For these reasons and because of its long track record the EFQM-based model is likely to gain more acceptance with project managers.

The literature on project success factors, surprisingly, outweighs that on project success criteria. Although quality was quoted as one of the success criteria, its parameters, such as 'meets requirements', 'happy users', 'happy team', also constituted project success criteria defined by Grude, Turner and Wateridge (1996). Success criteria appear to relate to both design/process quality and organisation quality. The link between project success factors and organisation quality is more visible and tangible. The softer issues leading to successful projects as identified by Pinto and Slevin (1988) such as top management support, personnel, communication, troubleshooting etc., are all building blocks of organisation quality (Basu 2004). These success factors also lead to the longer-lasting results or sustainability of project outcomes. The factors and arguments produced by other authors, such as Grude, Turner and Wateridge (1996), Hartman and Ashrafi (2001) and Cooke-Davies (2001), Jugdev and Muller (2005) and Shenhar, Dvir, Levy and Maltz (2001) also support this finding.

The purpose of project excellence and maturity models (see Chapter 6) is to enhance an organisation's ability to implement organisation strategy and project objectives through successful and consistent delivery of projects. The underlying theme and objectives of excellence models are therefore focused on the organisation quality in projects. Both OPM3 and CMMI have levels of maturity based on periodic assessments, OPM3 having three levels: knowledge, assessment and improvement, and CMMI having five levels: initial, repeatable, defined, managed and optimising. CMMI is aimed at IT organisations, but can be adapted to other project organisations. PEMM is a broad based approach to help companies plan and execute process based transformations, but it is too generic with a risk of inappropriate applications. The EFQM model was designed for operations management but it has also been applied to project organisations. Westerveld

(2003) attempted to modify the key characteristics of EFQM specifically for project management, which contains the basic ingredients of further enhancement.

All the above excellence and maturity models are good tools to capture a holistic snapshot of an organisation engaged in project management. However, these models do not appear to conduct a 'health check' of a project, nor do they contain any structured approach to move towards project excellence.

# CHAPTER 6

# OPERATIONAL EXCELLENCE CONCEPTS IN MAJOR PROJECTS

## INTRODUCTION

Due to the perception of the one-off unique quality of a project and the repetitive nature of operations, the traditional approach of project management has been consciously different from that of operations management. As supply chain management is inextricably linked with operations management, the mindset of project managers usually excludes the principle of supply chain management (Xue, Wang, Shen and Yu 2007). The primary objectives of project management (scope, time, cost and risk) are beginning to include quality as another parameter of objectives. Hence the objectives of project management (with the exception of scope and risk) are identical to those of supply chain management and operations management – that is quality, cost and time. Typically, a major project involves several stakeholders working together with controlled resources to deliver a completed project. A major project has many suppliers, contractors and customers; it has procurement and supply, demand planning and scheduling; it often lasts over several years and enjoys longer lead times. Therefore it can be argued that the management of major projects will benefit from adopting some customised supply chain management principles which will be discussed in this section.

## WHAT ARE OPERATIONAL EXCELLENCE CONCEPTS?

Before reviewing the applications of operational excellence concepts in projects it is useful to review the concepts themselves.

Operational excellence is demonstrated by results that reflect 'best in class' performance and sustained improvement over time in all areas of importance in an organisation and performance at a level that is at, or superior to, 'best in class' organisations. Common areas of importance are safety, product, quality, people and cost. The origin of operational excellence emerged from the application of performance improvement techniques, very often designated by three letter acronyms, such as TQM (total quality management) , BPR (business process re-engineering), JIT (just-in-time) and MRP2 (manufacturing resources planning) in manufacturing operations management (Oakland, 2003). However, with their broader applications to the service sectors, non-manufacturing functions and projects the focus is now shifted to process excellence. In the context of the dimensions of project quality and project excellence it is more appropriate to prefer the term operational excellence to remind ourselves the closeness of activities between operations and projects. There are three main concepts of operations excellence which are successfully being applied in managing project quality and project excellence. These are:

- Excellence models
- Supply chain management
- TQM, Lean and Six Sigma.

The role of excellence models in projects was reviewed in detail in Chapter 5. The review clearly indicated that an EFQM-based excellence model plays a vital role in the health check and holistic assessment of project management processes and provides a roadmap towards project excellence.

Chapter 1 also includes a good indication of the significance of supply chain management in managing a successful project. In a typical supply chain, raw materials are procured and items are produced at one or more factories, shipped to warehouses for intermediate storage and then shipped to retailers or customers. If you asked people involved in business to define the term supply chain you would get many different answers. Each definition would reflect the nature of the business and the inputs and outputs produced. For some, supply chain is related to purchasing and procurement, to others it is warehousing, distribution and transportation. Yet for others it would be sources of capital and labour. Supply chain management in operations must consider every organisation and facility involved in making the product and the costs involved in doing so. This also implies that the objective is to be cost-effective across the whole supply chain and providing customer satisfaction, which requires a system-wide approach to optimisation. In the context of managing a project the complexity of multi-tier contractors and suppliers and the requirements of key stakeholders are effectively achieved by applying the appropriate supply chain management principle in planning, procurement and delivery processes of projects. A new book (Basu, 2011b) covers how the benefits of supply chain management achieved in operations can be adapted and adopted to the advantage of managing project successes in more detail.

The success of TQM, Lean Thinking and Six Sigma in operations management cannot be disputed (Basu and Wright, 2003; Weinstein, Castellano, Petrick and Vokurka, 2008).

During the years following the Second World War, there was a rapid growth of advanced economies through industrialisation; but in the short term the focus seemed to be upon both increasing volume and reducing the cost. In general, improvement processes were ad hoc, factory-centric and conducive to 'pockets of excellence'. Then in the 1970s the holistic approach of TQM initiated the second wave of operational excellence. The traditional factors of quality control and quality assurance are aimed at achieving an agreed and consistent level of quality. However, TQM goes far beyond mere conformity to standard. TQM is a company-wide programme and requires a culture in which every member of the organisation believes that not a single day should go by within that organisation without in some way improving the quality of its goods and services. In order to complement the gaps of TQM in specific areas of operation excellence, high-profile consultants marketed mostly Japanese practices in the form of a host of three-letter acronyms (TLAs) such as JIT, TPM, BPR and MRPII. Total productive maintenance (TPM) has demonstrated successes outside Japan by focusing on increasing the capacity of individual processes. TQM was the buzzword of the 1980s but it is viewed by many, especially in the US quality field, as an embarrassing failure – a quality concept that promised more than it could deliver.

Six Sigma began back in 1985 when Bill Smith, an engineer at Motorola, came up with the idea of inserting hard-nosed statistics into the blurred philosophy of quality. In statistical terms, sigma ($\sigma$) is a measure of variation from the mean; thus the greater the value of sigma, the fewer the defects. Most companies produce results which are at best around four sigma or more than 6,000 defects. By contrast at the Six Sigma level, the expectation is only 3.4 defects per million as companies move toward this higher level of performance.

Although invented in Motorola, Six Sigma has been experimented with by Allied Signal and perfected at General Electric. Following the recent merger of these two companies, GE is truly the home of Six Sigma. During the last decade, Six Sigma has taken the quantum leap into operational excellence in many blue chip companies including DuPont, Ratheon, Ivensys, Marconi, Bombardier Shorts, Seagate Technology and GlaxoSmithKline.

The key success factors differentiating Six Sigma from TQM are:

- The emphasis on statistical science and measurement.
- A rigorous and structured training deployment plan (champion, master black belt, black belt and green belt).
- A project-focused approach with a single set of problem-solving techniques such as define, measure, analyse, improve, control (DMAIC).
- Reinforcement of the Juran tenets (top management leadership, continuous education and annual savings plan).

The Six Sigma programmes have moved towards the Lean Sigma philosophy, which integrates Six Sigma with the complementary approach of lean enterprise. Lean focuses the company's resources and its suppliers on the delivered value from the customer's perspective. Lean enterprise begins with lean production, the concept of waste reduction developed from industrial engineering principles and refined by Toyota (Womack and Jones, 1998). It expands upon these principles to engage all support partners and customers along the value stream. Common goals to both Six Sigma and Lean Sigma are the elimination of waste and improvement of process capability. The industrial engineering tools of lean enterprise complement the science of the statistical processes of Six Sigma. It is the integration of these tools in Lean Sigma that provides an operational excellence methodology capable of addressing the entire value delivery system. The predictable Six Sigma precisions combined with the speed and agility of lean produces definitive solutions for better, faster and cheaper business processes. Through the systematic identification and eradication of non-value-added activities, optimum value flow is achieved, cycle times are reduced and defects eliminated.

The dramatic bottom line results and extensive training deployment of Six Sigma and Lean Sigma must be sustained with additional features for securing the longer-term competitive advantage of a company. The process to do just that is FIT SIGMA (Basu, 2011a). The best practices of Six Sigma, Lean Sigma and other proven operational excellence best practices underpin the basic building blocks of FIT SIGMA.

Four additional features are embedded in the Lean Sigma philosophy to create FIT SIGMA (Basu, 2011a). These are:

- A formal senior management review process at regular intervals, similar to the sales and operational planning process.
- Periodic self-assessment with a structured checklist which is formalised by a certification or award, similar to the EFQM award but with more emphasis on self-assessment.
- A continuous learning and knowledge management programme.
- The extension of the programme across the whole business with the shifting of the theme of the variation control ($\sigma$) of Six Sigma to the integration of a seamless organisation ($\Sigma$).

## OPERATIONAL EXCELLENCE CONCEPTS IN PROJECTS

It is also evident that there is now increasing awareness amongst both practitioners (www. viasysweb.com, accessed 14/03/08) and academics (O'Brien, 2001; Adriti and Gunaydin, 1997; Tam and Hui, 1996) of applying appropriate supply chain principles and TQM in major undertakings. The most noticeable change is the introduction of ICT over the last three decades, with the market being enriched with faster and more comprehensive systems to improve the efficiency of supply chains from procurement to supplier relationships.

A literature search has revealed that there is only a limited amount of published work specifically focused on supply chain management in major projects. Recently some publications (Xue, Wang, Shen and Yu, 2007) have begun showing a recognition of supply chain management in projects, especially in Hong Kong and Taiwan. However, these publications appear to be dealing with a narrow segment of supply chain management in projects. The paper by Xue, Wang, Shen and Yu (2007) presented a concept of construction supply chain (CSC) management, and suggested two types of Internet-based coordination processes. One is a market mechanism for auction and contracting, while the other is the information hub for improving construction performance. The paper only focuses on tools in an Internet environment without pinpointing how the supply chain management processes can benefit a major project. Likewise, a paper by Chen and Chen (2005) deals with only one aspect of supply chain management in projects, such as payment conditions for contractors. Another publication by Yeo and Ning (2002) highlighted supply chain management good practices primarily in the procurement process of engineering and construction projects.

The piece by Huin (2004) attempts to encompass a broader area of supply chain management in projects. The research results in this paper show the benefits of enterprise resource planning (ERP) systems deployed in SMEs as contractors for large projects. SMEs appear to manage ERP systems. The conclusions are not convincing and are limited to the South East Asia region. An earlier paper by Boddy and Macbeth (2000) demonstrated good pointers of a collaborative relationship in managing projects. A study of 100 contracting companies involved in collaborative relationships with other organisations in managing projects, showed that only 46 per cent of these firms appeared to have succeeded in supply chain partnership. The collaboration by the successful group of companies demonstrated sustainable results in change management in projects specifically in four practices: resources, project goals, organisation structures and project control.

Ala-Risku and Karkkainen (2006) presented an empirical case study of a supply chain in a construction project. Supply chain principles, including short-term schedules, based on capacity analysis of resources were applied and thus reduced the lead time of delivery. The authors also suggested the transparency of information availability for improving the material logistics of construction projects.

Although there is a paucity of academic publications on supply chain management in projects, there are media reports highlighting the shortages, delays and financial losses experienced by major projects due to supply chain problems. For example, a recent publication by the Project Management Institute (2008) reported that Statoil ASA, the Norwegian Oil and Gas Company, wrote off the value of its participation in its South Pars gas field project by 2.2 billion kroner because of the delays and increased costs due to supply chain problems.

Operational excellence in projects is arguably more important now than ever. Leaders of major projects are now seeking project performance improvement tools and methodologies from proven practices of supply chain management. Manufacturing and service organisations tend to execute more of their activities in projects and programmes. Large-scale organisational change processes arising from mergers and acquisitions, restructuring and major IT projects, are nowadays carried out more efficiently as programme management (Artto, Martinsuo, Gemundsen and Murtoaro, 2009). Multinational construction contractors like Bechtel, Balfour Beatty and AMEC Group are embedding operational excellence functions (such as lean, Six Sigma, performance management) in their project and programme management organisation structure. Early research (Wright and Basu, 2008) has shown the activities related to operational excellence in projects which are generally in the domain of supply chain management.

The initiatives and processes in lean project management are deriving benefits from two sources. The first is the traditional approach of critical path scheduling (see Basu, 2008, p. 136) to optimise time for completion. The second advantage, from the lean tools applied in supply chain management, such as value stream and process mapping, is to reduce procurement lead time and wastes. The root cause of the above inefficiency lies in traditional project scheduling. The critical path keeps shifting because of the uncertainty of project work. Goldratt (1999) pointed out that the calculation of 'floats' can be misleading. The apparent buffer of time can evaporate due to preset times and allocation of resources. Building upon the concept of the critical chain, lean project management is developed.

Lean project management principles may have provided good measures to deal with the uncertainty of project work, and its apparent complexity seems to be pushing project managers towards the lean approaches of supply chain management. This lean thinking approach to minimise waste in the supply chain of projects is championed by the Lean Construction Institute (LCI) (www. leanconstruction.org, accessed 09/04/08). The goal is to build the project whilst maximising value, minimising waste and pursuing perfection for the benefit of all project stakeholders. Pinch (2005) explains that LCI aims are primarily focused on the reduction of waste, as defined by the seven categories of 'Mudas', caused by unpredictable workflow. This approach has been defined as 'lean construction'. Ballard (2001) has proposed a method of reducing cycle time in home-building projects within the context of even flow production. The key innovation is the formation of multi-craft teams to overlap activities in each phase of the project and also reduce activity durations through time studies.

Interest in Six Sigma is growing rapidly within the professional project management community, and the most common question arising from that group is reported as, 'How does Six Sigma relate to the project management body of knowledge (PMBOK)?' Gary Gack (http://software.isixsigma.com, accessed 13/02/08) concludes that Six Sigma and PMBOK do have connections, similarities and distinctions and, in the end, it is clear that Six Sigma complements and extends professional project management, but does not replace it. Both disciplines make important contributions to successful business outcomes. The core methodology of Six Sigma, DMAIC, is closely linked to the methodology, rigour and stages of life cycle of project management.

Even today, project managers are not comfortable with embracing Six Sigma in managing their projects. Their arguments in opposing the idea include that a project is unique and one-off so does not have a stable process, and that Six Sigma is only effective in repetitive, stable processes. A response to these doubts is that Six Sigma can be very effective if the tools and methodology are applied appropriately – i.e. fitness for purpose. Within projects there are many repetitive processes which form the basis of project estimating, or many processes are awaiting their design. In both situations DMAIC or DFSS (Design For Six Sigma) can be applied. However, the caveat is the *appropriateness* and for this reason Six Sigma methodology is more apposite for larger projects of a longer duration. The correct level of Six Sigma or FIT SIGMA (Basu and Wright, 2003) is also a good vehicle for developing and retaining members and leaders of a major project. A recent publication by Wright and Basu (2008) also shows how the principle of Six Sigma can be made to 'fit' to project management.

The methodology of DMAIC has added the rigour of the project life cycle to the implementation and closure of Six Sigma projects. Figure 6.1 shows the relationship between DMAIC with a typical project life cycle.

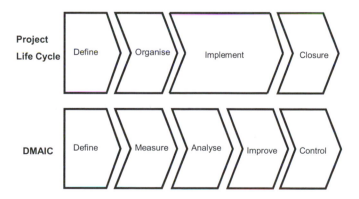

**Figure 6.1     Project life cycle and DMAIC life cycle (Basu, 2008)**

At present, project organisations are showing a positive interest in Six Sigma and courses and conferences (http://www.hau.gr/sitecontent/Six%20Sigma.pdf, accessed 14/03/08) are on offer for project members. Bechtel (www.bechtel.com, accessed 14/03.08) was one of the early users of Six Sigma in delivering their multinational projects. The investment of Bechtel in Six Sigma reached the break-even point in less than three years, and the overall savings have added substantially to the bottom line, while also benefiting customers. Some examples include:

---

**CASE EXAMPLES SIX SIGMA IN PROJECTS**

On a big rail modernisation project in the UK, a Bechtel team employed Six Sigma to minimise costly train delays caused by project work and reduced the 'break in' period for renovated high-speed tracks.

At a US Department of Defense site in Maryland, Six Sigma helped achieve significant cost savings by streamlining the analysis of neutralised mustard gas at a project to eliminate chemical weapons.

To speed up the location of new cellular sites in big cities, Bechtel developed a way to let planners use computers to view video surveys of streets and buildings, making it easier to pick the best spots.

In a mountainous region of Chile, Six Sigma led to more efficient use of equipment in a massive mine expansion, with significant cost savings.

---

A recent report by Holmes and Whelan (2009) supports the application of Six Sigma in major projects and shows that the implementation of Six Sigma in the London Underground Tube Lines project led to a project saving of £2.7 million.

## SUMMARY ANALYSIS

Table 6.1 summarises the key findings of the literature on the impact of organisational excellence concepts in project management.

There are significant potentials and benefits to be gained by adapting and adopting operational excellence concepts such as supply chain management (Ala-Risku and Karkkainen, 2006; Boddy and Macbeth, 2000), lean thinking (Pinch, 2005; Ballard, 2001) and Six Sigma (Wright and Basu, 2008; Bechtel, www.bechtel.com, accessed 14/03/08) in major projects. There are some publications showing the acceptance of supply chain management in projects, but applications of lean thinking and Six Sigma appear to be at their early stages.

**Table 6.1** **Key findings of the literature on operational excellence approaches in project management**

| Source | Key findings | Domain |
|---|---|---|
| O'Brien (2001) | Presented the importance of collaboration between suppliers in the supply chain of projects | Supply chain management Project management |
| Adriti and Gunaydin (1997) | Reported benefits from the application of TQM culture in construction projects | TQM Project management |
| Tam and Hui (1996) | Case study of the application of TQM in a major transport project in Hong Kong | TQM Project management |
| Xiaolong et al (2007) | Suggested Internet-based coordination processes based on experience in project supply chains in China | Supply chain management Project management |
| Chen and Chen (2005) | Supply chain management control to improve payment conditions for contractors | Supply chain management Project management |
| Yeo and Ning (2002) | Highlighted supply chain management good practices primarily in the procurement process of engineering and construction projects | Supply chain management Project management |
| Huin (2004) | Showed the benefits ERP systems deployed in SMEs as contractors for large projects | Supply chain management Project management |
| Boddy and Macbeth (2000) | Demonstrated good pointers of collaborative relationship in managing projects based on a study of 100 contractors involved in collaborative relationships | Supply chain management Project management |
| Ala-Risku and Karkkainen (2006) | The supply chain principles including short-term schedules based on capacity analysis of resources were applied and thus reduced the lead time of delivery | Supply chain management Project management |

**Table 6.1    *Concluded***

| Source | Key findings | Domain |
|---|---|---|
| Pinch (2005) | This lean thinking approach to minimise waste in the project supply chain was championed by the LCI primarily to reduce lead time and wastes | Lean thinking Project management |
| Ballard (2001) | Proposed a method of reducing cycle time in home-building projects within the context of even flow production | Lean thinking Project management |
| Wright and Basu (2008) | Showed how the principle of Six Sigma can be made to 'fit' to project management | Six Sigma Project management |
| Bechtel (www. bechtel.com) | The investment of in Six Sigma reached the break-even point in less than three years, and the overall savings have added substantially to the bottom line | Six Sigma Project management |
| Holmes and Whelan (2009) | The application of Six Sigma in London Underground Tube Lines generated a saving of £2.7 million | Six Sigma Project management |

Leading project contractors such as Bechtel, however, are also training their managers with operational excellence skills (such as managers educated as 'black belts'). In a major project or programme with a timespan of two years or more, it could be argued the activities, processes and objectives in the organisation could be closely related to those of operations management. This could be conducive to the application of operation excellence concepts. It is important to explore and validate these findings regarding operations excellence concepts in project quality and other findings in preceding chapters by field research.

## CONCLUSIONS

The success of operational excellence concepts, such as supply chain management, lean and Six Sigma/FIT SIGMA in the manufacturing and service sectors is well proven. The application of these concepts is still at an early stage as the field research described in Chapter 8 will indicate. However, for larger projects lasting over a longer period, which are being managed as an enterprise, the benefits of operational excellence concepts are gradually being realised to achieve project excellence. Large global project management contractors (e.g. Bechtel) have taken on board operational concepts as a competitive advantage to win contracts and deliver successful projects.

PROPOSITION 1 was developed and discussed in Chapter 2 and PROPOSITION 2 was developed and discussed in Chapter 4. Thus the new dimension of 'organisation quality' supported the definition and dimensions of project quality, as illustrated in Figure 2.1. As discussed in Chapter 5, sustainable outcomes of a project leading to project excellence requires more constructs in addition to the dimensions of project quality. Self-assessment by or based on an excellence model is one such construct. The analysis of Chapter 6 indicates that we also the we also need the input of operational excellence concepts.

The purpose of project excellence and maturity models (see Chapter 5) is to enhance an organisation's ability to implement organisation strategy and project objectives through a successful and consistent delivery of projects. The underlying theme and objectives of excellence models are therefore focused on the organisation quality in projects. Both OPM3 and CMMI have levels of maturity based on periodic assessments, OPM3 having three levels – knowledge, assessment and improvement – and CMMI having five levels – initial, repeatable, defined, managed and optimising. CMMI is aimed at IT organisations, but can be adapted to other project organisations. PEMM is a broad-based approach to help companies plan and execute process-based transformations, but it is too generic with a risk of inappropriate applications. The EFQM model was designed for operations management but it has also been applied to project organisations. Westerveld (2003) attempted to modify the key characteristics of EFQM specifically for project management, which contains the basic ingredients of further enhancement.

All of these four excellence and maturity models are good tools to capture a holistic snapshot of an organisation engaged in project management. However, these models do not appear to conduct a health check of a project, nor do they contain any structured approach to move towards project excellence. Although still in their infancy in the context of their applications in managing projects, operational excellence approaches such as TQM, Six Sigma, lean thinking and supply chain management appear to break ground in project management and show signs of bridging this gap of continuous improvement. Bechtel (www.bechtel. com, accessed 14/03/08) was one of the early users of Six Sigma in delivering their multinational projects. One fundamental tenet of Six Sigma is continuous training. The training should be supplemented by data sharing and collaboration amongst project partners. Publications on the project supply chain such as Boddy and Macbeth (2000) demonstrated good pointers of collaborative relationship in managing projects.

On the basis of the above analysis the third proposition has been derived:

> *PROPOSITION 3: The strategy of organisation quality in projects supported by periodic holistic assessments, operational excellence approaches and continuous training leads to project excellence.*

A conceptual model in Figure 6.2 illustrates the variable in the propositions and the links between them. The above model also offers a theoretical framework of the two dependable variables (project quality and project excellence).

An empirical study (Basu, 2010) with a mixed methodology approach (a questionnaire survey, partial least square modelling and case studies) supported the above three propositions and the model in Figure 6.2. The triangulation approach in this study also established that the weakness in one method is complemented by the strength of another. The comparison of findings from the three sources and their further analysis by triangulation congruency measures related to three propositions, lead to the following conclusions in search of project excellence:

- Organisation quality is an important dimension of project quality.
- People-related 'softer' project success criteria are closely related to organisation effectiveness or organisation quality.
- 'Softer' project success criteria may contribute to project excellence but these criteria or organisation quality alone do not lead to sustainable outcomes.

**Figure 6.2    Project quality and project excellence model**

- 'Project excellence comprising project quality' (containing three dimensions of quality including organisation quality) and two additional constructs (operational excellence concepts and self-ssessment and knowledge management) leads to the sustainability of outcome.

On the basis of the above conclusions the following definitions of project quality and project excellence are recommended:

*Project quality is the philosophy of the adherence of standards to fulfil acceptable delivery objectives throughout the life cycle of a project and there are three clear dimensions of project quality: design quality, process quality and organisation quality.*

*Project excellence is the delivery of sustainable outcomes to key stakeholders in the life cycle of the project, particularly during the final closure stage. This is achieved by the application of the three dimensions of project quality supported by operational excellence concepts and continuous learning.*

# CHAPTER 7

# HOW PROJECT QUALITY AND PROJECT EXCELLENCE ARE PRACTISED: AN EMPIRICAL STUDY

## INTRODUCTION

This chapter provides a review and analysis of the data obtained from the field research. The first part of the analysis focuses on the results from the survey and their relevance to research questions and propositions derived from the literature review. The second section deals with the significance of data in the conceptual model and causal modelling using partial least squares (PLS). This chapter deals with the quantitative aspects of the mixed methodology applied in field research, and the deductive approach applied here is aimed at testing the theoretical framework leading to the model in Figure 6.2. The empirical study also examines how project quality and project excellence are practiced in managing real-life projects. The results are further supported by two major case studies in Chapter 8.

## FIELD RESEARCH DESIGN

As indicated above, the major components of field research comprised semi-structure interviews, a questionnaire survey, a PLS modelling and case studies. From this research it became apparent that there were many different perspectives on this multidimensional issue ranging from (but without limitation to) the definition and dimensions of quality in project management, application of quality in projects, the impact of the critical criteria and factors relating to the success of projects and the role of project excellence and maturity models to the application of operational excellence approaches in project management. These perspectives and issues need to be tested by practical data.

The field research design was influenced by the review of literature both on the research topic and the published methods of research and comprised three stages.

- Stage 1: Semi-structured interviews with senior project and programme managers selected from the members of the Major Projects Association (MPA).

- Stage 2: Questionnaire surveys to members of the Association of Project Management (APM) and the Chartered Quality Institute (CQI) followed by a conceptual research model.
- Stage 3: Case studies of two comparable large projects based organisations and validation adapting the case study approach of Yin (2003) and Eisenhardt (1989). The case studies are described in Chapter 8.

Kvale (1983, p. 174) defines the purpose of the qualitative research interview as 'to gather descriptions of the life-world of the interviewee with respect to interpretation of the meaning of the described phenomenon'. The objective of gaining more insight of the research topic by semi-structured interviews with a list of themes or questions was also supported by King (2006). The first wave of data collection was through a selected group of interviewees (during august 2008) with knowledge and experience of major projects in the UK. This was chiefly aimed at gauging the level of interest and understanding of quality and excellence in managing major projects in the UK. These interviews included 16 senior project and programme managers from 15 organisations, with the majority representing their organisations in the MPA.

Following the semi-structured interviews, a questionnaire-based survey strategy was selected because this method provided access to a wide population in a highly economic way (Saunders, Lewis and Thornhill, 2007) and it enabled the collection of quantitative data for statistical analysis and causal modelling (Hair, Babin, Money and Samouel, 2003).

The questionnaire was developed in two stages. The initial version of the questionnaire was designed for a pilot survey with a sample of members from the APM. The structure and contents of the questionnaire were based on:

- Research questions;
- Three propositions derived after the literature review;
- Comments received during semi-structured interviews.

In general, the wording of questions in the questionnaire followed the '12 basic rules' of Openheim (2000) and questions were 'closed questions' with a multiple choice of response method which also allowed for additional comments. It comprised only 16 questions in 6 major sections, as follows:

- Project information: four questions – project's size, category and sector and quality budget;
- Quality definition: two questions;
- Quality in project management: three questions – responsibility and processes;
- Success criteria and success factors: two questions;

- Project excellence: two questions;
- Individual information: three questions – role and optional data for feedback.

Based on the feedback of the pilot survey the questionnaire was modified (see Appendix 1), with several questions rephrased for better clarity and a new question on quality budget added. The questionnaire was then sent to four Europe-based eminent academics in project management research for additional comments. The constructive feedback from one academic in particular helped to establish the 'content validity' of the questionnaire (Mitchell, 1996).

The refined questionnaire was then transcribed to an online format by using the 'www.hostedsurvey.com' facility. The refinement of the instrument was further ensured by two experienced colleagues who had successfully completed their research projects by using online survey. The online survey was a preferred choice because it was cost-effective, efficient and allowed participants' confidentiality, if preferred. The population of the survey were members of the CQI, MPA and APM.

The data from Excel was formatted for data compression and regression analysis by SPSS software and then in causal modelling by using the PLS technique originally developed by Wold (1985). Hulland (1999) and Fornell, Lorange and Roos (1990) recommend the PLS technique for causal modelling to deal with small data samples. The studies by Birkinshaw, Morrison and Hullard (1995) and Fornell, Lorange and Roos (1990) each present a single conceptual model for PLS regression analysis. Samouel (2008) explains that PLS is a method for constructing predictive models when the factors are many and highly collinear. The present research is intended to establish a predictive relationship of responses towards project quality and project excellence and also intended to support findings via literature review and qualitative analysis. When prediction is the goal and there is no practical need to limit the number of measured variables, PLS can be a useful tool (Chin, 1998). Furthermore, according to Hulland, Chow and Lam (1996) the use of PLS may be considered especially when the research situation demands the investigation of complex models in an explanatory rather than a confirmatory fashion. The PLS approach was therefore considered appropriate for this research.

In view of the practical implication of this research in major infrastructure projects which was further supported by semi-structured interviews, it was considered important to explore, explain and compare results from the questionnaire-based survey in the context of selected case studies of infrastructure projects.

The case study methodology (Yin, 2003; Eisenhardt, 1989) enables the study of both 'what' and 'how' questions in practical examples within a phenomenological framework. Yin (2003) suggests that the analysis of data leads to an analytical procedure (called pattern matching) which involves predicting a pattern based on propositions to explain what we expect to find in case studies. Thus it could be argued that the case study methodology would improve the reliability and robustness of results derived from the questionnaire-based data. According to Denscombe (2003), case studies encourage the use of multiple methods by incorporating a variety of sources and data as part of the investigation. The multiple methods used in this research so far were semi-structured interviews, a questionnaire-based survey, data analysis and causal modelling.

By virtue of the above rationale the two studies chosen for this research were Heathrow Terminal 5 Project (abbreviated as T5) and Channel Tunnel High Speed 1 Project (abbreviated as HS1). The study of the two cases is described in Chapter 8.

## SURVEY RESULTS

In this section results of both the semi-structured interviews and questionnaire survey are presented. As discussed earlier the output of the semi-structured interviews was used as the input to the questionnaire survey.

### Semi-structured Interviews

In line with the method of 'template analysis' (King, 2006) the key features of semi-structured interviews from each of the 16 participants were grouped in categories or themes, as shown in Table 7.1

**Table 7.1    Template analysis (King, 2006) of semi-structured interviews**

| Categories (themes) | Codes | Comments from interviewees (participants' accounts) |
|---|---|---|
| Definition of quality | DQ | 1. 'What concerns me most of all is that our clients ask for quality and safety standards but are more interested in costs'<br>2. 'We probably have all the tools, techniques, procedures and knowledge of programme management. You can always learn but our main focus should be to apply our knowledge and resources most effectively to deliver what the customer wants and also be profitable.'<br>3. 'I would like to see the worth of quality in this arena (major projects) and how others are thinking and applying … what is their passion.'<br>4. 'The general question is of assurance. How can I be sure that I am doing the right things?' |

**Table 7.1** *Concluded*

| Categories (themes) | Codes | Comments from interviewees (participants' accounts) |
|---|---|---|
| Project methodology and guidelines | PMG | 5. 'There are lots of things out there and we are trying to tap into and embed in our processes and procedures say PRINCE2. We have to cut our clothes according to our size.'<br>6. 'We are facing a big challenge in the area of document management and information management. In spite of IT and the Internet we seem to be a long way from sharing data with project partners.' |
| Success criteria and success factors | SCSF | 7. 'If it is numbers it is easy for engineers but we are not so good at softer issues. We are now focusing on softer skills, leadership, communication and that's where we are heading. Manpower planning and all people issues are big things for us.'<br>8. 'I would rate leadership, stakeholder management – especially at the beginning and end of the project – and communication within the team and contractors are some of the top success factors.'<br>9. 'Our challenge is how do we develop effective Project Leaders for mega events like London 2012?'<br>10. 'Our challenge is how to create an effective team and how can we move away from traditional 'contractual' team.' |
| Excellence models | EX | 11. 'I could get every gold award in the book if I have the budget, but is it worth it? It does not necessarily bring businesses – however an award every two years generates the "feel good factor".' |
| Operational Excellence concepts | OE | 12. 'We work in partnership ... and our objective is to deliver value for money for all customers.'<br>13. 'One of our major issues is whether there is a correlation between project performance and nature of contract.'<br>14. 'We know about Six Sigma, TQM, Lean and all that but are they not cost reduction tools for operations? We seem to be chasing contractors to reduce costs.' |
| Sustainable outcome | SO | 15. 'If we can manage softer issues with the team and customers, we are likely to get longer-lasting outcome. But it is easy to say and difficult to do. We may need processes to assess this as a success criteria.'<br>16. 'We tend to focus more on delivery time and budget. That's easy to measure, but customers and stakeholders are now expecting a legacy – what we leave behind when the project closes.' |

The semi-structured interviews not only helped to refine the questionnaire for the second wave of field survey, they also provided some useful pointers for continuing research in project quality and excellence. The pointers were based on both the codes in Table 7.1 and the interview notes. These pointers were:

- Project quality is primarily perceived as delivering what clients want supported by design quality (relevant code DQ);
- A dedicated quality manager is usually assigned to a major project (relevant code SCSF);
- Conformance to quality is mostly assured by gate reviews and periodic audits/health checks (relevant code PMG);
- About four out of five companies have their own project quality standards in place (relevant code PMG);
- Leadership, stakeholder management, communication and clear objectives are top project success factors (relevant code SCCF);
- Little use of OPM3 or CMMI maturity models but some interest in EFQM (relevant code EX);
- OE (operational excellence) in projects is in its infancy but some interest in Lean Thinking (relevant code OE);
- Concern about skills and resources and supplier partnerships (relevant code SO).

The results of the semi-structured interviews were verified during presentations and communications to the participative members of the MPA. It is to be noted that these results are exploratory and not conclusive.

## Survey Responses

The outputs of the semi-structured interviews and the pilot survey provided the inputs to finalise the design of the questionnaire for the online survey. The online questionnaire was made available to the members of the CQI in the March 2008 edition of the CQI Newsletter. At this juncture only six responses were received and these were incomplete. With the cooperation of the CQI and London Excellence, a list of UK members who were considered to be involved in project management was prepared, and the URL of the online questionnaire was emailed directly to 196 members. In addition, a direct email request was also sent to 8 members of the MPA and 11 members of the APM. Thus the total number in the mailing list was 215. As these 215 members were carefully selected from an experienced and homogeneous population for their involvement in managing projects in the UK, 'at least 95 per cent of the sample would represent the characteristics of the population' (Saunders, Lewis and Thornhill, 2007, p. 155). This represented a sample of 0.61 per cent out of a total population of approximately 35,000.

At the end of the data collection period 96 responses were collected. However, 23 responses were incomplete and the number of valid replies was 73. Taking into account these valid answers, the response rate was calculated to be 34 per cent of project and quality managers who received requests by direct email. Baruch (1999) conducted a study of 141 published papers to explore what should constitute reasonable response rates in academic studies. Based on the average of his empirical research, Baruch recommended an acceptable response rate for organisational participants as 36 per cent with a standard deviation of 13 per cent. The response rate of this research compared closely with Baruch's (1999) benchmark.

## Sample Size

The formula for estimating the sample size of a questionnaire survey as suggested by Hair, Babin, Money and Samouel (2003, p. 183) was adopted for this research. The impact of the sample size is reflected in the responses to questions using a scale of 1 to 5 (where 1 is 'not important' and 5 is 'most important'). The formula for the sample size is:

$$N = (DC \times V/DP)^2$$

Where,

N = sample size required
DC = Degree of confidence
V = Variability
DP = Degree of precision

The assumptions in this research included:

DC = 95 per cent degree of confidence represented by approximately two standard deviations.

As the standard deviations of different responses in the rating scale in the survey were not known, it was assumed that sample distribution was normal and in a scale of 1 to 5, the range is (5–1) or 4. The standard deviation of the rating scale was approximated by dividing the range of 4 by 4 (equals to 1), on the assumption that a normal distribution existed with a 95 per cent degree of confidence of +2 or –2 standard error.

Thus, V = Variability = 1

DP (the degree of precision) was set at 0.25 of a unit, i.e. a sample estimate should be accurate to 0.25 of a unit on the rating scale (Hair, Babin, Money and Samouel, 2003, p. 184).

Hence the required sample size $= (2 \times 1/0.25)^2 = 64$

The number of valid responses in the survey was 73, indicating an acceptable sample size.

The above analysis clearly shows that the sample size does not depend on the magnitude of the population (in this case, 35,000 members) but on the variability and accuracy of data.

Saunders, Lewis and Thornhill (2007, p. 466) suggest the sample size which might have some relationship with the extent and nature of population is given by the following formula:

$$n = p\% \times q\% \times (z / e\%)^2$$

Where

n is the sample size required
p% is the proportion belonging to the specified category
q% is the proportion *not* belonging to the specified category
z is the value corresponding to the level of confidence required
e% is the margin of error required.

Although the 215 members of the direct email request were carefully selected, it is difficult to precisely estimate the proportion of responses expected to have a particular category. As the specified category is project quality, it is expected that all members of APM and MPA should belong to the project category, and all members of CQI and London Excellence should belong to the quality category, and the majority of the total population should belong to the project quality category. The worst scenario is that 50 per cent of the sample will have the specified category, and a likely conservative scenario could be that 80 per cent of the sample should belong to the specified category.

Accordingly, assuming a 95 per cent level of confidence (corresponding z value being 1.96) and a 10 per cent sampling error, the sample sizes will be:

n for the worst scenario $= 50 \times 50 \times (1.96/10)^2 = 96$
n for a likely scenario $= 80 \times 20 \times (1.96/10)^2 = 61$

Saunders, Lewis and Thornhill (2007) also suggest an adjustment of the sample size relevant to the size of population as:

$$n' = n / (1 + n/N)$$

Where

n' is the adjusted sample size
n is sample size (as calculated above)
N is the total population

For a population of approximately 35,000 members, the adjustment will be negligible. Based on the formulae by Saunders, Lewis and Thornhill (2007) an acceptable sample size for the population of 35,000 could be 61.

Therefore, on the basis of the above analysis of sample sizes as suggested by both Hair, Babin, Money and Samouel (2003) and Saunders, Lewis and Thornhill (2007), the valid and usable 73 responses met the requirement of the acceptable sample size for this research. Furthermore, as highlighted by Tabachnick and Fidell (2007) and Hair, Babin, Money and Samouel (2003), a smaller sample size can be sufficient when there are many variables with high loadings (e.g. > 0.8).

## Descriptive Statistics

Having identified the valid responses, the normality of the data distribution was tested by using SPSS Version 16.0 software and the SPSS manual (Pallant, 2003). The shapes of the distribution have been assessed by two measures; Kurtosis for 'peakness' and Skewness for 'central symmetry'. When the values of Kurtosis and Skewness are within the limit of +/- 1.5, then the distribution of data could be assumed to be normal (Hair, Black, Babin, Anderson and Tatham, 2006, p. 80). Out of 72 items or scale in the questionnaire 65 items (90 per cent) showed a normal distribution tendency, with the values of Kurtosis and Skewness within the limit of +/- 1.5. The following seven items in Table 7.2 show the values of Kurtosis and Skewness above +/- 1.5.

**Table 7.2     Items with Kurtosis and Skewness outside the limit of +/-1.5**

| Items in questionnaire | Skewness | Kurtosis |
|---|---|---|
| *Q332 PRINCE2 | 1.54 | 1.16 |
| Q333 BS6079 | 2.87 | 7.76 |
| Q334 ISO 10006 | 2.99 | 8.31 |
| Q335 PMBOK/BOK | 3.38 | 10.99 |
| Q336 Company standards | −1,776 | −1.716 |
| Q511 OPM3 | 5.67 | 34.14 |
| Q512 CMMI | 2.72 | 6.37 |

* Q332 refers to the sub-question 2 of Question 3.3 (see Appendix 1).

Even with a relatively small sample size the distribution of most of the items (excluding Q336 Company standards) is reasonably normal.

This research is focused on large projects in the UK. Therefore, it is appropriate to analyse the profile of the projects from which responses were collected. As shown in Figure 7.1, 29 per cent of the ventures had spends of over £500 million and 66 per cent of those in this survey had spends of over £10 million. There is no clear definition of major projects in the '*Body of Knowledge*' by APM (2000). According to the Arup Group (www.arup.com/majorprojects, accessed 16/12/08), 'Major projects are substantial in value and complex in composition [they] involve multiple stakeholders'. For the purposes of this research it is assumed that schemes with investments of over £500 million are mega projects with characteristics closer to large infrastructure developments, while undertakings of over £10 million investment are major projects. With this argument, the responses represented mainly major projects but with only 29 per cent corresponding to large or mega projects.

The projects were also considered to be matured, as Figure 7.2 shows 67 per cent of the schemes were over two years old and only 10 per cent of projects were relatively new, having been running for under one year. Therefore, it is reasonable to suggest that most responses were based on the experience of matured projects.

It was also the intention to explore the type and industry sector represented by projects. The response data indicated that 28 per cent of replies came from public sector projects (not shown graphically). In addition, half of the projects in the survey (51 per cent) were engaged in major construction and transport infrastructure, and 18 per cent in information technology, as shown in Figure 7.3. The remaining (i.e. 'Other') 31 per cent comprised projects related to business transformation, major events and new product development. From the data based on the type and industry sector, it is indicative that half of the responses are more closely related to major infrastructure projects.

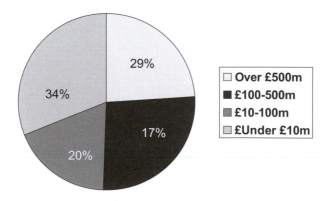

**Figure 7.1    The size of projects**

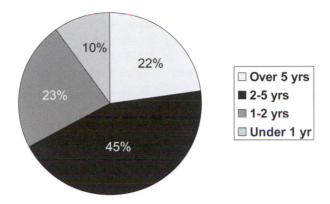

**Figure 7.2    The maturity of projects**

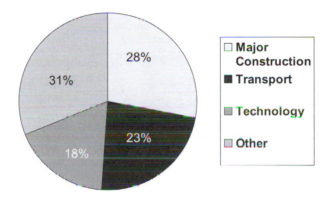

**Figure 7.3    Type of projects**

The participants represented the senior managers in project organisation structure. As Figure 7.4 shows, nearly two-thirds (66 per cent) of the respondents were either project/programme directors or project/quality managers, and 12 per cent represented team members. The remaining (i.e. 'Other') 24 per cent of members were secondary stakeholders or managers, though not directly involved in the day-to-day running of projects, and had either knowledge or interest in the management of projects.

From the above descriptive statistics, it can be argued that the survey covered a representative group of respondents with involvement in the specified category of research who were engaged in matured major projects, with nearly half of them in major construction and transport infrastructure. This is indicative that it is generally in congruence with the scope of the research.

However, it is also recognised that all respondents did not represent major infrastructure projects and it is considered a limitation of research for infrastructure projects only. If the sample size was larger further analyses and comparison of results by type and size of projects could have been investigated.

The survey also collected data for the quality budget in proportion to total project expenditures, and as Figure 7.5 shows, a high proportion of schemes (40 per cent) did not have a significant (less than 0.1 per cent) allocated budget for managing project quality. On the other hand, 35 per cent of ventures included quality budgets amounting to over 0.5 per cent of project costs. The role of quality in project management, as shown by its budget, was found to be varied and not fully recognised.

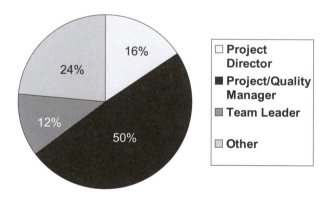

**Figure 7.4    Responses by position in organisation**

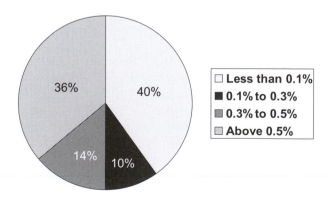

**Figure 7.5    Quality budget as a percentage of project cost**

## Unit of Analysis for Data Collection and Data Analysis

Yin (2003) suggests that the unit of analysis for observations and data collection should not be confused with the unit of analysis for research

According to Sekaran (2003) the unit of analysis for data collection is 'the level of aggregation of the data collected during the subsequent data analysis stage'. Therefore, the unit of analysis of data in this context can be on a number of levels such as an individual personal level, paired individuals, groups of individuals, organisation, industry or even a national level.

The unit of analysis for data collection and data analysis in the questionnaire survey of this research study was at the individual level, comprising project directors, project managers, quality managers or team members. The records collected from individuals were aggregated and analysed to reflect the data of project organisations.

The unit of analysis for data analysis in the case studies was based on two project organisations and the data were collected from individuals and project reports. The information provided by individuals from the same project organisation was aggregated or refined in agreement with Sekaran (2003). It could be argued that a firm is represented by individuals working in that organisation and therefore the aggregated data from individuals represented the project as the unit of analysis.

## ANALYSIS OF SURVEY RESULTS AND RESEARCH QUESTIONS

Responses were grouped in accordance with the four research questions. In the following section the results will be analysed in order of their link to these research questions.

Research question 1: What are the current processes of defining and measuring the dimensions of quality in various stages of project life cycle and what are the sustainable criteria?

There were two questions (Questions 2.1 and 2.2) related to the definition and dimension of project quality. The dimension of 'quality' relates to the specific focus or emphasis of any aspect of project quality

### Question 2.1 Project quality is defined as:

Table 7.3 shows the mean value and standard deviation of 73 responses related to the definition of project quality in a scale of 1 to 5, where 1 = not important and 5 = most important.

**Table 7.3    Definition of project quality**

| Criteria | Mean (scale 1 to 5) | Standard deviation | Rank |
|---|---|---|---|
| Meeting design specifications and requirements | 4.09 | 0.95 | 2 |
| Delivering project on time and within budget | 3.92 | 0.97 | 3 |
| Delivering what the client and sponsor want | 4.21 | 0.80 | 1 |
| Giving more emphasis on outcome than output | 3.38 | 0.79 | 4 |
| Giving more emphasis on sustainability and legacy | 3.15 | 0.95 | 5 |

These attributes of defining project quality were formulated in the light of the literature review and then formalised after semi-structured interviews . The criterion with the highest score was 'Delivering what the client and sponsor want', but the mean values were above average on all criteria (above the mid-value 3). The responses also indicated that the definition of quality was not standard amongst project members. In general, project quality was recognised as being more than 'important', with a mean score of 3.35 in a scale 1 to 5.

## Question 2.2 Primary focus on the dimension of quality

Table 7.4 shows the mean value and standard deviation of 73 responses related to the dimension of project quality in a scale of 1 to 5, where 1 = not important and 5 = most important.

**Table 7.4    The dimension of project quality**

| Criteria | Mean (scale 1 to 5) | Standard deviation | Rank |
|---|---|---|---|
| Design quality | 3.94 | 1.33 | 1 |
| Process quality | 3.83 | 0.79 | 3 |
| Organisation quality | 3.67 | 0.94 | 5 |
| Design and process quality | 3.82 | 0.84 | 4 |
| Design, process and organisation quality | 3.90 | 0.99 | 2 |

The questionnaire also included explanations for the dimensions of quality. The focus on design quality was considered to be highest in the batting order of the dimensions of quality. There is also a role of organisation quality with a score of 3.67 and all three dimensions (design, process and organisation) together ranked as second with a score of 3.9. It is also important to note that there was only a 7 per cent variation between the mean values of all five criteria.

Research question 2: What are the current methodologies and standard guidelines in project management, and what are the links between project success criteria and critical success factors?

There were three questions (Questions 3.1, 3.2 and 3.3) related to project methodologies and guidelines, and two questions (Questions 4. 1 and 4.2) concerned with project success criteria and critical success factors.

## Question 3.1 Quality responsibility in project organisation

As shown in Figure 7.6, the responsibility of quality is shared by the project manager (38 per cent) or the quality manager (32 per cent). It is also indicative that 36 per cent of projects with over 0.5 per cent of the project spend on the quality budget (see Figure 7.5), are likely to be larger and to have a dedicated quality manager.

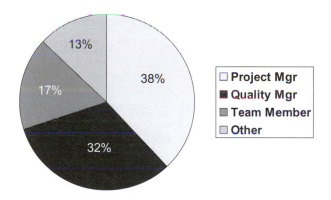

**Figure 7.6** **Quality responsibility in the project organisation**

## Question 3.2 Monitoring project quality

Table 7.5 shows the mean value and standard deviation of 73 responses related to the monitoring of project quality in a scale of 1 to 5, where 1 = not important and 5 = most important.

The use of Key Performance Indicators (KPIs) and independent auditing were the most preferred tools of monitoring project quality. It is indicative that 'gateway reviews' are supported by milestone tracking and KPIs. In spite of the highest ranking of KPIs in the survey, the balanced scorecard was positioned lowest. It can be argued that if the KPIs are based on the balanced scorecard principles, there could be opportunities for further improvement in the monitoring process of project quality.

**Table 7.5     Monitoring project quality**

| Criteria | Mean (scale 1 to 5) | Standard deviation | Rank |
|---|---|---|---|
| Use key performance indicators | 3.99 | 1.10 | 1 |
| Follow balanced scorecard principles | 3.01 | 1.29 | 5 |
| Use milestone tracking | 3.51 | 1.14 | 3 |
| Apply a 'health check' checklist | 3.04 | 1.23 | 4 |
| Apply independent auditing | 3.55 | 1.29 | 2 |

## Question 3.3 Application of Quality Standards and Guidelines

Table 7.6 shows the mean value and standard deviation of 73 responses related to the application of quality standards and guidelines in a scale of 1 to 5, where 1 = not important and 5 = most important.

Table 7.6    Quality standards in projects

| Criteria | Mean (scale 1 to 5) | Standard deviation | Rank |
|---|---|---|---|
| No formal quality plan | 1.80 | 1.50 | 2 |
| Quality plan based on PRINCE2 | 1.77 | 1.24 | 3 |
| Quality plan based on BS6079 | 1.23 | 0.62 | 6 |
| Quality plan based on ISO 10006 | 1.31 | 0,86 | 4 |
| Quality plan based on PMBOK/BOK | 1.29 | 0.89 | 5 |
| Company quality standards | 4.25 | 1.35 | 1 |

It is apparent that the most common method of written quality standards was company quality standards with a high mean score of 4.40, while the average score of the remaining criteria was only 1.52. It is also important to note that the use of published project methodologies (such as PRINCE2) in developing project quality standards was surprisingly infrequent.

## Question 4.1 Project success criteria

Table 7.7 shows the mean value and standard deviation of 73 responses related to the project success criteria in a scale of 1 to 5, where 1 − not important and 5 = most important.

Table 7.7    Project success criteria

| Criteria | Mean (scale 1 to 5) | Standard deviation | Rank |
|---|---|---|---|
| Meets budget | 4.34 | 0,72 | 2 |
| Delivered on time | 4.37 | 0.66 | 1 |
| Meets design requirements | 4.03 | 0.89 | 4 |
| Meets process requirements | 3.68 | 0.76 | 6 |
| Happy sponsors and clients | 4.15 | 0.96 | 3 |
| Happy users | 3.76 | 0.97 | 5 |
| Happy team | 3.41 | 0.91 | 8 |
| Sustainable outcome | 3.46 | 1.12 | 7 |

As discussed in Chapter 4, project success criteria relate closely to definitions of project quality (see Table 7.3 and 7.7). The success criteria applied in the sample of projects covered in the survey were found to be focused on traditional paradigms of project management, as demonstrated by the top three ranked criteria such as 'meets budget', 'delivered on time' and 'happy sponsors and clients'. Project managers appeared to be playing safe by keeping the customer happy and aiming to deliver the project on time and within budget. 'Sustainable outcome' and 'happy team' appeared to be of lower priority.

## Question 4.2 Project critical success factors

Table 7.8 shows the mean value and standard deviation of 73 responses related to the critical factors leading to successful projects in a scale of 1 to 5, where 1 = not important and 5 = most important.

Similar to the project success criteria, the span of the mean value was relatively narrow in project success factors, with the highest and lowest scores being 4.45 and 3.24. It is important to note that high-scoring factors such as 'project leadership', 'top management support', 'communication' and 'stakeholder management' are all people- and organisation-related 'softer' factors.

Research question 3: How can a holistic model measure the dimensions of quality of a project and also assess the overall effectiveness of a project and project organisation?

**Table 7.8    Project success factors**

| Criteria | Mean (scale 1 to 5) | Standard deviation | Rank |
|---|---|---|---|
| Sponsor and top management support | 4.44 | 0.68 | 2 |
| Project leadership | 4.45 | 0.73 | 1 |
| Stakeholder management | 3.89 | 1.00 | 5 |
| Communication and team-building | 4.27 | 0.71 | 3 |
| Appropriate tools and techniques | 3.38 | 0.97 | 7 |
| Appropriate quality plan | 3.24 | 0.90 | 8 |
| Planning and monitoring | 3.59 | 0.97 | 6 |
| Clear objectives | 4.10 | 0.84 | 4 |

There was one question (Question 5.1) related to models used in projects to assess the overall effectiveness both of projects and project organisation. Table 7.9 shows the mean value and standard deviation of 73 responses related to the application of excellence and maturity models in ventures using a scale of 1 to 5, where 1 = not important and 5 = most important.

**Table 7.9    Excellence and maturity models in projects**

| Criteria | Mean (scale 1 to 5) | Standard deviation | Rank |
|---|---|---|---|
| OPM3 model | 1.11 | 0.57 | 5 |
| CMMI model | 1.34 | 0.91 | 4 |
| EFQM-based excellence model | 2.56 | 1.63 | 1 |
| Customised checklist | 2.56 | 1.65 | 2 |
| Not used at all | 2.13 | 1.67 | 3 |

The use of project excellence and maturity models in project management was found be in its infancy. Only the EFQM-based excellence model and customised checklist were showing evidence of some application. CMMI was found to be used in various IT projects, but there was hardly any use of OPM3. This highlights a major gap in the area of managing project quality and excellence.

Research question 4: How practically are the operational excellence approaches likely to be used in project management and how do we relate the outputs of such approaches to project excellence?

There was one question (Question 6.1) related to the application of operational excellence concepts in projects. Table 7.10 shows the mean value and standard deviation of 73 responses related to the application of operational excellence in projects in a scale of 1 to 5, where 1 = not important and 5 = most important.

**Table 7.10    Operational excellence in projects**

| Criteria | Mean (scale 1 to 5) | Standard deviation | Rank |
|---|---|---|---|
| TQM | 2.87 | 1.36 | 1 |
| Six Sigma | 2.46 | 1.61 | 4 |
| Lean thinking | 2.76 | 1.39 | 2 |
| Supply chain management | 2.75 | 1.44 | 3 |
| Other | 1.23 | 0.82 | 6 |

Similar to project excellence models, the applications of operational excellence concepts in projects also scored lower values (below the mean score 3 in a scale 1 to 5). There was recognition of TQM, Six Sigma, lean and supply chain management in some major projects, but it appeared that many were still a long way from realising the full benefit of their application. This also highlights a major shortcoming in the area of managing project quality and excellence.

## PARTIAL LEAST SQUARES (PLS) MODELLING

The outputs from the analysis of the data from the questionnaire survey provided the inputs to the causal modelling by PLS analysis. These outputs included the reliability of scales and data, the underlying relationships among a set of related variables by the exploratory factor analysis and the limitations of the multiple regression analysis.

Structural Equation Modelling (SEM) techniques such as LISREL or AMOS estimate the causal relationship between variables by means of covariance analysis (Hair, Black, Babin, Anderson and Tatham, 2006). SEM encourages confirmatory rather than exploratory modelling; thus, it is suited to theory testing rather than theory development. The assumptions of covariance-based SEM include normally distributed data, independent observations, random sampling of data and a large sample size to validate testing and inference. This research study was conducted amongst qualified stakeholders of projects and the sample size (73) was relatively small, so the assumptions of normal distribution were not fully tested. Hence the data collected from the online survey was not considered appropriate for covariance analysis by SEM.

Hulland (1999) and Fornell, Lorange and Roos (1990) recommend the PLS technique for causal modelling to deal with small data samples. As Haenlein and Kaplan (2004) explain, PLS focuses on maximising the variance of the dependent variables explained by the independent ones instead of reproducing the empirical covariance matrix of SEM. This approach is also supported by Chin (1998) as PLS is primarily intended for causal-predictive analysis in situations of high complexity but low theoretical information. Furthermore, PLS can be used as an exploratory analysis tool to select suitable predictor variables. Unlike SEM models, PLS models do not require alternative models that are equivalent in terms of overall model fit (Chin, 1998). The underlying procedure of PLS follows a simple or multiple regression process, depending on the number of indicators hypothesised to influence the dependent variable. According to Samouel (2008), PLS is appropriate when:

- Data is non-normally distributed;
- Sample size is small;

- Theoretical model involves both formative and reflective constructs or Latent Variables (LVs);
- The main interest lies in prediction rather than theory testing.

Haenlein and Kaplan (2004) argue that PLS comes into its own principally in a situation in which covariance-based SEM tools reach their limit, namely when the number of indicators per LV becomes large.

Wetzel et al (2009) suggest that covariance-based SEM and components-based PLS path modelling should be regarded as complementary methods. They argue that under certain conditions, such as hierarchical construct models, PLS path modelling is likely to outperform covariance-based SEM.

On the basis of the above rationale, the PLS modelling approach was chosen for this research to compare the predictive results of the model with the research propositions.

Samouel (2008) also explains that the PLS model is estimated using an interactive Ordinary Least Square (OLS) like procedure, and the overall variance is used as the primary measure of model accuracy. The data are partitioned into blocks of attributes which are related to a specific construct of LVs (these are not measured directly, but are estimated in the model from measured variables). The estimation algorithm provides estimates of the parameters in each block sequentially and iteratively, until differences between successive iterations are minimised. The assessment of the estimated model comprises the following key steps:

1. Report model and interpret results
2. Assess the significance of loadings and path coefficients ('bootstrapping')
3. Assess validity and reliability of concepts (Average Variance Extracted [AVE] and internal consistency or composite reliability)
4. Assess predictive power ($R^2$) and predictive relevance ($Q^2$)
5. Modify/extend model based on experience or past research.

## The Conceptual Research PLS Model

As indicated earlier, the PLS approach was chosen for the conceptual research model (Figure 6.2) because the sample size of the online survey was relatively small, but another reason is also that it could be used for both reflective and formative indicators. According to Hulland (1999), there are two basic types of relationships between constructs and indicators (or measures) in a PLS model, viz. reflective indicators and formative indicators. Reflective indicators are believed to mirror the unobserved underlying constructs (also called LVs) with the construct giving rise to the observed measures (or indicators). In contrast, formative indicators define the construct. The measures or indicators derived or observed from the questionnaire survey replicate the relevant constructs in the model and thus are known as reflective indicators. The PLS model also contains two component models – the inner relation and outer relation models. According to Bagozzi (1994) this is equivalent to the measurement and structural components of covariance in SEM modeling. The PLS model shown in Figure 7.7 is based on the conceptual model.

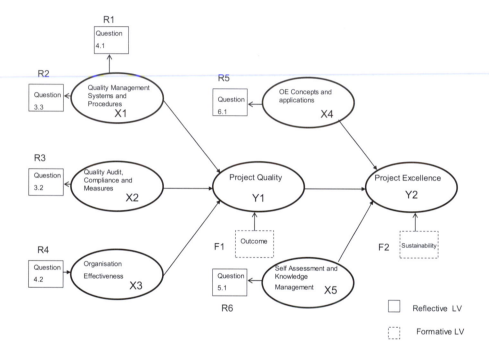

**Figure 7.7    Partial least squares model**

where:

    X1 = Quality management systems and procedures
    X2 = Quality audit, compliance and measures
    X3 = Organisation effectiveness
    X4 = Operational excellence concepts and applications
    X5 = Self-assessment and knowledge management
    Y1 = Project quality
    Y2 = Project excellence
    X1, X2, X3, X4 and X5 are exogenous variables
    Y1 and Y2 are endogenous variables

The equations showing the theoretical relationships of variables in the PLS model are:

$$Y1 = f(X1, X2, X3) + \varepsilon1$$
$$Y2 = f(Y1, X4, X5) + \varepsilon2$$

Where $\varepsilon1$ and $\varepsilon2$ are errors.

The outer relationships are specified in the outer or measurement model. These relationships are assumed to be between the LVs (e.g. X1 to X5) and reflective indicators (R1 to R6). Formative indicators (F1 and F2) of endogenous variables (Y1 and Y2) are also incorporated in the outer model. High co-relation is anticipated amongst reflective indicators, while formative indicators are expected to show low co-relation (Hulland, 1999).

Regression weights and correlation loadings are estimated for the PLS Model. Weights relate to formative indicators and loadings pertain to reflective indicators, which are equated to the regression and correlation coefficients respectively within the measurement equations. These represent the amount of alteration in the dependent variable for the unit change in the independent variables (Hulland, 1999). The PLS model is estimated by using an iterative OLS regression-like procedure. As Samouel (2008) describes, 'the data are partitioned into blocks of attributes which are related to specific LV. The estimation algorithm provides estimates of the parameters in each block sequentially and iteratively until differences between successive iterations are minimized'.

The *null hypothesis* is that there is no difference in the group statistics. Hair, Babin, Money and Samouel (2003) recommend that for each model an *alternative hypotheses* (opposite to null hypotheses) should be clearly stated in order to validate the model by rejecting null hypotheses. The alternative hypotheses for the PLS Model (Figure 7.7) are stated as follows:

- Hypothesis 1 (H1): Quality management systems and procedures has significant positive impact on project quality.
- Hypothesis 2 (H2): Quality audit, compliance and measures has significant positive impact on project quality.
- Hypothesis 3 (H3): Organisation effectiveness has significant positive impact on project quality.
- Hypothesis 4 (H4): Operational excellence concepts and applications' has significant positive impact on project excellence.
- Hypothesis 5 (H5): Self-assessment and knowledge management has significant positive impact on project excellence.
- Hypothesis 6 (H6): Project quality has significant positive impact on project excellence.

## MODEL EVALUATION

PLS-Graph software by Chin (2001) was used to replicate the model and also to evaluate the model. In SEM model-based studies, researchers aim to apply 'goodness of fit' measures, indicating how well a specified model reproduces the covariance matrix among indicator variables. It must also be noted that goodness of fit indices are sensitive to sample size (Hair, Black, Babin, Anderson and Tatham, 2006, p. 747).

According to Chin (1998), the PLS approach does not rely on distribution assumptions and traditional parametric-based goodness of fit techniques are not appropriate for model evaluation. Instead, Chin suggests the examination of path coefficients and the explanatory power of R square. Similar to multiple regression, R square is an estimate of the proportion of the variance of the dependent variable accounted for by the simulation. The software (PLS-Graph) carries out tests of significance for all path coefficients utilising 'one-tailed t-tests' and an alpha of 0.05 (Chin, 1998). The extent to which the indicators support their construct or latent variable is determined by the value of individual loading and the explanatory power of R square. Chin (1998) argues that most of the loadings (for reflective indicators) should be at least 0.60, showing that each indicator is accounting for 60 per cent or more of the variance of the underlying construct or LV.

The path coefficients give the direct effects and direction of relationship between the predictor construct and the predicted construct. Falk and Miller (1992) compare path coefficient to standard regression coefficient (or beta coefficient), and suggest that when this value is less than 0.015 or less than 1.5 per cent, the predictor construct is not making an important contribution to the variance in the predicted construct, and so the path should be eliminated. Path coefficient values above 0.2 are acceptable to be supportive of the construct (Chin, 1998). R square values of 50 per cent or above signify that the model is explained by 50 per cent or more of the data and results are then acceptable (Samouel, 2008; Chin, 1998).

In summary, the following benchmarks have been used to evaluate the fitness of the PLS model:

| | | |
|---|---|---|
| Loading | > 0.60 | (Outer model) |
| R square | > 0.50 | (Inner model) |
| Path coefficient | > 0.20 | (Inner model) |

A number of simulations were carried out with PLS-Graph software by using different combinations of indicators to test the robustness and fitness of the PLS model. In the light of the fitness indicators above, models with two combinations of indicators (viz. 32 indicators and 26 indicators) were shortlisted for further analysis.

The path cocoefficients of the models with 32 and 26 indicators are summarised in Table 7.11 and R square values in Table 7.12.

**Table 7.11    Path coefficients in PLS path modelling**

| Paths | Path coefficients with 32 indicators | Path coefficients with 26 indicators |
|---|---|---|
| H1: Quality systems to project quality | 0.530 Supported | 0.388 Supported |
| H2: Audit and measures to project quality | 0.196 Supported | 0.044 Partly supported |
| H3: Organisation effectiveness to project quality | −0.253 Not supported (negative coefficient) | 0.473 Supported |
| H6: Project quality to project excellence | 0.047 Partly supported | 0. 195 Supported |
| H4: OE concepts to project excellence | 0.442 Supported | 0.411 Supported |
| H5: Self-assessment and knowledge management to project excellence | 0.409 Supported | 0.269 Supported |

*Source*: PLS-Graph simulation.

**Table 7.12    R square value**

| Endogenous variable | R square with 32 indicators | R square with 26 indicators |
|---|---|---|
| Project quality | 0.279 Not supported | 0.771 Supported |
| Project excellence | 0.604 Supported | 0.617 Supported |

*Source*: PLS-Graph simulation.

As shown in in the above table (Table 7.12), the path between the endogenous variables (project quality to project excellence) is showing a path coefficient of 0.47 with 32 indicators and 0.195 with 26 indicators. However, all paths from exogenous variables showed values above 0.2 except for 'audit and measures' to 'project quality' for the model with 26 indicators. Furthermore, as shown in Figure 7.8b and Table 7.12, R square values for both the dependent variables with 26 indicators are 0.771 for project quality (acceptable) and 0. 617 project excellence (acceptable). $R^2$ value for project quality in the model with 32 indicators was 0.279 (partly acceptable).

A comparison of the mean values of loadings, path coefficients and R square values for models with 32 and 26 indicators are shown in Table 7.13.

**Table 7.13    Mean values of loadings, path coefficients and R squares**

| Parameters | Model with 32 indicators | | Model with 26 indicators | |
|---|---|---|---|---|
| | Mean | Std deviation | Mean | Std deviation |
| Loadings | 0.761 | 0.16 | 0.876 | 0.09 |
| Path coefficients | 0.230 | 0.29 | 0.297 | 0.02 |
| R squares | 0.441 | 0.25 | 0.694 | 0.15 |

*Source*: PLS-Graph simulation.

The mean values of loadings, path coefficients and R square and their standard deviations indicate that with comparison to the model with 32 indicators, the fitness indicators of the model with 26 indicators are more significant and acceptable.

The interdependency of three exogenous constructs of project quality was tested by the PLS model with 26 indicators by estimating the path coefficients between them as shown below. These estimates (see Table 7.14) are comparable to standardised regression coefficients (Hair, Black, Babin, Anderson and Tatham, 2006) and indicate that the construct 'Organisation effectiveness' is closely correlated to 'Quality systems' but not with 'Audit and measures'.

**Table 7.14    The interdependency of three constructs of project quality**

| Paths | Path coefficients with 26 indicators |
|---|---|
| Quality systems to audit and measures | 0.531 |
| Quality systems to organisation effectiveness | 0.936 |
| Audit and measures to organisation effectiveness | 0.051 |

*Source*: PLS-Graph simulation.

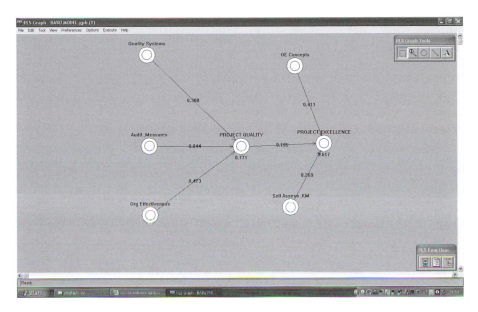

**Figure 7.8a   PLS model and results with 26 indicators (toggled)**
*Source*: PLS-Graph simulation.

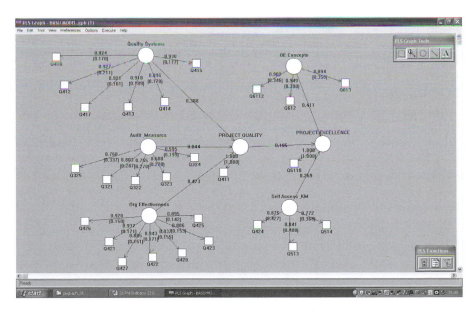

**Figure 7.8b   PLS model and results with 26 indicators**
*Source*: PLS-Graph simulation.

Samouel (2008) suggests that in assessing the statistical significance of loadings and path coefficients, the 'bootstrapping' technique should be used. According to Chin (1998), this bootstrapping method represents an inferential approach for estimating the precision of the PLS estimates, where N samples are created in order to obtain N estimates for each parameter in the PLS model. Each sample is created by testing with replacements from the original set. For each of the sample the bootstrapping value is calculated. The mean of the bootstrapping values are calculated as a proxy for the overall population mean, and their standard deviations and standard errors are also determined. The bootstrapped t-statistic, with (N–1) degrees of freedom (N = number of samples) is then generated and used to test the null hypothesis (the significance of loadings and paths). As it is explained by Hair, Black, Babin, Anderson and Tatham (2006, p. 367), t-statistic assesses the statistical significance of the difference between two sample means for a single dependent variable.

Chin (1998) suggests the significance ($\alpha$) level as 0.05 for 'one-tailed t-tests', which corresponds to 1.96 as the critical value of t-static. On the basis of this benchmark one path ('audit and measure' to 'project quality') is not significant, one path ('OE concepts' to 'project excellence') is highly significant, and other paths are moderately significant. However, t-statistic values of all loadings (including the loadings of indicators reflected by 'audit and measure') are highly significant, with values above 1.96. It is therefore indicative that with a limitation for the path coefficient related to one construct (viz. 'audit and measure') the results of the PLS model with 26 indicators (see Figure 7.8a) are statistically important.

## CONCLUSIONS

This empirical study demonstrates that an example of PLS modelling can be used at least in a predictive sense in a complex project management environment. Only reflective sets of measures were created to estimate the underlying constructs, and the model appeared to be less problematic with the absence of formative indicators. The model also helped to establish the relationship between constructs as posited by the alternative hypotheses of the model and the research propositions. The iterative approach of PLS modelling enabled the establishment of a robust model with a strong causal relationship without the use of the confirmatory factor analysis. All alternative hypotheses, with the exception of Hypothesis 2, have been well supported by the model. It can be argued that additional indicators are required to reflect the construct 'Quality audit, compliance and measures', which is relevant to Alternative Hypothesis 2, to improve the result from 'partly supported' to 'supported'. A recent research on structural equation modelling by Temme, Paulssen and Dannewald (2008) concluded that the inclusion of 'attitudes' as an additional latent variable in a travel mode choice model led to improvements in terms of both model fit as well as explanation.

The results of the PLS model with 26 indicators do support that 'organisation effectiveness' has a direct effect and significant relationship (path coefficient 0.473) with 'project quality'. This supports the first proposition that 'organisation quality' is an important dimension 'project quality'. The results of the model with 26 indicators also demonstrate that 'softer' or people related issues of success factors (such as 'Q 421: Sponsor and top management support', 'Q422: Project leadership' and 'Q423: Stakeholder management') are significant components of the construct, 'organisation effectiveness' as given by their loadings above 0.88. This supports the second proposition. The model also shows that 'organisation quality' alone does not lead to the 'sustainability of outcome'. However, it indicates that 'project excellence' comprising 'project quality' (containing 'organisation effectiveness') and two additional latent variables (viz. 'operational excellence' concepts and 'self-assessment and knowledge management') leads to 'project excellence'. This supports the third proposition.

All three propositions derived in this research are supported by the PLS model.

The analysis of data from the questionnaire-based survey and PLS modelling do direct the research to a number of useful pointers, as discussed above. Sekaran (2003, p. 308) suggests that data analysis and interpretation of field research may be most meaningfully explained by referring to a business project. The results will be examined further in the light of two case studies in Chapter 8.

# CHAPTER 8

# HEATHROW TERMINAL 5: CASE STUDY

## INTRODUCTION

The next two chapters present the descriptions, data collections and analyses of two case studies on major infrastructure projects: Heathrow Terminal 5 and the Channel Tunnel Rail Link High Speed 1 (also referred to as T5 and HS1). Broadly similar major infrastructure projects in recent years in the UK include Wembley Stadium, High Speed 1 Channel Tunnel Rail Link, Heathrow Terminal 5, London 2012 Olympic Games and Crossrail Project. The best practices and learning from two major infrastructure projects (viz. Heathrow Terminal 5 and Channel Tunnel High Speed 1) were presented at two closely connected MPA seminars during the first quarter of 2008. As a consequence some of the 'elite interviewees' who were members of MPA suggested a comparative study of these two high-profile projects. After reporting on these two cases, a comparison of the best practices of each is made, and used to test the three research propositions and also to explain the findings from the questionnaire-based survey and PLS modeling (see Chapter 7). Chapter 9 ends with the development of the Assessing Project Excellence (APEX) model.

According to Yin (2003) and Eisenhardt (1989), case studies are the preferred strategies of research on social science topics, especially for 'how' and 'why' questions, as well as enabling the researcher to focus on a contemporary phenomenon within a real-life environment. This is also supported by Robson (2002) who defines a case study as 'a strategy for doing research which involves an empirical investigation of a particular contemporary phenomenon within its real life context'. The chosen case studies of Heathrow Terminal 5 (T5) and the Channel Tunnel Rail Link High Speed 1 (HS1) projects are both related to the contemporary phenomenon of efficient transport in a real-life environment. As indicated earlier, the five exogenous constructs as an output from the PLS modelling provided an input to case studies around these constructs. Therefore the case studies are presented and analysed around the five exogenous constructs of the conceptual model (see Figure 6.2). These are:

- Quality management systems and procedures
- Quality audit, compliance and measures (to be reported in subheadings as quality audits and compliance, and performance management)[1]
- Organisation effectiveness
- Operational excellence concepts and applications
- Self-assessments and knowledge management

## CASE STUDY 1: HEATHROW TERMINAL 5 PROJECT (T5)

### Project Background

Heathrow Terminal 5 opened on 27 March 2008 with the very public outcry of the failure of its baggage system. In analysing the root causes of the operational failure during the handover of the project, there are likely to be technical and human errors for both British Airways (BA) and the British Airports Authority (BAA); nevertheless, some of the exemplary best practices and initiatives of the T5 project should not be underestimated or overlooked.

BAA's Terminal 5 (T5) programme at London Heathrow Airport is currently one of Europe's largest construction projects. It is expected to cater for approximately 30 million passengers a year and provide additional terminal and aircraft parking capacity. T5 is also expected to feature a world-class transport interchange connecting road, rail and air. The facility represents a £4.3 billion investment for BAA.

The mission and key objectives of the project included:

- To set new standards in delighting the traveller at T5;
- To develop and deliver T5 to new industry standards of health safety and security;
- To earn the proactive support and trust of key stakeholders;
- To leave behind a legacy of quality.

The need for supplier partnerships in line with the T5 Agreement and the complexity of rail, road, construction and systems requirements of the project were additional project objectives. To achieve these challenging targets in money and programme, BAA had to consider a novel contracting and procurement strategy

---

1　　The addition of another exogenous construct (viz. performance management) in case studies is in line with the conclusions on additional latent variables by Temme, Paulssen and Dannewald (2008). The gap identified in the construct 'Audit and measures' by the PLS analysis has provided a substantive input to case studies for further investigation by an additional construct.

supported by a performance management system and an audit process. The best practices and learning points of the T5 agreement and balanced scorecard-based performance management system have been well documented (Basu et al 2009), but best practices and learning points can also be derived from other constructs of project quality and project excellence.

## Quality Management Systems and Procedures

Quality strategy and procedures contribute to the Quality Management System (QMS) framework to set and deliver quality requirements by systematically integrating quality planning, quality assurance, quality control and quality improvement processes in a project. Figure 8.1 shows the structure of QMS adopted in the T5 project.

- *Quality planning*: sets quality objectives and necessary procedures to deliver and assure the objectives and requirements are met.
- *Quality assurance*: puts in place processes and procedures which provide assurance that quality requirements will be met. Quality assurance at the beginning of a project is more cost-effective than control measures used at later stages.
- *Quality control*: focused on verifying quality requirements and standards.
- *Quality improvement*: focuses on increasing the ability to meet quality objectives and requirements, and leads project quality to project excellence.

The primary focus of quality in the T5 project was the quality assurance of suppliers governed by the quality requirements specification and team execution

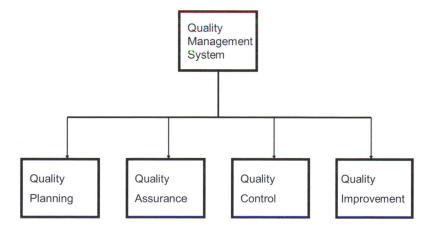

**Figure 8.1    Structure of the T5 quality management system**
*Source*: Terminal 5 Project.

plan. A formal document was drawn up for the quality requirements specification defining quality principles, policies and requirements for both the T5 project teams and first-tier suppliers. The execution planning processes were outlined in another formal document to address key management questions including, 'Is work complete at handover?'.

The quality control of the T5 project was focused on periodic audit, a well-designed performance monitoring system supported by key indicators and measures and an inspection and test plan when work was completed. Figure 8.2 shows an overview of the quality assurance and control processes of the T5 project.

The quality improvement process was driven by audit reports and performance management RAG (red, amber and green) reports.

The quality procedures were continuously reviewed, with a formal structure of forums which allowed the information and decision process to be cascaded up and down the project quality organisation. The forums also enabled behavioural changes through the participation of quality personnel and leaders at all levels at relevant stages of the review process. Table 8.1 summarises the purpose and membership of the different quality forums in the T5 project.

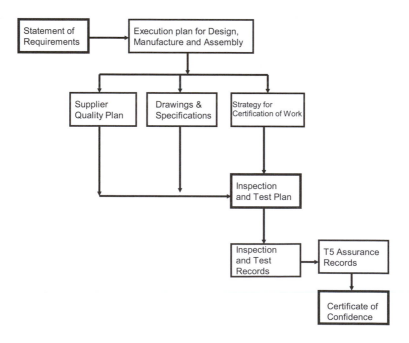

**Figure 8.2    The T5 quality assurance and control process**
*Source*: Terminal 5 Project.

**Table 8.1     Purpose and membership of quality forums**

| Forum | Purpose | Membership |
|---|---|---|
| Weekly buildings quality leadership team | Feedback and address issues from right first time workshops and work through other behaviour change opportunities and challenges (i.e. communications campaign etc.) | Buildings quality leaders supported by members of the team |
| Fortnightly buildings quality community of practice | Share information, make decisions and have key debates and discussions | Buildings co-ordinator representatives plus members of building quality team |
| Monthly T5 quality co-coordinators meeting | To get quality co-coordinators on the same page, ensure consistency of reporting forum to share ideas and implement updated/new quality processes | Quality co-coordinators representatives from across the project |
| Monthly T5 quality steering committee | To inform and make quality decisions across T5 | Project leaders and quality leaders from across the project |

*Source*: Terminal 5 Project.

## Quality Audit and Compliance

Both audits and health checks have two primary objectives (Wateridge, 2002). The first is to ensure that the project is running satisfactorily according to the procedures and criteria. The second is to learn from practices of a completed project in order to improve the management of future schemes. Regardless of whether the project audit is conducted mid-term or at its conclusion, the procedure is similar and there is no shortage of audit processes or checklists. However, the audit and self-assessment practices of the T5 project have created a fresh approach involving all key stakeholders.

In the T5 project audits were carried out broadly in two areas – product audit and process audit. Product audits were aimed to review the status and readiness of product specifications by project teams (e.g. rail, systems, baggage, energy centre, airfield, site and logistics etc.) and product areas (e.g. structure and fabric, rail systems, passenger equipment, utilities, civil and earthworks and so forth.).

Process audits aimed to review the process conformance by project teams to provide assurance for gateway decisions. In addition, as shown in Figure 8.3, the audit activities were extended to supplier assessment and failure investigation.

Three levels of audit processes were applied for conducting product/process compliance audits on the T5 project, and also to ensure quality and environment, health and safety audits:

- **Level 1 audits**: designed for auditing the majority of smaller projects (*c*.300).
- **Level 2 audits**: designed for auditing the top 30 projects as agreed by the T5 quality management executive.
- **Level 3 audits**: conducted on critical projects by the full-time quality management team.

The levels of audit engagement were determined by the Quality Management Executive (QME) which comprised the engineering director, construction director and quality director. As shown in Figure 8.4, the QME assessed the level of engagement according to the importance and priority of sub-projects by taking into account the type of commercial contract, the business risk, supplier performance data and engineering criticality results.

The audits were conducted each month, and the selection of assessments at each level depended primarily on the decisions made during 'milestone review meetings' ('gateway decisions') for process compliance and 'readiness for key construction events' for product compliance. The robustness of the T5 audit processes is underpinned by the decisions made by the QME to determine appropriate levels, risk focus, safety, gateway decisions and readiness for key construction events. The audit results are also linked to performance management and improvement priorities.

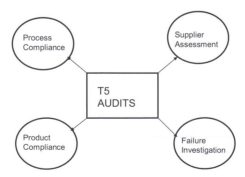

**Figure 8.3    Types of T5 audit**
*Source*: Terminal 5 Project.

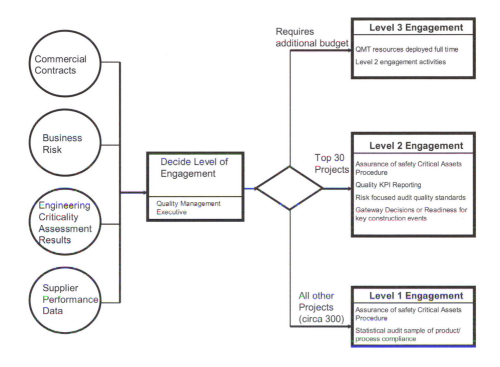

**Figure 8.4 Level of T5 audit engagement**
*Source*: Terminal 5 Project.

Each audit was led by an appointed auditor who was responsible for the detailed planning of the appraisal, involving the audit manager as appropriate. Guidance and reference documents were used in planning the different types of assessment. The requirement for the pre-audit meeting was agreed between the auditor and the auditee. Pre-audit meetings proved to be helpful to both parties as they provided the auditee with a copy of the checklist in advance.

In addition to publishing ongoing audit results, there was also an annual overview of these results which were published along with KPI findings. A sample annual audit results overview (23/03/05 to 29/03/06) included:

- 71 product audits completed
- 66 process audits completed
- 9 readinesses for key stage events completed.

The report also showed red, amber and green findings. For example, process audits included 58 red findings and 133 amber findings. The audit findings were categorised, and reported with green status and typical assurance requirements, as shown in Table 8.2, as an example of product audits for 2005/6.

**Table 8.2    Example of T5 product audit**

| Finding category | Typical assurance requirements | Audits reported green status (%) |
|---|---|---|
| Assurance from supplier audits | Supplier audit schedule has been agreed, planned audits carried out, findings analysed | 37 |
| Work is protected | Products are protected in accordance with planned arrangements | 72 |
| Verified and certified | Inspection and tests have been completed and certificates of compliance have been issued | 62 |
| Production and conformance controlled | Methods statements, inspection and test plans and production control procedures are implemented and non-conformance identified | 21 |
| Samples and benchmarks agreed | Samples, benchmarks and prototypes have been submitted and agreed | 69 |
| Verifications planned | Inspection and test plans meet the requirements of T5 quality management specification | 45 |
| Supply chain management | Lower-tier suppliers have been evaluated and purchasing information includes requirements for approved product, records, processes and equipment | 62 |
| Process approach | The T5 project management system is used as appropriate and T5 quality plan agreed | 51 |
| Requirements managed | Requirements have been established, agreed and communicated | 62 |

*Source*: Terminal 5 Project.

The audit results were also supported by specific recommendations to address non-conformance issues such as:

- Suppliers need to ensure that they audit their own activities in order to provide an adequate level of assurance for both on- and off-site activities.
- Project teams need to enhance supervision to ensure that production and conformance controls are implemented as planned.

The objective of auditing was not just to generate findings, but to bring about improvement in compliance with project requirements. Most of the findings relating to process non-compliance fell into the amber category. Red risks were very serious and this category was not used lightly; the failing was deemed sufficiently serious that project management considered stopping production until corrective action was taken. These findings were notified to appropriate project leaders as soon as possible in advance of the formal audit reports. Data received from auditees in response to audit findings were reviewed by the auditor or the audit manager. After satisfactory mitigation, the result was communicated to the action owner and then the audit finding was considered closed.

### Performance Management

The performance management system of T5 (Little, 2005) is underpinned by well designed KPIs and measures. As shown in Figure 8.5, there are 5 KPIs, 10 key measures and 37 performance data.

The KPIs are selected as high-level quality indicators to steer the major project objectives and requirements. The KPIs, supported by linked key measures, provide overall snapshots to direct the project through enablers, monitoring progress or assuring results. The performance data are the metrics which are measured for each

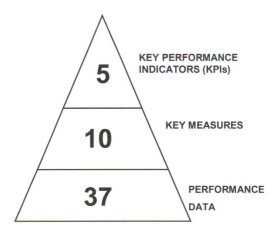

**Figure 8.5    The T5 metrics triangle**
*Source*: Terminal 5 Project.

part of the project by team members, including suppliers, to monitor performance as a target or planned versus actual. Finally, the key measures are the chosen ten measures to be reported and published regularly.

Table 8.3 shows an example of metrics for the manufacturing and assembly stage of the project. Each KPI is linked to relevant key measures and each key measure is supported by a number of performance data.

It is important to recognise that all metrics must be tried and tested with worked out examples. In addition they should be validated by collecting trial data under different conditions before they are communicated to the project team. It is helpful to provide a guidance note for each metric which can then be explained

**Table 8.3    The relationships between key performance indicators, key measures and performance data**

| Key performance indicators | Objectives | Key performance measures | Number of performance measures |
|---|---|---|---|
| 1. Verifications planned and work supervised | Plan to get it right first time (RFT) | 1. Inspection and test plan agreed<br>2. Supervisors RFT trained | 6 |
| 2. Benchmarks agreed | Making quality standards visible and achievable | 3.Samples/ benchmarks agreed | 4 |
| 3. Inspected and protected | Keep work free from error and damage | 4. Inspections meeting benchmarks and quality standards<br>5. Checks showing work and assets are protected | 2 |
| 4. Compliance assured | Provide team assurance that the brief is met | 6. Non-conformance report resolution and cost (NCRs)<br>7. Team certificates of compliance issued | 13 |
| 5. Handover agreed and work complete | Ensure assets are fully integrated and maintainable | 8. Handovers accepted<br>9. O&M manuals accepted<br>10. Maintenance work plans accepted | 12 |

*Source*: Terminal 5 Project.

to team members in workshops to gain their understanding and acceptance. A similar process was followed for T5 performance metrics and a Quality KPI Workbook was prepared. The workbook contained a description and definition of each indicator and measure supported by guidance notes and individual or team responsibilities. For example, each of the KPIs and performance measures (also called data table heading) were supported by guidance notes for data collection and reporting as shown in Table 8.4 for the KPI Verifications planned and work supervised.

In order to clearly assign responsibility and accountability for each KPI, a simple RACI (responsible, accountable, consult and inform) format was used. Each team member or leader, either as an individual or as a team, was aware of their role as a sponsor (responsible), owner (accountable), contributor (consult) or participant (inform). The roll-out and implementation of the balanced scorecard-based performance management for the T5 project was enabled and enhanced by two major initiatives of the project. These were the 'T5 Agreement' and 'Four-tiered approach of quality culture'. As part of the 'T5 Agreement' contractors were responsible for the relevant key performance measures.

**Table 8.4    Guidance notes for KPI: verifications planned and work supervised**

| Performance measures (data table heading) | Guidance notes |
|---|---|
| Inspection and test plans scheduled | Enter the total number of plans required |
| Inspection and test plans due | Enter the accumulative number of plans due to date |
| Inspection and test plans agreed | Enter the accumulative number of plans agreed by team. Refer to CP4 and T5- XXX-QA-00002 for details |
| Supervisors mobilised | Enter the accumulative number of supervisors mobilised |
| Supervisors RFT trained | Enter the accumulative number of supervisors RFT trained |
| Verifications planned and work supervised RAG status | R: ITP or training › 6 weeks late A: ITP or training 0–6 weeks late G: ITP and training meeting target for work in progress |

*Source*: Terminal 5 Project.

Each project team (such as airfield, baggage, rail and so on) recorded, measured and monitored each performance measure and, on a monthly basis, the 10 key performance measures were reported as a balanced scorecard (Kaplan and Norton, 2004). Table 8.5 shows an example of a balanced scorecard.

**Table 8.5    T5 balanced scorecard for December 2007. All figures are percentages**

| Project team | Inspection and test plan agreed | Supervisors RFT trained | Samples/benchmarks agreed | Inspections meeting quality Standards | Checks showing work is protected | NCRs closed | Team certificates of compliance issued | Handover accepted | O&M manuals accepted | Maintenance integration work plans accepted |
|---|---|---|---|---|---|---|---|---|---|---|
| Airfield | 100 | 100 | 100 | 98 | 98 | 97 | 100 | 100 | 84 | 100 |
| Land campus | 93 | 74 | 86 | 87 | 78 | 92 | 86 | 100 | 29 | 100 |
| Completions | 100 | 100 | 100 | 88 | 72 | 92 | 100 | 100 | 51 | 0 |
| Baggage | 100 | 100 | 100 | 76 | 100 | 83 | 67 | 100 | 84 | 100 |
| Rail | 100 | 100 | 100 | 100 | 100 | 100 | 100 | 100 | 100 | 100 |
| TTS | 98 | 100 | 100 | 73 | 71 | 62 | 100 | 0 | 0 | 0 |
| **Overall T5** | **99** | **99** | **99** | **87** | **86** | **92** | **99** | **100** | **66** | **100** |

*Source*: Terminal 5 Project.

The overall T5 results for key performance measures are also presented graphically as the quality management profile, as shown in Figure 8.6.

The key performance measures provide a snapshot of the operation of each project team which were also highlighted by RAG colour codes according to their status with regard to targets. However, improvement projects were acted upon more by individual performance measures at the specific project level. The most significant contributors to improvement projects were Non-conformance reports (NCRs). There were nine performance measures related to NCRs as part of one KPI, viz. compliance assured. These measures enabled the quantification of a part of 'cost of poor quality' (COPQ) given by estimated cost of NCRs. Root cause analyses by type of non-conformance and supplier led to continuous improvement in design, processes and savings. Figure 8.7 shows an example of NCR report analysis.

# Programme
# Quality Management Profile

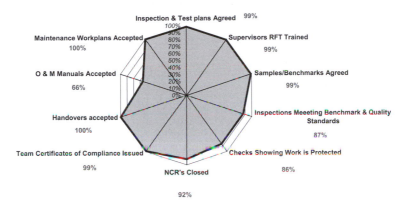

**Figure 8.6     T5 quality management profile**
*Source*: Terminal 5 Project.

**Figure 8.7     Sample NCR report analysis**
*Source*: Terminal 5 Project.

Overall *c*.6000 non-conformance reports were raised on T5, but the accumulative cost of non-conformance was only 0.6 per cent of the budget. Analysis of the data showed that 70 per cent of the total cost of non-conformance resulted from just 150 reports. A no-blame culture resulted in the speedy and effective resolution of all issues.

As discussed above, KPIs and key measures of the T5 project were customised to meet the requirements of the T5 Agreement and the complexity of the project spanning across rail, road and air infrastructures. However, the key balancing principles of the four aspects (financial, customer, internal processes and learning and growth) of the Kaplan and Norton balanced scorecard (Kaplan and Norton, 2004) have been incorporated in the T5 KPIs as shown in Figure 8.8.

In the Kaplan and Norton balanced scorecard, the enabling or leading indicators are 'Financial' and 'Learning and growth'. In the T5 balanced scorecard, the enabling indicators are 'Benchmarks agreed' (which also include some financial benchmarks) and 'Verifications planned and work supervised' (containing supervisors training). As regards the lagging or results indicators, 'Handover agreed and work complete' in T5 relates to the 'Customer' aspect of Kaplan and Norton, while the T5 KPIs, 'Inspected and protected' and 'Compliance ASSURED' relate to the 'Internal process' aspect of Kaplan and Norton.

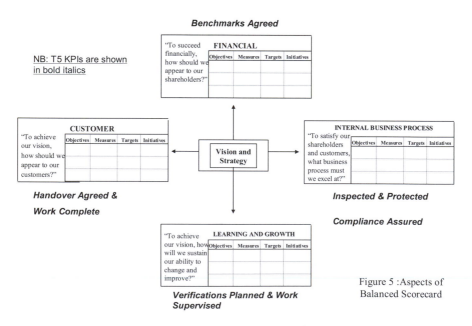

**Figure 8.8    The T5 balanced scorecard**
*Source*: Based on Kaplan and Norton (2004).

On a closer analysis, all the key measures as a group in each of the T5 KPIs do not conform to a specific aspect of the Kaplan and Norton balanced scorecard as shown in Figure 8.8. For example 'Total estimated cost of NCRs', which is a key measure of the KPI 'Compliance assured' also relates to the financial aspect. The matching of the T5 metrics is more appropriate at the level of key measures, as shown in Table 8.6.

**Table 8.6    T5 key measures in the aspects of the balanced scorecard**

| Kaplan and Norton balanced scorecard aspects | T5 balanced scorecard examples of key measures |
|---|---|
| Financial | Samples/benchmarks agreed<br>Total estimated cost of NCRs |
| Customer | Handovers accepted RFT<br>Outstanding work items closed<br>O&M manuals accepted<br>Maintenance work plans accepted |
| Internal processes | Inspections meeting benchmark and quality standards<br>Checks showing work is protected<br>NCRs raised<br>NCRs closed<br>Team certificates of compliance issued |
| Learning and growth | Inspection and test plans agreed<br>Supervisors RFT trained |

*Source*: Present research.

Arguably there are some gaps in the T5 KPIs and key measures related to the 'Financial' and 'Growth' (innovation) aspects, but the manufacturing and assembly stage KPIs would not be expected to address this.

The metrics of the T5 balanced scorecard have been designed to reflect specific requirements of the project as enablers, as well as showing results leading to continuous improvement. The experience of the project team indicates that NCR-related data has been most effective in the identification of the cost of poor quality, to improve design and processes by analysing root causes by task or supplier, and also to attract the attention of the project board.

It is evident from preceding analysis that the fundamental principles of the balanced scorecard have been gainfully adopted and customised to the performance management systems of T5, in order to meet the specific requirements of this complex major project. The best practices of project performance management arising from this case study include:

- Encouraging supplier partnership and proactive involvement of contractors in monitoring and improving project quality and conformance to standards.
- Providing indicators and measures within three main themes as enablers, monitoring progress and showing results along the project life cycle, right up to the handover and completion of work.
- The metrics and processes are validated and then embedded by extensive discussions with stakeholders followed by documentation, communication campaign and training workshops.
- The ongoing testimony of NCRs, supported by the estimation of the cost of non-conformance and improvement projects based on root cause analysis, is a strong point of the process and opens up opportunities for Six Sigma and innovation.
- Suppliers should be empowered to own the monitoring and improvement process using their performance data. Metrics should be customised within the framework of the Kaplan and Norton balanced scorecard.

This case study is an important first step in providing support towards measuring and improving quality standards in major projects. An initial research (Basu, 2008) indicates that in spite of formal quality plans supported by PRINCE 2 and ISO 9000, many projects managed to 'tick many boxes' but failed to deliver expected quality criteria. The performance management system of the T5 project, having learnt from other major ventures, has established a 'best practice' of the application of a balanced scorecard approach in major projects by involving key stakeholders and contractors.

The efficacy of the T5 performance management system complements the audits and also underlines the gap in the five exogenous constructs of the conceptual model (see Figure 6.2). In addition it bolsters the need for performance management as an additional construct. This is in agreement with the conclusions on additional latent variables by Temme, Paulssen and Dannewald (2008).

## Organisation Effectiveness

The T5 project was given the go ahead on 20 November 2001 after 46 months of a public enquiry and consultation, the longest in British history. The project leadership was taken up by BAA (the owner/operator of Heathrow Airport) and Terminal 5 was built for British Airways as the project client and customer. During the long enquiry period, BAA went through training initiatives on other airport projects (such as Hong Kong airport) and previous large-scale infrastructure projects (such as the Jubilee Line Extension and the Channel Tunnel).

Figure 8.9 shows the high-level organisation structure of the T5 Project and the structure of quality management within this organogram.

Although BAA already possessed core project teams and technical leadership formed by their own employees, the project deployed around 100 key contractors and consultancy firms including three major contractors. Fundamental to the success of the supplier partnership was the T5 Agreement. The idea was to free consultants and contractors from the financial risk and in return empower them to manage and mitigate this risk. To this end, BAA took out a single insurance policy to cover the whole of the multibillion pound project. For the workers too, the project set the benchmark for construction pay. The ideas for this agreement emerged while plans for T5 were being scrutinised under the long-running public enquiry. As a result of the T5 agreement, each contractor must be totally open in their business dealings and firms like Balfour Beatty and Crown House shared information with each other, even though they were working on different parts of the project.

The head of quality, as part of the technical leadership department of BAA, was responsible for enabling and assuring the process quality of the scheme. Project group leaders of four main project groups were responsible for delivering the product quality of the completed work.

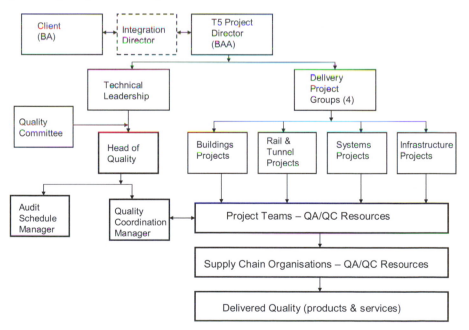

**Figure 8.9    T5 project organisation structure**
*Source*: Terminal 5 Project.

Each project group (such as rail and tunnel) had its own quality coordinators who worked alongside the quality coordination manager, who in turn reported to the head of quality. As part of the T5 agreement, suppliers within supply chain organisations provided QA/QC (quality assurance/quality control) resources who liaised with quality coordinators of the respective project teams. The audit schedule manager reported to the head of quality and managed both multidiscipline audit teams and independent surveillance teams. In order to clearly assign responsibility and accountability for each function, a simple RACI (responsible, accountable, consult and inform) format was used. Each team member or leader, whether as an individual or as a team, was aware of their role as either a sponsor (responsible), owner (accountable), contributor (consult) or participant (inform).

The role of the integration director appeared to be complex. This position was reported to be responsible for assuring 'cost, time, quality and safety' at Terminal 5 and also to manage the integration of 100 IT systems to airport operations, flight information boards, human resources information and administration systems (T5 Supplement, December 2006). To supervise the integration, a separate test centre was constructed and a series of trial runs were planned to ensure that all passenger services worked on the day T5 opened. There were also five large-scale passenger trials to 'flood' T5 with 2000 people acting as travelling passengers. The integration director was also the managing director of Heathrow airport, and acted as the link between the T5 project management (BAA) and client (BA).

In spite of these preparation plans, Terminal 5 opened on 27 March 2008 with the very public failure of its much-lauded baggage system. The terminal's sole resident, British Airways (BA), had failed to properly prepare its employees for the handover of 70 per cent of its operations to the new building. With staff unable to get into position to carry out their tasks, it was not long before the baggage system choked and had to be shut down. According to one newspaper report,

> *BA and BAA ran 75 trials with a total of 15,000 would-be passengers, yet due to the need to keep the rest of organisation running concurrently, only 50 (5%) or so of the baggage handlers were fully trained on T5 equipment. Training for the majority of the 6,500 BA employees involved a day tour of the terminal and a couple of hours of watching reels about the impact of the change.* (Financial Times, *5 April 2008*)

## Operational Excellence Concepts and Applications

The literature review clearly indicated the benefits of applying operational excellence concepts in major projects. These concepts include TQM, Six Sigma, Lean Thinking and supply chain management.

The T5 project did not apply the Six Sigma approach. It is arguable that if Bechtel had been chosen as a major contractor, then the likelihood of applying Six Sigma in T5 would have been high, and this could have enhanced the interface between BAA and BA during the launch of T5. Limited green belt training workshops were conducted for Heathrow operations but these were not extended to the T5 project teams. The presence of a TQM culture was evident in the four-tier approach to training but it was different from the rigour of Six Sigma deployment. A feasibility study of the application of EFQM was conducted at the early stage of the project and then aborted. This study report was not available for this research, and the reason for the failure to apply EFQM was not explained.

The much-applauded T5 Agreement made with suppliers underpins some key ingredients of both Lean Thinking and supply chain management in major projects. A supply chain management function was incorporated into the T5 Project organisation to make the best of the supplier partnership in the procurement of supply and services. In addition, this T5 Agreement:

- had an emphasis on teamwork and joint problem solving;
- had a joint risk management, problem solving and planning infrastructure;
- stated that the suppliers' profits were ring-fenced on top of openly audited costs, eliminating claims for extra payments;
- was deliberately written in a non-adversarial style.

Furthermore, in spite of its size, T5 had links with lean and agile development, as shown in the following examples:

- *The use of prototyping activities*. The roof of the T5 building, with a span of 150 metres, is one of the largest in Europe. BAA decided to trial the erection off-site, documenting the lessons learnt, leading to a three-month schedule saving when the roof was erected *in situ*. This use of prototyping is one of the core techniques of agile thinking.
- *The use of Lean principles*. Work on the site was arranged according to a 'demand-led' or 'pull' system, where materials are delivered on a just-in-time basis. This constitutes one of the central tenets of Lean Thinking.
- *The use of iterative techniques*. By using an expert joint review team, BAA is able to give approval for the construction of a feature to start before its design is complete. This is similar to agile software-development techniques where expansion starts before all the requirements are known.

## Self-assessments and Knowledge Management

There were no specially designed self-assessment checklists in the T5 project to identify gaps, quality processes and required skill levels. A copy of the audit checklist was sent in advance to the auditee by the auditors, and the pre-audits following the checklist were the only considered form of self-assessment. This process was limited to the compliance of audit requirements, and therefore did not offer a comprehensive self-assessment method. The absence of an EFQM-based evaluation process also showed the weakness and vulnerability in quality procedures in areas which were not covered by quality KPIs or audits.

As described earlier, the training and communication aspects of the T5 project were enabled and enhanced by its two major initiatives. These were the T5 Agreement and the four-tiered approach of quality culture. As a result of the T5 Agreement, BAA shouldered the financial risk and expected the consultants and suppliers to work together. People from all stakeholders were encouraged to raise issues at the earliest opportunity. This in turn enhanced the reporting and discussions on performance and non-conformance issues. 'When you align people's objectives, stuff happens. The agreement has allowed us to work with our consultants and suppliers in a refreshing new way', observed Andrew Wolstenholme, the T5 project director.

As shown in Figure 8.10, an interrelated four-tier approach (Millard, 2005) of embedding quality culture to project team members and suppliers was introduced in 2005.

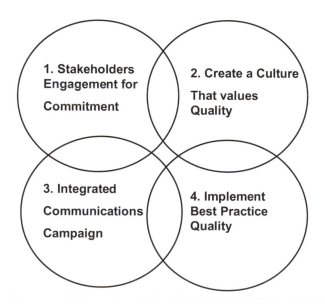

**Figure 8.10   The T5 four-tier approach**
*Source*: Terminal 5 Project

This four-tier approach is an ongoing process and is primarily driven by focussed discussion groups and workshops. The stakeholders engagement and commitment process is supported by the project executive commitment to engage with project leadership and suppliers (principals), and to introduce a RFT quality concept to ensure their buy-in and commitment. The culture and behaviour change process has been iterative, comprising regular workshops, briefing, awareness and feedback on quality KPIs and an RFT behavioural change programme. Quality certificates were awarded for site supervisors, and eventually site workers, who attended RFT workshops. This was further supported by the third-tier communication campaign, which included quality logo branding, quality commitment workshops, quality booklets, a quality walkabout and quality awards and posters. The fourth tier on quality best practice started with research and interviews with experts to establish best practices and align them with quality KPIs. This was followed by supervisor training and workshops to ensure understanding and ownership from supervisors.

There was a common safety education programme that aimed to make every individual accountable for safety. Everyone on site, from designers and managers, to supervisors and operatives, was given training on how to work safely. The project was supported by a journal called *T5* which published selected articles to communicate general progress and best practices. The project team also shared best practices with industry (namely the BMW Mini plant in Oxford), professional bodies (the Major Projects Association) and major infrastructure projects (the Channel Tunnel Rail Link High Speed 1 Project).

# CHAPTER 9

# CHANNEL TUNNEL RAIL LINK HIGH SPEED 1 PROJECT (HS1): CASE STUDY

## PROJECT BACKGROUND

In 1996, London and Continental Railway (LCR) was awarded the concession to build the Channel Tunnel Rail Link (CTRL) which was later known as the High Speed 1 (HS1) project. Union Railways (UR) was allocated the responsibility to act as the client or sponsor of the project, and Rail Link Engineering (RLE) was appointed as project manager. RLE was a consortium of construction companies formed between Arup, Bechtel, Halcrow and Systra.

HS1 is the first new railway in England for over 100 years and the first high-speed railway (capable of 300 kmph) ever in the UK. It comprises 100 kilometres between London and the Channel Tunnel near Dover, with three stations and two depots. At the height of construction in 2001, the combined workforce of UR and RLE was over 1000, and at the closure stage the figure was 350. The completed £5.8 billion project (excluding the regeneration budget) opened on time and within budget. The scheme was split into two areas. Section 1 was started in 1998 and runs between the Channel Tunnel and Ebbsfleet (near Gravesend) in Kent. It completed on time and on budget in 2003. Section 2 comprised primarily the activities in the north to south network from St Pancras, and was delivered for commercial operation to Eurostar on 14 November 2007.

The original objectives of the project included:

- To provide the main high-speed railway link between Britain and continental Europe.
- To provide the transport spine and stimulus to the rejuvenation of the derelict inner city areas around Stratford and Kings Cross.

### Quality Management Systems and Procedures

The project sought to ensure that quality was built in from the start. A project-specific quality strategy, designed from existing best practices of the member companies of the consortium, was submitted within the agreed three months of the award of the concession. The knowledge and experience of project methodology (e.g. PRINCE2 and PMBOK) of the partners in the consortium was incorporated into documents as appropriate.

The quality approach of RLE (the project manager), was part of the overall execution plan drawn up by UR (the client). The HSE strategy as shown in the documentation structure is given in Figure 9.1.

The quality strategy aimed to ensure that quality was defined and measurable, and that processes were established and implemented to ensure and demonstrate conformance. The approach included audits and surveillance activities as an independent check to ensure that the defined requirements of the client were achieved. The UR execution strategy was directly linked to a separately specified Health, Safety and Environment (HSE) plan of the project. The HSE strategy ensured that all relevant statutory safety and environmental requirements were met with due regard so that risks were reduced to a level that was as low as reasonably possible.

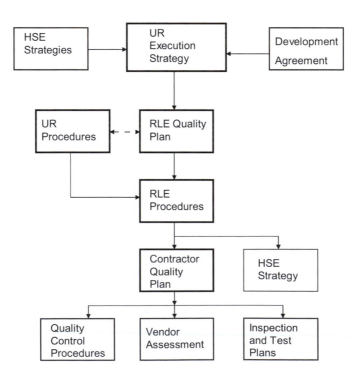

**Figure 9.1    HS1 quality management documents structure**
*Source*: High Speed 1 Project.

The quality policy statement established the project's quality commitments including compliance with ISO 9001, and the quality strategy established the compliance with development agreement requirements. The RLE quality plan was underpinned by detailed procedures and instructions and contractor quality plans. RLE procedures were drawn up in compliance with UR procedures where appropriate. These documented processes included:

- RLE procedures to ensure self-certification by contractors
- Audit programmes
- Procedures for process quality control
- Vendor assessment
- Inspection and test plans.

The RLE head of quality was responsible for monitoring all aspects of the above strategy and systems, in addition to managing the overall audit process. The head of quality had direct access, if necessary, to the managing director of UR. As project manager, RLE certified that all the works specified in the contract were completed, so that two weeks later the works were taken over by UR, the client. This Client Acceptance Process (CAP) was controlled by UR's procedures. Based on the fulfilment of the CAP, the head of quality certified compliance to achieve Permit to Use (PtU).

## Quality Audit and Compliance

Three types of audit processes were applied for when conducting the management systems audit on the HS1 project. An additional aim was to ensure quality and environment, health and safety audits as follows:

- **Level 1 audits**: designed for auditing management systems related to RLE senior management and major contractors. Auditors were drawn from RLE, UR and the contractor's corporate organisations.
- **Level 2 audits**: designed for auditing management control systems related to subcontractors and associated RLE middle management. Auditors were drawn from contractors and RLE.
- **Central audits**: conducted by internal auditors of RLE for auditing design and procurement processes.

Each type of audit has well-defined practices supported by detailed process charts in three key stages (Rail Link Engineering, 2005):

- Programming and planning
- Execution
- Follow-up and close out.

Figure 9.2 shows a simplified flow diagram of the key stages of the audit process for all three types of audit.

The programming and planning of each type of audit starts with a 12-month audit programme at the beginning of each year, and auditors are nominated from each discipline. A Consolidated Audit Plan (CAP) for assessment every three months is e-mailed to interested parties. The plans are updated regularly at the monthly audit coordination meetings. Appropriate checklists are prepared and audit briefs are issued 30 days before each appraisal. The auditors attend a pre-closing meeting to review and agree audit findings and prepare Corrective Action Requests (CARs) and observations of good practice. A CAR form comprises three parts: section A is for recording agreed findings, section B deals with corrective deeds while section C concerns the action taken. The follow-up and closure stage includes closing meetings where corrective procedures in section B are agreed, and in subsequent closing meetings the 'action taken' box in section C is monitored and completed.

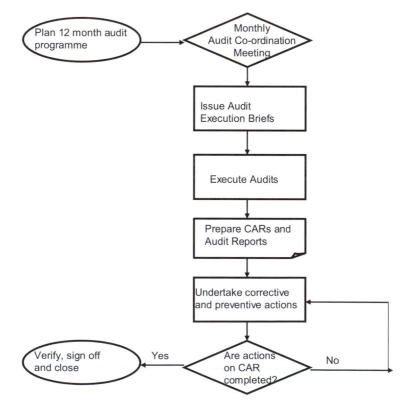

**Figure 9.2    A simplified flow diagram of the HS1 audit process**
*Source*: High Speed 1 Project.

The audit process is supported by a number of well-designed documents and forms. These include:

- *CAP*: the planned dates of three monthly audits are transferred from the annual audit plan to the CAP. The dates are shown on a three-month calendar in the CAP which also contains details on the company or site for audit, the persons responsible and duration.
- *Audit brief*: 30 days prior to the planned audit date, the audit brief is agreed and issued. This remit covers the scope of the audit for systems/process, product and management and takes into account the progress of work and any issues at the time of audit.
- *Audit checklist*: there are pre-designed checklists and guidelines for each type and stage of the audit, but specific checklists are prepared or updated that are appropriate to the brief and scope. The list is prepared in a simple format containing item, requirement, document reference, code (e.g. N – Nonconformity, A – Acceptable, O – Observation), and finding.
- *CAR*: as indicated earlier, this is an important document to record and monitor audit results during the execution and closure stages of the audit and contains three sections (A, B and C).
- *Observation record*: this is used for recording observations particularly related to points of good practice.
- *Audit report*: each audit is supported by a summary audit report with notes on CARs, observations and an annotated checklist of questions. The audit report is agreed for issue within 15 days of closing meetings.

The robustness of HS1 audit processes is underpinned by the involvement of the project team (RLE), client (UR) and major contractors. Government-appointed contactors and auditors (e.g. Mott McDonald) are also involved in 'spot auditing'. The key indicators from the audit reports compare and validate the relevant recorded KPIs and thus ensure the monitoring and evaluation of management systems in place and the general progress of the project.

During the sign-off at each stage of the project, the detail specifications and documents were checked by a compliance review group. This group was made up of representatives of RLE, UR, Network Rail and Eurostar. Compliance data and documents were stored in a specially designed database called DOORS (Dynamic Object Orientated Requirement System). As well as providing access to procedures, it also contained a mass of technical information to assist the team in working efficiently. Compliance data with agreements with key stakeholders were monitored by the UR executive every six months.

It is evident from the preceding analysis that the fundamental principles of project audits and health checks have been gainfully adopted and customised to the monitoring and evaluation management systems of HS1, in order to meet the specific requirements of this complex major project. The best practices of project audits and health checks arising from this case study include:

- Assessing the need of auditing management systems and project progress to design audit processes at appropriate levels. This covers the project teams, major contractors and subcontractors.
- Detailed design and documentation of audit processes supported by process charts, a checklist, audit brief, audit notification and audit forms.
- Involvement of key stakeholders in the audit process including government, client, project teams and contractors. This has the effect of thus encouraging the supplier partnership and the proactive involvement of contractors in monitoring and improving project quality and conformance to standards.
- Audit processes and checklists to span across the key aspects of project deliverables including health and safety, environment, quality, design and procurement.
- Aligning the audit processes with the project execution strategy, executive reports, health checks and EFQM-based self-assessment.

This case study is an important first step in providing support towards measuring, monitoring and improving safety and quality standards in major projects. The audit strategy and processes of the HS1 project, having learnt from other major undertakings, have established a 'best practice' of the application of monitoring and evaluation of management systems in major projects. This has been done by involving major stakeholders and contractors.

## Performance Management

The performance management processes of the HS1 project are centred round key progress reports (e.g. the URN executive report and the RLE progress report). These accounts applied selected KPIs to monitor performance in safety, progress, costs, risks and quality assurance and audits.

Safety was given the highest priority in project management and safety measures were dealt with first. Two KPIs for safety were Accident Frequency Rate (AFR) and Lost Time Accidents (LTA). Both AFR and LTA indicators were measured by the project group and also by site, electrical, rail and plant, and were reported for the period and cumulative. As an example, the executive report ending May 2007 stated that 53.3 million site hours were expended during which LTA was only 194 and AFR was 0.21.

The performance management systems operated continuously from the start of the project. A project-specific management system was designed from existing best practices of the member companies and was submitted to the government. The design standards and processes were developed and discussed between the client (UR) and project management (RLE) and were referred to as the project progressed.

As indicated above, the project applied selected KPIs in the monthly reports and these were jointly reviewed by the client and project manager. The key performance indicators are listed in Table 9.1.

The monthly reports, including the above KPIs, were compiled by both RLE and UR from their databases and earned value analysis. The reports and KPIs were not identical and were prepared from two different data sources. When these accounts are reviewed jointly, they are both beneficial in that they identify more gaps for improvement, but also disadvantageous due to the problems created in the reconciliation from different data sources. It is evident that the systems and KPIs were not structured around the four aspects of the balanced scorecard. A balanced scorecard approach was applied to one single project (Contract 430 Section 1 by Skanska). Massive data were collected and monitored for concrete cover details, but the approach failed because it was too detailed, and it was not extended to the whole project.

**Table 9.1    HS1 key performance indicators**

| |
|---|
| Programme progress |
| Planned % complete |
| Actual % complete |
| Installation release notices (plan vs. actual) |
| Compliances (% sign off) |
| No. of permits to use (PtU) deliverables |
| Safety and environment |
| Accident frequency rate (AFR) |
| Lost time accident (LTA) |
| Closure of environmental NCRs |
| Risk management |
| Top risks this period |
| Top risks last period |
| Quality |
| Non-conformance reports (NCRs) |
| Overdue corrective action requests (CARs) |
| Six Sigma cost savings |
| Costs |
| Budget variance |
| Cost forecasting |
| Cost performance (earned value analysis) |

*Source*: High Speed 1 Project.

The absence of a balanced scorecard-based performance management system in HS1 shifted the dependence of performance monitoring to the rigorous and frequent audit processes at various levels. This apparent weakness of the performance management system supports the rationale for a well-designed performance management system as an additional construct for the conceptual model.

## Organisation Effectiveness

When the LCR was awarded the concession to build the Channel Tunnel Rail Link (CTRL), the UK Parliament provided the framework of the project in December 1996. As indicated earlier, the core organisation structure (see Figure 9.3) is underpinned by the client and project manager relationship and roles. LCR allocated the responsibility to UR to act as a client for the CTRL project. UR then appointed RLE as the project manager of CTRL. The two entities, UR and RLE, worked in partnership to deliver the project.

Each of the consortium members of RLE (viz. Arup, Bechtel, Halcrow and Systra) possessed specific expertise, and together they covered the skills necessary for the design, development, procurement, construction and commissioning of the railway and associated infrastructure. UR as the client provided the interface with key stakeholders who were the parties affected by the CTRL, including the

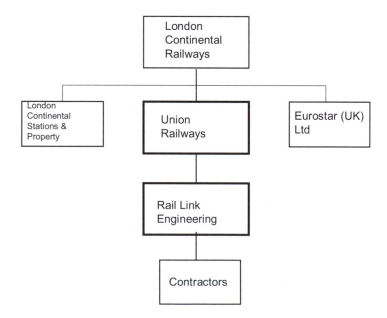

**Figure 9.3    CTRL HS1 core organisation structure**
*Source*: High Speed 1 Project.

government, planning authorities, statutory environmental agencies, highway authorities and ultimately, the operators (Eurostar and Network Rail). RLE constituted the interface with contractors and suppliers.

UR and RLE jointly established a project structure whereby each entity had a clearly defined role and responsibility. This approach prevented duplication and ensured a partnership approach, evidenced by the joint mission statement and objectives signed by both parties. UR and RLE possessed a combined workforce of around 350 full-time employees. UR staff were recruited over a number of years to fulfil the requirement of project delivery, while RLE staff were drawn from the parent companies as and when required. The two organisations were virtually mirror images of each other with clear lines of communication (see Figure 9.4).

The government project representatives had members of its team located in the project head office near St Pancras, and also had access to construction sites and to project information on the designated intranet. The co-location allowed continual and informal contact with 'opposite numbers', supported by meetings and correspondence as necessary.

Although there was no general partnership concurrence made with contractors (just like the T5 agreement), formal agreements with each contractor were drawn up following the legal framework of New Engineering Contracts 2 (NEC). These contracts included the so-called 'Z clauses' of NEC, such as Z16 for transferring

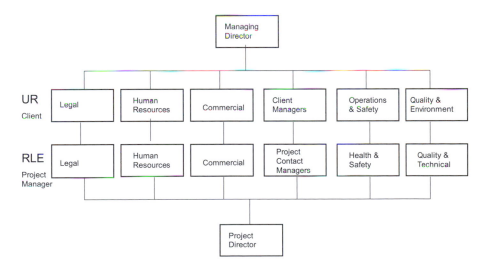

**Figure 9.4    CTRL HS1 detail organisation structure**
*Source*: High Speed 1 Project.

work scope to others in the event of non-performance by the contractor. A culture of openness and transparency had been developed by providing common access to project documents through the 'InfoWorks' electronic document storage and management system.

The strong points of the HS1 project organisation effectiveness are centered on the clear role and partnership between UR as Client and RLE as Project manager, and the interfaces with stakeholders by UR. The roles of UR and RLE are summarised in Table 9.2.

**Table 9.2    Roles of client (UR) and project manager (RLE) in HS1**

| Union Railways (UR) roles | Rail Link Engineering (RLE) roles |
|---|---|
| Client | Project manager |
| Preparation of client brief and preliminary design | Detailed design and engineering of client brief |
| Management of stakeholder interfaces | Management of contractors and construction interfaces |
| Land acquisition programme | Procurement |
| Compliance to client brief | Project management of construction |
| Budget and overall contingency | Project delivery and operation |

*Source*: High Speed 1 Project.

Dealing with stakeholder interfaces (including 14 local authorities and 6,500 neighbours) of the railway project was a complex undertaking by UR. The client and stakeholders had numerous activities to assume both during and after RLE completed their work. In order to manage this, UR developed the project's Integrated Client Programme (ICP). The ICP was a programme of high-level activities that involved interfaces between the project and stakeholders including Eurostar, London and continental stations and properties. On a four-weekly basis the activities in the programme were reviewed with stakeholders and then updated as necessary. On 14 November 2007 the Queen formally opened the high speed line of HS1 from St Pancras. By this date, only three contracts worth £50 million out of a total £5.2 billion were not fully closed due to the fact that work for 'snag lists' arising from IPC reviews was still in hand.

## Operational Excellence Concepts and Applications

Bechtel was the first major engineering and construction company to adopt Six Sigma, a data-driven approach to improving efficiency and quality, in major projects. On big rail modernisation projects in the UK, including the HS1 project,

Bechtel teams used Six Sigma to minimise costly train delays caused by project work, and in so doing reduced the break-in period for renovated high-speed tracks.

The introduction of Six Sigma to the HS1 project delivered both cost savings and programme benefits. The Six Sigma programme trained 23 black belts and around 250 green belts and yellow belts. A further 100+ senior managers were educated to act as champions in improvement projects. Over 500 such improvement projects were completed, which in turn led to a cost saving/avoidance of at least £40 million. These projects covered and benefited a wide range of activities across the whole of HS1 undertaking including numerous architectural, civil and railway construction endeavours. Consequently this had the effect of ensuring timely third-party methodology approvals, facilitating procurement, accelerating drawing reviews and allowing the timely generation of construction record documentation. It is evident that some of the improvement projects, such the reduction of lead time in methodology approvals and drawing reviews, also applied Lean Thinking concepts.

UR and RLE jointly submitted qualification reports to the British Quality Foundation (BQF) for an EFQM Award. These documents were submitted in two sections – Part 1 comprising enabling factors (such as leadership, policy and strategy, people, partnership and resources and processes) and Part 2 detailing results factors (such as people, customers, society and KPIs). The proposal was assessed externally by qualified EFQM assessors from the BQF and the HS1 project received the EFQM Award in 2007. The evaluation revealed more strong points of the project in the realm of the enabling factors but weaker aspects in the results factors. The HS1 project also received the 'Project of the Decade' award in February 2008 from the London Transport Awards.

The application of supply chain management concepts was relatively limited in the HS1 scheme. Individual contractors managed their own supply chain and procurement. The benefits of a single supplier and centralised procurement (for example for lining segments) were achieved in the tunnelling project.

## Self-assessments and Knowledge Management

As part of the HS1 audit strategy, pre-audit health checks were conducted by site teams using the same audit brief and checklist. These pre-audits helped the preparation of the appraisal at each site, and also ensured that the auditees completed the outstanding section B (for agreed corrected action) of CAR forms with scheduled completion dates.

In addition to the pre-audit health checks, the project team (RLE), client (UE) and contractors developed a self-assessment culture as part of their qualification for EFQM accreditation. However, there was no specially designed checklist for self-assessment, only the EFQM criteria were applied. Following appropriate training, periodic health checks were carried out for both enabling and performance criteria of EFQM, and the HS1 project was awarded the British Quality Foundation Excellence Award in 2007. Self-assessment was used primarily to meet EFQM requirements but not to identify skill gaps for people development.

When project leaders identified the need to recruit a new member to the team, suitable candidates from member companies were sought. All positions had job descriptions detailing education, skills and experience requirements. The member companies had extensive people resources worldwide and a wide range of specialist skills were available when needed. A survey in early 2007 showed that 23 nations were represented in the venture. According to an internal report, the project worked in excess of 82 million hours without any time lost due to industrial relation disputes.

A clear distinction was made between training specific to the delivery of the endeavour, which was funded by the project and training for personal development, and career progression which remained the responsibility of member companies. A good example of project-specific education was the comprehensive approach to health and safety training including site inductions. Instruction in Six Sigma was given to 250 people who were also empowered to identify problems, create a business case, investigate the difficulties and instigate improvements.

Member companies of RLE had their own process for dialogue and sharing best practices. For example, Bechtel used an employee forum with the minutes made available on their own Bechtel intranet. Arup employed a similar process known as 'Airtime'. Presentations were regularly given by leaders on the progress of the project with a summary of successes and the challenges that ahead.

Even after the opening of St Pancras on 14 November 2007, HS1 maintained a skeleton project team for over six months to ensure the legacy and sustainable outcome of the scheme.

## A COMPARATIVE ASSESSMENT OF THE T5 AND HS1 PROJECTS

Both Heathrow T5 and the Channel Tunnel Rail Link HS1 projects have enjoyed high-profile media and public attention in recent years in the UK, and showed some remarkable similarities in their project background and project management best practices. For example, both schemes went through several years of public review before approval. Both were major infrastructure projects comprising rail, roads, buildings and systems linking London with the outside world. HS1 was split into two major aspects: Section 1 (between the Channel Tunnel and Ebbsfleet) and Section 2 (north to south network from St Pancras). Similarly, T5 was also divided into two phases: the T5 A and B buildings as Phase 1 and the T5 C building as Phase 2. Both were mega projects with multibillion pound spends (HS1 had £5.8 billion and T5 with £4.3 billion). Section 2 of HS1 was completed with the opening by the Queen at St Pancras on 14 November 2007, and then a few months later, the Queen opened Heathrow Terminal 5 on 27 March 2008.

With this similar background, what is the comparative assessment of project quality and excellence-related best practices between these two projects? Also, under the six components of project quality and excellence, how do these case studies help to explain and support the research questions?

In line with the conceptual research model and further analysis of the two case studies, a checklist for the Assessment of Project Excellence, named APEX, has been developed under the six major constructs/components/categories of project quality and excellence as follows:

1.  Quality management systems and procedures
2.  Quality audits and compliance
3.  Performance management
4.  Organisation effectiveness
5.  Operational excellence concepts and applications
6.  Self-assessments and knowledge management.

As shown in Table 9.3, each component comprises five questions or items in the checklist. This checklist has been carefully constructed on the basis of findings from the literature review, field research and case studies.

**Table 9.3    Assessment of Project Excellence (APEX) checklist**

| Descriptions | Poor 1 | Fair 2 | Good 3 | Very good 4 | Excellent 5 |
|---|---|---|---|---|---|
| **Quality management systems and procedures** | | | | | |
| 1.1. Formal quality management systems and procedures for the project team are in place | ☐ | ☐ | ☐ | ☐ | ☐ |
| 1.2. Formal quality management systems and procedures for suppliers/contractors are in place | ☐ | ☐ | ☐ | ☐ | ☐ |
| 1.3 Project team members and suppliers are trained and they understand and accept quality management systems and procedures | ☐ | ☐ | ☐ | ☐ | ☐ |
| 1.4 Quality management systems and procedures follow the guidelines of project methodology of PRICE2 or PMBOK or BS6079 or ISO 10006 | ☐ | ☐ | ☐ | ☐ | ☐ |
| 1.5 Quality management systems and procedures are applied effectively in project management by team members and suppliers. | ☐ | ☐ | ☐ | ☐ | ☐ |
| **Quality audit and compliance** | | | | | |
| 2.1 Formal quality audit procedures are in place covering design conformance, process conformance and supplier deliverables | ☐ | ☐ | ☐ | ☐ | ☐ |
| 2.2 Audit processes are explained and communicated to project teams and suppliers before the commencement of an audit | ☐ | ☐ | ☐ | ☐ | ☐ |
| 2.3 Audit team includes members from quality, safety, project team, contractors and users as appropriate | ☐ | ☐ | ☐ | ☐ | ☐ |
| 2.4 Audit process is supported by well-designed documents, check lists, documents, reports and continuous improvement | ☐ | ☐ | ☐ | ☐ | ☐ |
| 2.5 Compliance of requirements of the project brief is carried out with the client at key stages of project sign-off by using an agreed format of key operational requirements | ☐ | ☐ | ☐ | ☐ | ☐ |
| **Performance management** | | | | | |
| 3.1 Performance management system is structured around the principles and four aspects of the balanced scorecard | ☐ | ☐ | ☐ | ☐ | ☐ |
| 3.2 The key performance indicators reflect both enabling and delivered measures | ☐ | ☐ | ☐ | ☐ | ☐ |
| 3.3 Performance management system spans across project groups and key suppliers | ☐ | ☐ | ☐ | ☐ | ☐ |
| 3.4 Performance management system is aligned with gateway or milestone reviews | ☐ | ☐ | ☐ | ☐ | ☐ |
| 3.5 Performance management system is aligned with audit, self-assessment and continuous improvement | ☐ | ☐ | ☐ | ☐ | ☐ |

| Descriptions | Poor 1 | Fair 2 | Good 3 | Very good 4 | Excellent 5 |
|---|---|---|---|---|---|
| **Organisational effectiveness** | | | | | |
| 4.1 Organisation structure includes steering team (project board), project teams and support team with a dedicated quality manager and budget for quality | | | | | |
| 4.2 High priority is given for client relations and stakeholder management | | | | | |
| 4.3 The coordination of contractors and subcontractors is ensured by supplier partnership agreements | | | | | |
| 4.4 There is a defined role of HR supported by job descriptions of project team members and RACI is used for relevant tasks related to the work breakdown structure | | | | | |
| 4.5 Softer critical success factors such as leadership, communication and user involvement are embedded in organisation culture | | | | | |
| **Operational excellence concepts** | | | | | |
| 5.1 Proactive application of Six Sigma concepts in a cost-effective programme | | | | | |
| 5.2 Recognition of the supply chain management principles, with dedicated resources if appropriate, in procurement, forward planning and supplier partnership | | | | | |
| 5.3 Appropriate application of maturity or excellence models such as EFQM | | | | | |
| 5.4 Proactive application of Lean Thinking in minimising non-value-added activities and process cycle times | | | | | |
| 5.5 Evidence of processes and initiatives to instil TQM culture (especially if Six Sigma is not applied) within project teams and suppliers | | | | | |
| **Self-assessment and knowledge management** | | | | | |
| 6.1 In line with quality audit, performance management and maturity or excellence models there is evidence of well-structured checklists for holistic health checks | | | | | |
| 6.2 Evidence of regular self-assessment to identify and follow up areas of continuous improvement | | | | | |
| 6.3 Continuous education and training to share and enhance skills, process and systems knowledge of project team members and suppliers | | | | | |
| 6.4 Well-designed and managed media such as website, newsletter and billboards to communicate best practices and key messages | | | | | |
| 6.5 There is evidence of proactive planning and communication processes to achieve -asting outcomes and legacy | | | | | |

Legend:

Score

T5 project     114 (76%)

HS1 project     121 (81%)

*Source*: Present research.

There are 30 questions in total (5 questions in each category) which are ranked on a scale of 1 to 5 where 1 = not important and 5 = most important. The overall figures (out of the maximum grade of 130) for the T5 and HS1 projects were 114 (76 per cent) and 121 (81 per cent) respectively. The average scores in each category for both projects are shown in Table 9.4 and presented graphically in Figure 9.5. These results will be called APEX Scores.

**Table 9.4      APEX Scores for T5 and HS1 projects**

| Category | T5 project | | HS1 project | |
|---|---|---|---|---|
| | Total | Average | Total | Average |
| Quality management systems and procedures | 20 | 4 | 21 | 4.2 |
| Quality audit and compliance | 20 | 4 | 24 | 4.8 |
| Performance management | 23 | 4.6 | 14 | 3.0 |
| Organisational effectiveness | 21 | 4.2 | 22 | 4.4 |
| Operation excellence concepts | 13 | 2.6 | 20 | 4.0 |
| Self-assessment and knowledge management | 17 | 3.4 | 19 | 3.8 |
| **Overall** | **114 (76%)** | **3.80** | **121 (81%)** | **4.05** |

*Source*: Present research.

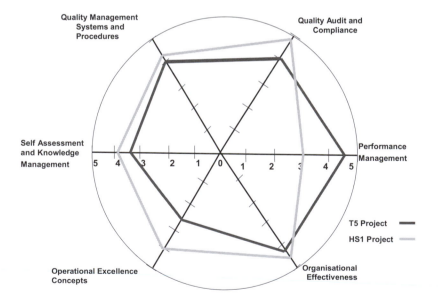

**Figure 9.5      The APEX chart of T5 and HS1 projects**
*Source*: Present research.

The rationale of scoring and the specific strengths of the T5 and HS1 projects are discussed in the following section under the six major constructs/components/ categories of project quality and excellence.

## Quality Management Systems and Procedures

Both the T5 and HS1 projects had well-structured and documented quality management guidelines to cover quality planning, quality assurance, quality audit and control and quality improvement of project teams as well as suppliers. As indicated in the case study, the primary focus of quality in the T5 project is the quality assurance of suppliers governed by the quality requirements specification and team execution plan. Furthermore, the quality procedures were continuously reviewed with formally structured forums which allowed the information and decision process to be cascaded up and down the project quality organisation.

In the HS1 undertaking, a project-specific quality management system was designed from existing best practices of the member companies of the consortium. The Bechtel experience of PMBOK and Arup's knowledge of PRINCE2 were reported to be incorporated in detail procedures. The quality policy statement also established that the project's quality commitments were in compliance with ISO 9001 in the development agreements of contractor quality plans.

This constitutes a strong area of both projects, and thus the scores varied between 'very good' and 'excellent'.

## Quality Audit and Compliance

The processes and execution of the HS1 project excelled in the area of quality audit and compliance. As indicated earlier, the fundamental principles and best practices of project audits and health checks have been gainfully adopted and customised to the monitoring and evaluation management systems of HS1, in order to meet the specific requirements of this complex major undertaking.

The T5 project also exercised a robust audit process at three levels. As indicated earlier, the robustness of the T5 Audit processes was underpinned by the decisions made by the quality management executive to determine the appropriate levels, risk focus, safety, gateway decisions and readiness for key construction events. The audit results were also linked to performance management and improvement priorities.

This also represents a strong area for both projects. The HS1 scheme in particular demonstrated additional strength and rigour in assessing compliance and was, on the whole, an outstanding example of project audit and compliance.

## Performance Management

The T5 project demonstrated excellent processes and key performance indicators, incorporating a balanced scorecard approach in managing project performance. This is an exceptional example of the application of a properly designed performance management system in a complex project. As indicated earlier, the best practices of project performance management arising from this case study included the encouragement of the supplier partnership, and the proactive involvement of contractors in monitoring and improving project quality and conformance to standards.

Performance management forms a relatively weak area for the HS1 project. Key performance indicators were focused on monitoring time, cost and safety and were not based on a balanced scorecard approach. The emphasis appeared to be more on control after the event (supported by an excellent audit process), rather than assurance and prevention of non-conformance.

Thus this represents is a strong area for T5 and but a weak zone for HS1.

## Organisation Effectiveness

This is another strong field for both projects. The organisation structure of both the T5 and HS1 projects included a steering team (project board), project teams and a support team with a dedicated quality manager and budget for quality.

An additional strong point of the T5 project was its T5 agreement, which was fundamental to the success of the supplier partnership. It appeared that BAA, with its established capital projects department, was in a better position to sustain good relationships with major contractors. The HS1 venture, although not so robust in its supplier partnership agreement, had a consortium under the umbrella of RLE. A major asset of the HS1 organisation was the role of UR as client acting as an effective interface with powerful customers like the government, Rail Track/Network Rail and Eurostar. It can be argued that in the case of the T5 project, the role of the integrator director as the interface between BAA and BA did not work well, and could be a contributing factor to the problems at the T5 terminal during the early stage of its operations.

This is an area where both projects scored very well and could do even better by complementing and emulating each other.

## Operational Excellence Concepts

There was evidence of the excellent application of Six Sigma and EFQM in the HS1 project. As described earlier, Bechtel teams used Six Sigma to minimise costly train delays caused by project work and thus reduced the break-in period for renovated high-speed tracks. The introduction of Six Sigma to the HS1 project delivered both cost savings and programme benefits.

The application of supply chain concepts could be further improved in the HS1 project, while supply chain management was a particularly strong suit in the T5 venture. As indicated earlier, a supply chain management function was incorporated into the T5 project organisation to make the best of supplier partnership in the procurement of supply and services. However, T5 missed the opportunity of applying Six Sigma and EFQM, although the culture of Lean Thinking was evident.

Hence, this is an area where the HS1 project was significantly stronger than that of T5.

## Self-assessment and Knowledge Management

Both T5 and HS1 showed workable processes of periodic self-assessment (prior to the audit schedules) and training programmes. This self-assessment was arguably more structured in the HS1 project with the support of checklists from EFQM.

The T5 project introduced an interrelated four-tier approach of embedding a quality culture to project team members and suppliers. In the HS1 plan, training specific to the delivery of the scheme was funded by the project, and education for personal development and career progression remained the responsibility of member companies. Both projects also established their own process for dialogue and sharing best practices. This then can be seen as a good area for both projects.

## APEX MODEL

As discussed above, one significant practical outcome of this research is the development of an APEX (Assessing Project Excellence) model. Qureshi et al (2009) conclude that by conducting an empirical study and checking the impact, a simplified excellence model has the potential to be used as a framework to assess project management performance. The 30 questions in this model have been derived from this research, and supported by the best practices of the T5 and HS1 projects. The questions are comprehensive regarding project quality and excellence, but they are not so exhaustive that they could claim to carry out a holistic assessment of all aspects of project management; it is not intended as a substitute for EFQM or a CMMI type of assessment. However, it is simple, interactive and user-friendly and focused on self-assessment. Even the organisations planning to apply for accreditation by external excellence and maturity models can benefit from using APEX as a first step towards achieving project excellence goals.

The guidelines for considering each question is given in Appendix 1. These guiding principles are focused primarily on major projects and there could be variations depending on the type and size of a scheme. As described by Grude, Turner and Wateridge (1996), the results can be analysed individually, both within and between groups. When analysing within groups, it likely that, in spite of guidelines, there could be variations in the scoring of each question. This variance can be calculated as follows (Grude, Turner and Wateridge 1996):

$$\text{Variance V} \quad = \quad \Sigma \, (x - X)^2 \, / \, N$$

Where

x is the individual score
N is the number of people in the group
X is the mean score for the question, $X = \Sigma \, x \, / \, N$.

When there is a high variance – two or greater according to Grude, Turner and Wateridge (1996) – there is major disagreement among members and the reason for such divergence should be explored. However, the intention of this model is a qualitative exercise to encourage self-assessment, and not to achieve quantitative results focusing on statistics and parameters such as confidence limits.

In order to ease the scoring and assessment process, APEX™ has been developed and is described in Appendix 2.

## EXPLORATORY AND EXPLANATORY FINDINGS

As indicated earlier, the two case studies adopted both exploratory and explanatory approaches (Yin, 2003). The findings from the exploratory approach identified the best practices followed in the T5 and HS1 projects and responded to 'what' questions, while the exploratory approach responded to 'how' questions and established its results from the questionnaire survey and PLS modelling. Tables 9.5 and 9.6 respectively summarise the main findings from the exploratory and explanatory approaches.

It is to be noted that the strengths of T5 were the gaps in HS1 and, likewise, the strong processes of HS1 were missing in T5. According to Yin (2003), exploratory objectives of case study research relate to the exploration of a phenomenon through 'what' questions, and also develop hypotheses or propositions by analytical induction. Eisenhardt (1989) emphasises the importance of the development of theory in exploratory studies, while Marshall and Rossman (1989) support the need for a better understanding of processes in exploring case studies. The exploratory objectives in this research were focused on seeking and understanding best practices relevant to research questions in the T5 and HS1 projects. A comprehensive list of best practices emerged by adopting the strengths from both the T5 and HS1 projects.

**Table 9.5    Summary of exploratory findings**

| Case study | Main strengths | Main gaps |
|---|---|---|
| Terminal 5 | Balanced scorecard-based performance management system Suppler partnership and T5 agreement Supply chain management in major projects | Weak client role (British Airways) in project organisation Absence of EFQM and Six Sigma |
| High Speed 1 | Strong client role (Union Railways) in project organisation Application of EFQM and Six Sigma in major projects Retaining a follow-up project team after the formal opening of St Pancras | Absence of balanced scorecard-based performance management system Less formal application of supply chain management |

**Table 9.6    Summary of explanatory findings**

| Constructs | Terminal 5 | High Speed 1 |
|---|---|---|
| Quality management systems | Well-structured and documented quality management guidelines to cover quality planning, quality assurance, quality audit and control and also quality improvement of the project teams as well as suppliers | Well-structured and documented quality management guidelines to cover quality planning, quality assurance, quality audit and control and also quality improvement of the project teams as well as suppliers |
| Audit and compliance | A robust audit process at three levels | Excelled in the area of quality audit and compliance |
| Performance management | Demonstrated excellent processes and key performance indicators incorporating a balanced scorecard approach in managing project performance | Key performance indicators were focused on monitoring time, cost and safety and not based on a balanced scorecard approach |
| Organisation effectiveness | The organisation structure included steering team, project teams and support team with a dedicated quality manager and budget for quality supported by T5 agreement for supplier partnership | The organisation structure included steering team, project teams and support team with a dedicated quality manager and budget for quality |
| Operational excellence concepts | Supply chain management as a particularly strong area | Evidence of excellent application of Six Sigma and EFQM |
| Self-assessment and knowledge management | Workable processes of periodic self-assessment, prior to the audit schedules, and training programmes | Workable processes of periodic self-assessment, prior to the audit schedules, and training programmes and a strong client relationship to sustain longer-term outcomes |

There are no fixed recipes for building or comparing explanations (Yin and Heinsohn, 1980). According to Campbell (1975) and Yin (2003), the search for enlightenment from cases is a kind of pattern matching process. Saunders, Lewis and Thornhill (2007) explain Yin's pattern matching (2003) and suggest the need to establish a conceptual framework, and then test the adequacy of that framework in case studies. In this research, the conceptual research model (see Figure 6.2) was taken as the conceptual framework for the pattern matching and explanation building of constructs. For three constructs – quality management systems, audit and compliance and organisation effectiveness – the pattern of processes and their implications in both the T5 and HS1 projects matched well. The pattern also compared closely for self-assessment and knowledge management. This matching of constructs strengthens the internal validity of the conceptual model. Two other constructs – performance management and operational excellence concepts – were 'complemented' in two projects. In other words, the strength in one project in these two constructs appeared as gaps in the second one. Yin and Heald (1975) applied aggregation of factors of case studies to explain urban decentralisation. The aggregate of combined factors from the T5 and HS1 projects in all six constructs provides explanations and logical patterns to support the requirements of the constructs for project quality and project excellence.

The above pattern matching and explanation building processes have helped to link the case study data to support the propositions. The resulting constructs of the conceptual model (see Figure 6.2) are summarised below:

- The matching of four constructs in case studies – quality management systems, audit and compliance, organisation effectiveness and self-assessment and knowledge management – supports the corresponding constructs in the conceptual model.
- The strength of the construct operational excellence concepts in HS1 supports the corresponding construct in the model. It is argued (Holmes and Whelan, 2009) that the absence of Six Sigma in T5 might have contributed to the problems during the opening of the terminal.
- The strength of the construct performance management in T5 underlines the gap in the construct quality, compliance and measures in the conceptual model (see Figure 6.2). This supports the rationale for an additional construct in the model.

## CONCLUSIONS

The case studies of the T5 and HS1 projects have contributed not only in explanatory analyses of research questions and propositions in the present research, but also to the knowledge and best practices in project quality and excellence. The key conclusions include:

- Both projects are contemporary flagship schemes in building sustainable transport infrastructures in south-east England and show remarkably comparable project characteristics.
- The case studies have explained the definition and dimension of qualities, and also the impact of the application of excellence models and operational excellence concepts in major projects. These examples and explanations have helped to answer four research questions and also to support three propositions.
- The best practices of both projects have identified their strong points and shortcomings in the components of project quality and excellence. These strengths and gaps appeared to complement each project. For example, the T5 venture could have improved its organisation effectiveness by adopting a more robust client role as occurred in the HS1 project, and could have significantly benefited by the application of operational excellence concepts such as Six Sigma and EFQM. Likewise, the HS1 project could have gained from the application of the balance scorecard-based performance management system and supplier partnership (i.e. the T5 Agreement) and supply chain management that occurred in the T5 project.
- The case study of T5 in particular has supported the need for an additional construct (performance management) in line with the conclusions on additional latent variables by Temme, Paulssen and Dannewald (2008).
- The case studies have helped to develop a 6-category and 30-question-based, simple but effective process called APEX to assess the key constructs of project quality and excellence. This self-assessment process could be used as the first step of a 'health check' to identify strengths and weaknesses in managing quality and excellence in a major project.

The analysis of the practical data of both T5 and HS1 projects has helped to support the conceptual model (Figure 6.2) and the findings of the results from semi-structured interviews, questionnaire survey and PLS modeling. Furthermore these case studies have identified practical pointers to the success of future major infrastructure projects such as HS2 and London Airport extensions.

# CHAPTER 10

# IMPLEMENTATION: HOW TO MAKE PROJECT QUALITY AND PROJECT EXCELLENCE HAPPEN

## INTRODUCTION

In the preceding chapters, the importance of appropriate strategy and practices for assessing project quality and excellence has been further supported by field research. The results of the research have also identified and verified some specific strengths and weaknesses of current practices related to quality and excellence in major projects. There is little argument that the management of all major projects needs further improvement, and therefore the recommendations arising from the findings and conclusions of this study should add value to the knowledge and business of project quality management.

In this chapter a summary of key recommendations is presented and these are also reflected in the checklist in the APEX model (see Appendix 2). The recommendations are followed by an implementation plan of managing quality in major project.

## RECOMMENDATIONS

These recommendations are aimed at all types of major projects including infrastructure projects.

### Quality Management Systems and Procedures

Formal quality management systems and procedures for the project team should be in place before the implementation phase of the project. The quality management systems and procedures for suppliers/contractors should also be established. Quality management systems and procedures should follow the guidelines of the project methodology of PRINCE2 or PMBOK, and also the proven practices of company standards and delivered projects. The training programmes in both T5 and HS1 have helped to inculcate quality management systems, beyond just ticking boxes, to project team members.

In fact, both project team members and suppliers should be trained as well as ensuring that they understand and accept quality management systems and procedures. It is also important that these quality management systems and procedures are applied effectively in project management, both by team members and suppliers.

## Quality Audit and Compliance

Formal quality audit procedures should be in place covering the three realms of design conformance, process conformance and supplier deliverables. It is vital that audit processes are explained and communicated to project teams and suppliers before the commencement of any audit.

Audit teams should include members from the areas of quality, safety and the project team, in addition to contractors and users as appropriate.

The audit process should be well supported by effectively designed documents, checklists, reports and continuous improvement.

It is also important that compliance with the requirements of the project brief is carried out with the client at key stages of project sign-off by using an agreed format of key operational requirements

## Performance Management

A performance management system should be structured around the principles and four aspects of the balanced scorecard. The key performance indicators should reflect both enabling and delivered measures.

It is vital that a performance management system spans across project groups and key suppliers. It must be aligned with gateway or milestone reviews (MSP, 2007) and also with audit, self-assessment and continuous improvement.

## Organisational Effectiveness

Organisation structure should include the steering team (project board), project teams and a support team with a dedicated quality manager and budget for quality. This budget for quality should be above 0.5 per cent of the project spends as found in T5 and HS1 projects.

It is critical that high priority is given for client relations and stakeholder management (such as the HS1 organisation). The coordination of contractors and subcontractors should be ensured by supplier partnership agreements (such as the T5 agreement).

HR should have a clearly defined role supported by job descriptions of project team members. The RACI process is used for relevant tasks related to work breakdown structure.

It is important to recognise that softer critical success factors such as leadership, communication and user involvement are embedded in organisation culture.

## Operational Excellence Concepts

Proactive application of Six Sigma concepts should be pursued as a cost-effective programme. Even if there is no formal application of Six Sigma, there should be evidence of processes and initiatives in order to instil a TQM culture within project teams and suppliers.

Secondly, there should be a clear recognition of the supply chain management principles, with dedicated resources if appropriate in procurement, forward planning and supplier partnership.

Also important is the appropriate application of maturity or excellence models such as EFQM or IPMA.

Finally it is vital to demonstrate the proactive application of lean thinking in minimising non-value-added activities and process cycle times.

## Self-assessment and Knowledge Management

In line with quality audit, performance management and maturity or excellence models, there is evidence of the value of well-structured checklists to perform holistic health checks. The APEX (Assessing Project Excellence) model should also be considered to complement these health checks.

There should be evidence of regular self-assessment to identify and follow up areas of continuous improvement. Moreover, continuous education and training need to occur in order to share and enhance the skills, process and systems knowledge of project team members and suppliers.

It is also necessary to have a budget and appropriate resources to ensure the application of well-designed and managed media such as a website, newsletters and billboards. All of these methods can be employed to communicate best practices and key messages.

For major infrastructure projects, there should be a separate group installed at least six months before the project closure focusing on longer-lasting outcomes and legacy for cultural, economic and environmental objectives. This group should also continue its activities with the operational team a few months after the project closure.

## IMPLEMENTATION

The above recommendations provide foundations of a quality management strategy in managing projects. These are based upon the guidelines in PMBOK (2008) and PRINCE2 (2009) and tempered by a literature review, field research and case studies. Regardless of the quality programme that a project organisation may choose to adopt, a selection of a structured approach will be essential to make things happen. 'Quality is not something you install like a new carpet or a set of book shelves. You implant it. Quality is something you work at. It is learning process' (Deming, 1986). We should acknowledge that owning the best of golf clubs does not make one a Tiger Wood, nor by borrowing the racket of Pete Sampras does one win a Wimbledon title. The success depends on the skills of the players, developed by rigorous training and practice. Therefore, it goes without saying that the employees from the top to bottom of a project organisation, especially the key players, should be provided with the right level of education and training to ensure that their knowledge and understanding for the tools and techniques of quality management are appropriate for the specific process and application.

Here we provide a proven pathway, primarily based on the case studies of T5 and HS1, for implementing a quality management programme in major projects from the start of the initiative to the closure of the project, embedding the change to a sustainable organisation-wide culture. The framework of a quality management programme is shown in Figure 10.1 and described below. Note the emphasis on each step of the programme could vary depending on the type, size and complexity of the project.

### Step 1: Develop a Quality Management Organisation and Plan

A key task for the project board is to appoint an independent quality manager reporting to top management as early as possible. The following mega projects all had an independent quality function set up either at the initiation phase or at the design and appraisal phase of the project:

- In Channel Tunnel the quality director reported directly into the chief executive and this allowed an independent reporting on the overall performance of both British and French project teams.
- In HS1 a Quality and environment director reported directly to the managing director of the client organisation (Union Rails).
- In Heathrow Terminal 5 the head of quality was independent of production issues and also monitored performance of contractors.

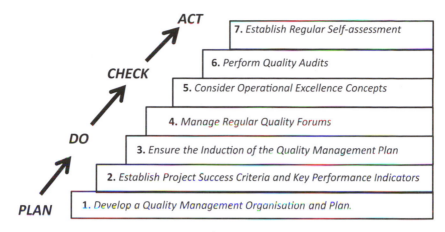

© Ron Basu

**Figure 10.1    Framework of a project quality strategy implementation**

- In Dutch High Speed Line also quality was an independent function which monitored both the QC and QA activities.

Our experience is that it is essential to allocate a quality budget (over 0.5 per cent of project spends) and convince the CEO and at least a third of the board with the scope and benefits of project quality, before launching the quality management plan. The success rate of a 'back door' approach without the endorsement of the key players cannot be guaranteed. If a quality is not wholly supported by senior management it is not a recommended strategy. In cricketing terms a CEO can open the batting, but a successful opening stand needs a partner at the other end. Senior management can learn from the experience of established major projects, and indeed there can well be mutual benefits for the project organisations organisation through an exchange of visits. A new project organisation also benefits from quality management experience of members recruited from successfully completed major projects. During the development of the management awareness phase it is useful to produce a board report or 'white' paper summarising the findings and benefits of a quality management plan. There are useful guidelines in ISO 10005 (International Standards Organisation, 2005) to justify the vital needs of a quality plan for the benefit of top management:

a) to show how the organisation's quality management system applied to a specific case;
b) to meet statutory, regulatory or customer requirements;
c) in developing and validating new products or processes;
d) to demonstrate, internally and/or externally, how quality requirements will be met;

e) to organise and manage activities to meet quality requirements and quality objectives;

f) to optimise the use of resources in meeting quality objectives;

g) to minimise the risk of not meeting quality requirements;

h) to use as a basis for monitoring and assessing compliance with the requirements for quality;

i) in the absence of a documented quality management system.

The objectives of a quality management plan should aim to provide assurance that assets are safe, reliable and meet quality requirements (product quality) and also to work efficiently and effectively so that products are delivered on time and budget (process quality). An implicit objective is also to ensure that the requirements are understood and accepted by key stakeholders (organisation quality).

The quality systems requirements are clearly documented as a quality plan for the first-tier suppliers and an essential document to accompany the invitation to tender. The key requirements should include:

1. The first-tier suppliers should implement within four weeks of the starting date a quality management system based on the best practices of ISO 100005 and ISO 9001.

2. In addition the first-tier suppliers should conform to specific project quality requirements of the client determined from the operational criticality, functional safety and the risk that the development and installation of the system may present to the timescale and cost of the project.

3. The first-tier suppliers shall set out a plan to demonstrate how their quality management system integrates with the client's requirements and provide quality management inductions to its subcontractors and suppliers.

4. The first-tier suppliers shall participate with the client in regular quality forums, quality audits and provide periodic progress reporting of quality management activities.

5. The first-tier suppliers shall appoint a quality manager who is a key person as a condition of contract and will be independent of the design and construction functions.

6. The inspection and test activities of the first-tier suppliers shall demonstrate compliance with the client's and also regulatory requirements. Certificates of compliance shall be issued to confirm that the plan has been actually implemented.

The core requirements of the quality plan for the first-tier suppliers should also be embedded into the main quality plan of the client. In preparing the quality plan the specific roles and responsibilities of each quality requirement, both within the project organisation and external stakeholders, should be clearly stated.

An example of a quality management plan is shown in Appendix 3.

## Step 2: Establish Project Success Criteria and Key Performance Indicators

As discussed in Chapter 4, the success criteria should of the project should be agreed with the sponsor and key stakeholders at the start of the project. Grude, Turner and Wateridge (1996) suggest success criteria in generic categories as follows:

- Commercial success
- Meets user requirements
- Meets budget
- Happy users
- Achieves purpose
- Meets timescale
- Meets quality
- Happy team.

If the above categories are further grouped into the 'four perspectives' of the balanced scorecard (Kaplan and Norton, 1996) these could as shown below:

- Financial perspectives
  - Commercial success
  - Meets budget
- Customer perspectives
  - Meets user requirements
  - Achieves purpose
- Internal processes perspective
  - Meets timescale
  - Meets quality
- Learning and growth perspective
  - Happy users
  - Happy team

It is a good practice to identify and agree with key stakeholders KPIs grouped into the four perspectives of the balanced scorecard (see Table 8.7). The metrics of project success criteria should be at two levels. At the top level they may be called Key performance measures which are reviewed during milestone review meetings. The second level metrics known as KPIs support the key performance measures and are reviewed during quality forums. Key performance indicators should include metrics to assess training, safety and environment standards. First-tier suppliers should be empowered to own the monitoring and improvement process using their performance data.

## Step 3: Ensure the Induction of the Quality Management Plan

Having developed the quality management plan and KPIs the next stage is to ensure that key stakeholders understand and agree with the requirements in the plan and the metrics. The induction programme could be conducted on two levels. First a half-day workshop to introduce the plan and indicators to the project board and the senior members of the first-tier suppliers. This should be followed by a number of one-day workshops for team members from the client organisation and major suppliers. It expected that the details of the both the quality plan and KPIs, with omissions and inclusions, would be refined during the induction sessions.

Without the induction workshops the key stakeholders are not likely to buy-in to the quality plan and the indicators. Consequently in spite of the existence of a well-designed quality plan with KPIs the quality management processes in the project could result as an imposed 'ticking boxes' exercise.

## Step 4: Manage Regular Quality Forums

Induction workshops are one-off at the early stage of the project while quality forums should be conducted at regular intervals, usually every month, during the total life cycle of the project. Quality forums are organised and led by the quality managers and participants include project manager, team leaders and quality leaders, from both the client and major suppliers. The agenda of a quality forum could include:

- Critical assets
- Key performance indicators
- Non-conformance reports
- Inspection and test plans
- Acceptance reports
- Self-certification by suppliers.

A quality forum is a vital component of organization quality in managing projects. It not only ensures communications and agreement of key stakeholders of quality issues from the same page but also helps to inculcate a quality culture across the project organisation.

## Step 5: Consider Operational Excellence Concepts

As discussed in Chapter 6, there are three main concepts of operations excellence which are successfully being applied in managing project quality and project excellence, and these are:

- Excellence models
- Supply chain management
- TQM, lean and Six Sigma.

Excellence models form a part of regular self-assessment and are covered in Step 7. Supply Chain Management (SCM) can reside as function on its own but it is important to establish a close interface between SCM and quality management, especially related to the procurement of goods and services. All invitations to tenders and contract should conform the quality management plan described in Step 1 above.

TQM, lean and Six Sigma are interrelated concepts and inextricably linked to the management of quality in projects. These concepts are now merged into Lean Sigma or FIT SIGMA initiatives and as discussed in Chapters 7 and 8 the application of Lean Sigma or FIT SIGMA in projects is at an early stage. In larger projects lasting over two years the initial investment of training black belts and green belts is justifiable without any dispute. When a Lean Sigma or FIT SIGMA programme is fully embedded in a major project it not only identifies and delivers data-driven projects within the project, it also enhances the organisation quality and improves communications amongst key stakeholders.

## Step 6: Perform Quality Audits

A quality audit process ensures the conformance and compliance of standards established by the quality management plan and KPIs. An additional aim is to ensure environment, health and safety requirements. The audit process of the High Speed 1 project (see Chapter 9) is a benchmark of best practices where three types of audit processes were applied:

1. Level 1 audits: designed for auditing quality management systems related to senior management and major contractors. Auditors were drawn from both the client and first-tier suppliers.
2. Level 2 audits: designed for auditing quality management control systems related to subcontractors and associated middle management. Auditors were drawn from contractors and the client.
3. Central audits: conducted by internal auditors of the client for auditing design and procurement processes.

Each type of audit has well-defined practices supported by detailed process charts in three key stages, such as programming and planning, execution, follow-up and close out. The audit process is supported by a number of well-designed documents and forms as described in Chapter 9

## Step 7: Establish Regular Self-assessment

The regular review of KPIs can only identify the measurable quality standards. Even quality audits can help to flag the conformance of the quality management plan and inspection test results. There are many intangible parameters of quality and enablers of project success that cannot be easily detected by KPIs or audit reports. These include leadership, project strategy, partnerships with suppliers, motivation of team members and stakeholders engagement to name a few. Therefore it is important to establish a holistic self-assessment checklist and regular review process to pinpoint gaps and training requirements related to intangible factors. The checklist can be derived from EFQM or even P3M3, as discussed in Chapter 5. However, it is strongly recommended that the checklist should be adapted to the specific requirements of the project. The APEX model (see Appendix 2) could be a starting point to establish the checklist for self-assessment. The review should be carried out every three or four months.

The outcome of the self-assessment is to identify gaps mainly in intangible enablers and also assess skills and training requirements to address these gaps. A well-designed and administered self-assessment process acts as a powerful tool towards achieving sustainable outcomes leading to project excellence.

It is to be noted that more effort and management time are required to develop the implementation at the early stages of the project life cycle. Step 6 may precede Step 5 if there be doubts about the timing of operational excellence. During the execution and closure stages the deliverables of the quality plan must be overseen by the client quality team, although the quality assurance requirements are largely ensured by the self-certification process of the first-tier suppliers, as illustrated in Figure 10.2.

## WAY FORWARD

It is hoped that the ideas, processes, recommendations and implementation plan presented in this book will assist the project leaders and quality managers to manage quality beyond the generic guidelines available in PMBOK (2008), PRINCE2 (2009) and ISO 10005 (International Standards Organisation, 2005). The field research and case studies are supporting data to validate the contents of this book. An outline of an implementation plan is also provided in this chapter to assist the practitioners beyond the guidelines in bodies of knowledge. However, it a part of a continuous learning process aiming towards further improvement and it is recognised that 'the devil is in the detail'.

It is important to note that the results of the field research reported in this book have some limitations especially related the scope of quality, assumptions and responses from the online survey.

Project Board Objectives

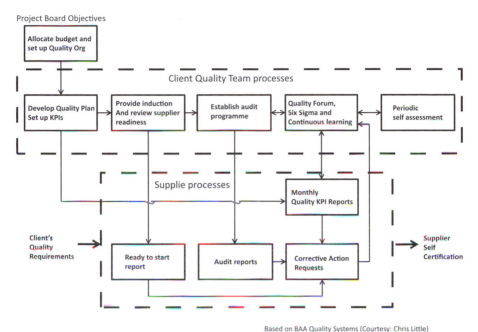

Based on BAA Quality Systems (Courtesy: Chris Little)

**Figure 10.2    An example of quality management processes in a major project**

The scope of this book is primarily focused on major and contemporary infrastructure projects in the UK. It is expected that the general conclusions of this research could be extended judiciously to other major projects in the UK. However, it is questionable whether these same conclusions should equally apply in the context of another culture. For example, the organisation quality strategy of the London 2012 Project may not be comparable to that its predecessor, the Beijing 2008 Olympic Project. Accordingly replication studies across different countries, sectors and types of projects are encouraged.

Another area of constraint is the assumption of keeping the factors related to cost, time, risk and safety as independent of project quality and excellence. As such, no specifically designed constructs related to these factors are included in the instruments of this research. There are some academic publications examining the links between cost and quality (Abdelsalam and Gad, 2009), between safety and quality (Ling. Liu and Woo, 2009), between risk and quality (Zou, Zhang and Wang, 2007) and time and quality (Luu, Kim, Tuan and Oguntana, 2009). Further studies could address this limitation. They would need to assess the impact of the recommendations of this research – in relation to project quality and project excellence – on the opportunities and risks in the three key domains of cost, time and safety.

The next area of limitations concerns the sample and responses from the online survey. For example, 34 per cent of the projects in the sample were under £10 million and so not considered as 'major' projects. Furthermore, 49 per cent of the projects were related to 'technology and other' and thus not categorised as infrastructure or construction projects. The qualification of a major project as 'spends over £10 million' is far removed from the billions of pounds being spent on infrastructure projects. The sample size of 73 responses has satisfied the minimum requirement (Hair, Babin, Money and Samouel, 2003; Saunders, Lewis and Thornhill, 2007) and also the reliability of the PLS model. However, it is still considered a small sample from a relatively large population of practioners in project and quality management in the UK. Given a larger sample size, further analyses and comparison of results by type and size of projects could have been investigated. Furthermore, the outcomes related to project quality and project excellence from two consumer/passenger-focused projects such as T5 and HS1 could have been tested. This could be achieved by a carefully designed questionnaire-based survey on passengers at Heathrow and St Pancras respectively.

The construct for 'Quality Audit, Compliance and Measures' in the existing PLS model (Figure 7.8b) was partly supported by PLS-Graph simulations. The case studies of HS1 and T5 demonstrated the strong presence of both audit and compliance and performance management within this construct. Further research can be carried out by incorporating two latent variables (e.g. 'audit and compliance' and 'performance management') supported by additional reflective indicators to replace this construct in the PLS model.

An important area to explore will be the validation of findings and conclusions across other types of major projects in the UK, especially major ICT projects. The research can also be extended to encompass different cultural environments in Europe, North and South Americas, Africa, Australia, the Middle East and Asia. Even though the fundamentals of the project quality and excellence model may prevail, there are bound to be many specific requirements related to the type of projects as well as local priority and culture.

The scope of research can be expanded by including constructs related to cost, time and risk to incorporate a conceptual research model on project quality and project excellence. A quantitative model of cost–benefit analysis could also constitute an area of further research.

The case studies supported the rationale of including performance management as an additional construct to complement the gap in the construct quality audits, compliance and measures in the PLS model (see Figure 7.8b). Although the rationale for an additional construct is in agreement with Temme, Paulssen and Dannewald (2008), further research is recommended in the PLS model with an additional construct to bolster this finding.

The 'softer' issues relating to organisation quality and organisation effectiveness also need further investigation. For example the issues of emotional intelligence (Goleman, 1996) and organisation intelligence (Dulewicz and Higgs, 2005) could be further explored.

Further research could also be extended to explore the 'nine schools of thought' in project management research (Anbari, Bredillet and Turner, 2008) and to include business as an additional school as follows:

| School | Metaphor | Key idea | Came to prominence | Influence |
|--------|----------|----------|--------------------|-----------|
| Business | The project as an enterprise | Deliver values and sustainable outcomes to stakeholders | Late 2000s | Organisation quality, supply chain and operational excellence |

As a final thought, the book has, by virtue of its subject matter, read rather like a technical report at times. So in closing, I would like to offer you by contrast a little literary analogy. If we consider that *design quality* and *process quality* are like sections of a piece of prose then organisation quality is the poetry of project management. By extension *project excellence* creates a lasting epic poem. So my advice to you is, plan a project in prose, practise in poetry and excel by delivering an epic poem.

# ONLINE QUESTIONNAIRE

## SECTION 1: INTRODUCTION

### 1.1 Would you describe the size of your project/programme as:

Duration

- Over 5 years
- 2–5 years
- 2 years
- Under 1 year

Budget

- Over £1 billion
- £500 million–£1 billion
- £100 million–£500 million
- £10 million–£100 million
- £1 million–£10 million
- Under £1 million

### 1.2 Would you classify your project/programme primarily as:

- Major construction
- Transport
- Advanced technology
- Information technology
- Business transformation
- Major event
- New product delivery
- Other

If Other please specify

## 1.3 Would you describe your project/ programme in:

- Manufacturing sector
- Building industry
- Service sector
- Public sector
- Public–private partnership
- Other

## 1.4 What is the budget for quality management allocated to each project (as percentage of total project spend) £:

- No budget
- Less than 0.1%
- 0.1–0.3%
- 0.3–0.5%
- Above 0.5%

## SECTION 2: DEFINITION OF QUALITY

## 2.1 In the context of your project/programme you would define project quality as:

(Show in a scale from 1–5, where 1 = not important, 2 = somewhat important, 3 = important, 4 = very important, 5 = most important.)

- Meeting the design specifications and requirements
- Delivering project/programme on time and within budget
- Delivering what the client and sponsor want
- Giving more emphasis on outcome than output
- Giving more emphasis on sustainability and legacy
- Other

If Other please specify

Comments

## 2.2 In the context of your project/programme your primary focus on the dimensions of quality is:

(Show in a scale from 1–5, where 1 = not important, 2 = somewhat important, 3 = important, 4 = very important, 5 = most important.)

- Design quality
- Process quality
- Organisation quality
- Design and process quality
- Design, process and organisation quality
- Other

If Other please specify

(*NB*: Design quality relates to product and specifications, process quality relates to service and conformance and organisation quality relates to people and longer-term outcomes.)

Comments

## SECTION 3: QUALITY IN PROJECT MANAGEMENT

## 3.1 In the project organisation project quality is the responsibility of:

- Project manager
- Dedicated quality manager
- Project planner
- External auditor
- Team members
- Not defined
- Other

If Other please specify

Comments

### 3.2 Pinpoint how you monitor project quality and performance

(Show in a scale from 1–5, where 1 = not important, 2 = somewhat important, 3 = important, 4 = very important, 5 = most important)

- Use key performance indicators (KPIs)
- Follow balanced scorecard principle
- Use milestone tracking
- Apply 'health check' checklist
- Apply independent auditing
- Other

If Other please specify

Comments

### 3.3 You set the quality standards and guidelines in your project/programme by:

(Please choose only ONE option and show in a scale from 1–5, where 1 = not important, 2 = somewhat important, 3 = important, 4 = very important, 5 = most important)

- No formal quality plan
- Quality plan based on PRINCE2
- Quality plan based on BS 6079
- Quality plan based on ISO 10005
- Quality plan based on PMBOK/BOK
- Company quality standards
- Other

If Other please specify

Comments

## SECTION 4: PROJECT SUCCESS CRITERIA AND FACTORS

### 4.1 For the last most significant project/programme in which you have been involved please rate important criteria of success:

(Show in a scale from 1–5, where 1 = not important, 2 = somewhat important, 3 = important, 4 = very important, 5 = most important)

- Meets budget
- Delivered on time
- Meets design requirements
- Meets process requirements
- Happy sponsors and clients
- Happy users
- Happy team
- Sustainable outcome
- Other

Comments

### 4.2 For the last most significant project/programme in which you have been involved please rate important factors of success:

(Show in a scale from 1–5, where 1 = not important, 2 = somewhat important, 3 = important, 4 = very important, 5 = most important)

- Sponsor and top management support
- Project leadership
- Stakeholder management
- Communication and team building
- Appropriate tools and techniques
- Appropriate quality plan
- Planning and monitoring
- Clear objectives
- Other

Comments

## SECTION 5: PROJECT EXCELLENCE AND MATURITY

### 5.1 Have you used in the significant projects in which you have been involved to assess project effectiveness or excellence:

(Show in a scale from 1 -5, where 1= not important, 2= somewhat important, 3= important, 4= very important, 5 = most important)

- OPM 3 model
- CMMI model
- EFQM based excellence model
- Customised checklist
- Other
- Not used at all

If Other please specify

Comments

## SECTION 6: OPERATIONAL EXCELLENCE IN PROJECTS

### 6.1 For the significant projects/programmes in which you have been involved you have applied operational excellence (OE) initiatives such as:

(Show in a scale from 1–5, where 1 = not important, 2 = somewhat important, 3 = important, 4 = very important, 5 = most important)

- Total quality management
- Six Sigma
- Lean thinking
- Supply chain management
- Other

If Other please specify

Comments

## SECTION 7: CONCLUSION

Thank you for your cooperation and contribution to our research.

### 7.1 Would you describe your role in the project/programme as:

- Project/programme sponsor
- Project/programme director
- Project/programme manager
- Team leader
- Team member
- Stakeholder
- Other

### 7.2 If you would like a feedback:

- Name:
- Address:
- Telephone:
- Email:

### 7.3 Would you like to participate in a face-to-face interview?

- Yes
- No

# GUIDELINES FOR APEX (ASSESSING PROJECT EXCELLENCE)

## CRITERIA 1 QUALITY MANAGEMENT SYSTEMS AND PROCEDURES

### 1.1 Formal quality management systems and procedures for the project team are in place

*Poor*: There is no formal quality management system or procedures are in place for the project team members.

*Fair*: Although there is no formal quality management system, there are selective procedures related to safety standards for critical processes in place for the project team members.

*Good*: Written documents on quality management and procedures for quality standards, roles and responsibilities, and guidelines for safety in project management processes are available for specific projects for the project team members.

*Very good*: A well-structured and well-written document on quality management systems and procedures is in place to cover requirements of quality planning, quality assurance, quality improvement and quality control for specific projects for the project team members.

*Excellent*: A well-structured and well-written document on quality management systems and procedures is in place for the project team members to cover requirements of quality planning, quality assurance, quality improvement and quality control for specific projects and there is proactive emphasis on its appropriate application.

## 1.2 Formal quality management systems and procedures for suppliers/contractors are in place

*Poor*: There is no formal quality management system or procedures for project teams in place for major suppliers and contractors.

*Fair*: Although there is no formal quality management system there are selective procedures related to safety standards for critical processes in place for major suppliers and contractors.

*Good*: Written documents on quality management and procedures for quality standards, roles and responsibilities, and guidelines for safety in project management processes are available for specific projects for major suppliers and contractors.

*Very good*: A well-structured and well-written document on quality management systems and procedures is in place for major suppliers and contractors to cover requirements of quality planning, quality assurance, quality improvement and quality control for specific projects.

*Excellent*: A well-structured and well-written document on quality management systems and procedures is in place for major suppliers and contractors to cover requirements of quality planning, quality assurance, quality improvement and quality control for specific projects and there is proactive emphasis on its appropriate application.

## 1.3 Project team members and suppliers are trained and they understand and accept quality management systems and procedures

*Poor*: Even if there is a formal quality management system the document of quality management system is in name only and there is no training programme to roll out the systems and procedures.

*Fair*: There is a formal quality management system in place but there are only limited ad hoc training activities to team members and suppliers. There is no evidence that team members or suppliers understand the system.

*Good*: There is a formal quality management system in place and it is supported by regular training programmes to team members and suppliers. There is evidence that team members or suppliers understand the system but the acceptance is limited.

*Very good*: There is a formal quality management system in place and it is supported by regular training to team members and suppliers. There is evidence that team members or suppliers understand and in general accept the system.

*Excellent*: There is a formal quality management system in place and it is supported by regular training to team members and suppliers. There is evidence that team members or suppliers understand and fully accept and apply procedures.

## 1.4 Quality management systems and procedures follow the guidelines of project methodology of PRINCE2 or PMBOK or BS6079 or ISO10006

*Poor*: Even if there is a formal quality management system the document for the quality management system does not follow the methodology of quality and project management available in formal documents like PRINCE2

*Fair*: Even if there is a formal quality management system, the document for the quality management system loosely follows the methodology of quality and project management available in formal documents like PRINCE2

*Good*: There is a formal quality management system in place and the document for the quality management system in general follows the methodology of quality and project management available in formal documents like PRINCE2 or the document is based on own company standards.

*Very good*: There is a formal quality management system in place, the document for the quality management system in general follows the methodology of quality and project management available in formal documents like PRINCE2 or the document is based on own company standards as appropriate for specific projects.

*Excellent*: There is a formal quality management system is place, the document for the quality management system is developed specific to the project, drawing on best practices of methodology from formal documents like PRINCE2 and also own company quality standards and proven projects.

## 1.5 Quality management systems and procedures are applied effectively in project management by team members and suppliers

*Poor*: Even if there is a formal quality management system it is in name only, and the procedures and guidelines document of quality management system are not applied in project management by team members and suppliers.

*Fair*: Even if there is a formal quality management system, the procedures and guidelines document of quality management system are only occasionally applied in project management by team members and suppliers.

*Good*: There is a formal quality management system and the procedures and guidelines document of the quality management system are applied in project management by team members and suppliers, although its effectiveness is not uniform in all project teams and suppliers.

*Very good*: There is a formal quality management system and the procedures and guidelines document of the quality management system are applied in project management by team members and suppliers, its effectiveness is in general uniform in all project teams but not with all suppliers.

*Excellent*: There is a formal quality management system, the procedures and guidelines document of the quality management system are applied in project management by team members and suppliers and are uniformly effective in all project teams and with all suppliers.

## CRITERIA 2 QUALITY AUDIT AND COMPLIANCE

### 2.1 Formal quality audit procedures are in place covering design conformance, process conformance and supplier deliverables

*Poor*: There are no formal quality audit procedures in place for the project team members to cover design and process conformance and supplier deliverables.

*Fair*: Although there are no formal quality audit procedures there are selective procedures related to safety standards for critical processes and selective design specifications are in place for the audit team members.

*Good*: Written documents on quality audit procedures for design and process conformance and supplier requirements are available for selective aspects of projects and major suppliers.

*Very good*: Well-structured and well-written documents on quality audit procedures are in place to cover requirements of design conformance, process conformance, health, safety and environment standards and requirements for all suppliers.

*Excellent*: Well-structured and well-written documents on quality audit procedures are in place to cover requirements of design conformance, process conformance, health, safety and environment standards and requirements for all suppliers and there is proactive emphasis on its appropriate application.

## 2.2 Audit processes are explained and communicated to project teams and suppliers before the commencement of audit

*Poor*: Even if there is a formal quality audit system the document of quality audits is in name only and there is no training programme to roll out the systems and procedures.

*Fair*: There is a formal quality audit system in place but only limited ad hoc training to team members and suppliers. There is no evidence that team members or suppliers understand the system.

*Good*: There is a formal quality audit system in place and it is supported by regular training to team members and suppliers. There is evidence that team members or suppliers understand the system but the acceptance is limited.

*Very good*: There is a formal quality audit system in place and it is supported by regular training to team members and suppliers. There is evidence that team members or suppliers understand and in general accept the system.

*Excellent*: There is a formal quality audit system in place and it is supported by regular training to team members and suppliers. There is evidence that team members or suppliers understand and fully accept and apply procedures. Audit schedules and protocols are communicated to auditees in advance.

## 2.3 Audit team includes members from quality, safety, project team, contractors and users as appropriate

*Poor*: Even if there is a formal quality audit system there is no defined team to carry out quality audit.

*Fair*: There is a formal quality audit system in place but there are only limited ad hoc team members to carry out the audit. There is no evidence that team membership extends to suppliers.

*Good*: There is a formal quality audit system in place and it is supported by a regular core audit team of the quality department. There is evidence that team membership may include project teams and suppliers.

*Very good*: There is a formal quality audit system in place and it is supported by a regular core audit team of the quality department. There is clear evidence that team membership includes the participation of project teams, contractors and users as required.

*Excellent*: There is a formal quality audit system in place and it is supported by a regular core audit team derived from the quality department, safety, project teams, contractors and users. There is clear evidence that team membership is finalised depending on the audit and may also include independent auditors.

## 2.4 Audit process is supported by well-designed documents, checklists, documents, reports and continuous improvement

*Poor*: There are no formal quality audit procedures in place and there is no evidence of appropriate documents to support them.

*Fair*: Although there are no formal quality audit procedures there are selective documents related to safety standards for critical processes and selective design specifications and process requirements.

*Good*: Written documents on quality audit procedures for design and process conformance and supplier requirements are supported by checklists and some selective post-audit forms.

*Very good*: Well-structured and well-written documents on quality audit procedures are in place to cover requirements of design conformance, process conformance, health, safety and environment standards and requirements for all suppliers. These are supported by checklists and post-audit forms.

*Excellent*: Well-structured and well-written documents on quality audit procedures are in place to cover requirements of design conformance, process conformance, health, safety and environment standards and requirements for all suppliers, there is proactive emphasis on its appropriate application. These are adequately supported by well-designed documents, checklists, documents, reports and continuous improvement.

## 2.5 Compliance of requirements of the project brief is carried out with the client at key stages of project sign off by using an agreed format of key operational requirements

*Poor*: There are no formal quality audit procedures in place for assessing the compliance requirements at key stages of project sign-off.

*Fair*: Although there are no formal quality audit procedures for compliance of requirements, there are selective procedures related to safety standards for critical processes and assess the compliance of selective design specifications.

*Good*: Written documents on quality audit procedures, compliance of requirements for design and process conformance and supplier requirements are available for selective aspects of projects and major suppliers.

*Very good*: Well-structured and well-written documents on quality audit procedures for compliance of requirements are in place to cover requirements of design conformance, process conformance, health, safety and environment standards and requirements for all suppliers. The verification of compliance is carried out at key stages of the project.

*Excellent*: Well-structured and well-written documents on quality audit procedures for compliance of requirements are in place to cover requirements of design conformance, process conformance, health, safety and environment standards and requirements for all suppliers. The verification of compliance is carried out at key stages of the project. This is supported by a database which is validated regularly.

## CRITERIA 3 PERFORMANCE MANAGEMENT

### 3.1 Performance management system is structured around the principles and four aspects of the balanced scorecard

*Poor*: There is no formal performance management system in place for the project team members.

*Fair*: Although there is no formal performance management system there are selective performance indicators related to safety standards, cost and time for critical processes in place for the project team members.

*Good*: Written documents on performance management for quality standards and key performance indicators are available for specific projects for the project team members but they do not follow the four aspects of the balanced scorecard.

*Very good*: A well-structured and well-written document on performance management systems is in place to cover requirements, safety and quality and quality standards based on the principles of the balanced scorecard for the project team members.

*Excellent*: A well-structured and well-written document on performance management system is in place to cover requirements, safety and quality and quality standards based on the principles of the balanced scorecard for the project team members and key performance indicators also include suppliers.

## 3.2 The key performance indicators reflect both enabling and delivered measures

(NB Enabling measures indicate how the project is managed and delivered measures indicate the results and outcome)

*Poor*: Even if there is a formal performance management system the document for the performance management system is in name only and there is no performance indicator to accurately define enabling and delivered measures.

*Fair*: There is a formal performance management system in place but the performance indicators are related to delivered measures for safety, cost and time only.

*Good*: There is a formal quality performance system in place and it is supported by mainly delivered measures. There are also some enabling measures which are assessed during periodic audits.

*Very good*: There is a formal quality performance system in place and it is supported by delivered measures and some enabling measures. There is evidence that that these measures are regularly monitored.

*Excellent*: There is a formal quality performance system in place and it is supported by comprehensive delivered measures and some enabling measures. There is evidence that these measures are regularly monitored and enabling measures are also assessed by periodic audits or health checks.

## 3.3 Performance management system spans across project groups and key suppliers

*Poor*: Even if there is a formal performance management system there is no participation amongst project team members to review the key performance indicators.

*Fair*: There is a formal performance management system in place but this is limited to ad hoc team members to review data. There is no evidence that team membership extends to suppliers.

*Good*: There is a formal performance system in place and it is supported by a regular core performance team of the quality department. There is evidence that team membership may include project teams and suppliers.

*Very good*: There is a formal performance management system in place and it is supported by a regular core performance team of the quality department. There is clear evidence that team membership includes the participation of project teams, contractors and users as required.

*Excellent*: There is a formal quality audit system in place and it is supported by a regular performance team derived from the quality department, safety, project teams, contractors and users. There is clear evidence that team membership is extended to other stakeholders as required.

### 3.4 Performance management system is aligned with gateway or milestone reviews

*Poor*: Even if there is a formal performance management system the system is in name only with periodic publication of performance reports. The reports are seldom reviewed.

*Fair*: There is a formal performance management system in place with periodic publication of performance reports. The reports are reviewed on ad hoc basis without reference to gateway or milestone reviews.

*Good*: There is a formal performance management system in place with periodic publication of performance reports. The reports are regularly reviewed with occasional reference to gateway or milestone reviews.

*Very good*: There is a formal performance management system in place with periodic publication of performance reports. The reports are regularly reviewed and are aligned with gateway or milestone reviews.

*Excellent*: There is a formal performance management system in place with periodic publication of performance reports. The reports are regularly reviewed and are aligned with gateway or milestone reviews. The reviews are supported by action plans for continuous improvement.

### 3.5 Performance management system is aligned with audit, self-assessment and continuous improvement

*Poor*: Even if there is a formal performance management system the system is in name only with periodic publication of performance reports. The reports are seldom reviewed.

*Fair*: There is a formal performance management system in place with periodic publication of performance reports. The reports are reviewed on ad hoc basis without reference to audits, self-assessment and continuous improvements.

*Good*: There is a formal performance management system in place with periodic publication of performance reports. The reports are regularly reviewed with occasional reference to audits, self-assessment and continuous improvements.

*Very good*: There is a formal performance management system in place with periodic publication of performance reports. The reports are regularly reviewed and are aligned with audits, self-assessment and continuous improvements.

*Excellent*: There is a formal performance management system in place with periodic publication of performance reports. The reports are regularly reviewed and are aligned with audits, self-assessment and continuous improvements. The reviews are supported by action plans for continuous improvement.

## CRITERIA 4 ORGANISATIONAL EFFECTIVENESS

### 4.1 Organisation structure includes a steering team (project board), project teams and support team with a dedicated quality manager and budget for quality

*Poor*: There is no formal organisation structure with the steering team, project team and support team in place for the project.

*Fair*: There is a formal organisation structure in place for the project but the role of quality manager is not defined.

*Good*: There is a formal organisation structure with a steering team, project team and support team in place for the project and the role of quality management is assigned to a project manager or team members.

*Very good*: There is a formal organisation structure with a steering team, project team and support team in place for the project and the role of quality management is assigned to a quality manager but the quality budget is not well-defined.

*Excellent*: There is a formal organisation structure with a steering team, project team and support team in place for the project and the role of quality management is assigned to a quality manager. The quality budget is over 0.5 per cent of project spends.

## 4.2 High priority is given for client relations and stakeholder management

*Poor*: Even if there is a formal organisation structure with steering team, project team and support team in place for the project there is no assigned role for client relations and stakeholder management.

*Fair*: There is a formal organisation structure in place for the project but the role of client manager is not defined. Discussion with stakeholders and client is carried out by ad hoc meetings.

*Good*: There is a formal organisation structure with a steering team, project team and support team in place for the project and the role of client and stakeholder management is assigned to a project manager.

*Very good*: There is a formal organisation structure with a steering team, project team and support team in place for the project and the role of client and stakeholder management is assigned to a client manager.

*Excellent*: There is a formal organisation structure with a steering team, project team and support team in place for the project and the role of client and stakeholder management is assigned to a client director as part of the steering team. High priority is given to client relations and stakeholder management.

## 4.3 The coordination of contractors and subcontractors is ensured by supplier partnership agreements

*Poor*: Even if there is a formal organisation structure with a steering team, project team and support team in place for the project there is no consistent service level or partnership agreement with contractors.

*Fair*: There is a formal organisation structure in place for the project but the formal service-level agreements are limited to major contractors. The subcontractors are managed by first-tier contractors.

*Good*: There is a formal organisation structure with a steering team, project team and support team in place for the project and there are service-level agreements with all contractors and suppliers.

*Very good*: There is a formal organisation structure with a steering team, project team and support team in place for the project and there are service-level agreements with all contractors and suppliers. There are partnership agreements with major suppliers.

*Excellent*: There is a formal organisation structure with a steering team, project team and support team in place for the project and there are service-level agreements with all contractors and suppliers. There are partnership agreements with major suppliers. The coordination of contractors and subcontractors is ensured by supplier partnership agreements.

## 4.4 There is a defined role of HR supported by job descriptions of project team members and RACI is used for relevant tasks related to work breakdown structure

*Poor*: Even if there is a formal organisation structure with a steering team, project team and support team in place for the project there is no assigned role for HR.

*Fair*: There is a formal organisation structure in place for the project but the role of HR is assigned to a project manager supported by an administration staff.

*Good*: There is a formal organisation structure with a steering team, project team and support team in place for the project and the HR manager reports to the project manager. There are formal job descriptions of team members.

*Very good*: There is a formal organisation structure with a steering team, project team and support team in place for the project and the HR manager reports to the project manager. There are formal job descriptions of team members with clear responsibilities related to work breakdown structure.

*Excellent*: There is a formal organisation structure with a steering team, project team and support team in place for the project and the role of HR management is assigned to a HR director as part of the steering team. There are defined job descriptions of project team members and RACI is used for relevant tasks related to work breakdown structure.

## 4.5 Softer critical success factors such as leadership, communication and user involvement are embedded in organisation culture

*Poor*: More focus is on delivering on time and budget and there is little emphasis on softer critical success factors such as leadership, communication and user involvement.

*Fair*: Although there is more focus is on delivering on time and budget and there is also some emphasis on softer critical success factors such as leadership, communication and user involvement.

*Good*: Although there is more focus is on delivering on time and budget and there is also adequate emphasis on softer critical success factors such as leadership, communication and user involvement.

*Very good*: Equal emphasis on cost, time and quality. Proactive initiatives are in place to ensure softer critical success factors such as leadership, communication and user involvement and they are embedded in organisation culture.

*Excellent*: Equal emphasis on cost, time and quality. Proactive initiatives are in place to ensure softer critical success factors such as leadership, communication and user involvement.

## CRITERIA 5 OPERATIONAL EXCELLENCE CONCEPTS

### 5.1 Proactive application of Six Sigma concepts in a cost effective programme

*Poor*: There is no application of Six Sigma concepts.

*Fair*: Although there is no formal application of Six Sigma there is evidence of the application of selective Six Sigma tools.

*Good*: Although there is no formal application of Six Sigma programme or organised training there is evidence of the application of selective Six Sigma tools and ad hoc projects.

*Very good*: Formal application of Six Sigma programme and training in place and there is evidence of some DMAIC-based projects.

*Excellent*: Formal application of Six Sigma programme and training in place and there is evidence of many DMAIC-based projects, savings and data-driven culture.

### 5.2 Recognition of the supply chain management principles, with dedicated resources if appropriate, in procurement, forward planning and supplier partnership

*Poor*: There is no conscious application of supply chain principles.

*Fair*: Although there is no formal application of supply chain management there is evidence of the application of selective supply chain principles in procurement.

*Good*: Although there is no formal application of supply chain management with dedicated resources there is evidence of the application of supply chain principles in procurement and supplier partnership.

*Very good*: Formal application of supply chain management with dedicated resources is in place, showing some improvement in procurement and supplier partnership.

*Excellent*: Formal application of supply chain management with dedicated resources is in place showing significant results in managing procurement, forward planning and supplier partnership.

## 5.3 Appropriate application of maturity or excellence models such as EFQM

*Poor*: There is no conscious application of maturity or excellence models such as EFQM.

*Fair*: Although there is no formal application of maturity or excellence models such as EFQM there is evidence of the application of selective self-assessment.

*Good*: Although there is no formal application of maturity or excellence models such as EFQM there is evidence of the application of self-assessment based on the EFQM or CMMI format.

*Very good*: Formal application of maturity or excellence models such as EFQM or CMMI is in place with a holistic approach showing some improvement in overall performance.

*Excellent*: Formal application of maturity or excellence models such as EFQM or CMMI is in place with a holistic approach showing significant improvement in overall performance. Achieved performance excellence awards.

## 5.4 Proactive application of lean thinking in minimising non-value-added activities and process cycle times

*Poor*: There is no conscious application of lean thinking principles.

*Fair*: Although there is no formal application of lean thinking principles there is evidence of the application of selective lean principles in procurement.

*Good*: Although there is no formal application of lean thinking principles with dedicated resources there is evidence of the application of lean principles in procurement and non-value-added processes.

*Very good*: Formal application of lean thinking principles with dedicated resources is in place showing some improvement in procurement and non-value-added processes.

*Excellent*: Formal application of lean thinking principles with dedicated resources is in place showing significant improvement in procurement, process cycle time and non-value-added processes.

## 5.5 Evidence of processes and initiatives to instil TQM culture (especially if Six Sigma is not applied) within project teams and suppliers

*Poor*: There is no conscious application of TQM initiatives.

*Fair*: Although there is no formal application of TQM initiatives there is evidence of the application of selective TQM principles in procurement and project teams.

*Good*: Although there is no formal application of TQM initiatives with dedicated resources there is evidence of the application of TQM principles in project teams and suppliers.

*Very good*: Formal application of TQM initiatives (or Six Sigma) with dedicated resources is in place showing continuous improvement in processes.

*Excellent*: Formal application of TQM initiatives (or Six Sigma) with dedicated resources is in place showing continuous improvement in processes. There is evidence of TQM culture amongst project teams and suppliers.

## CRITERIA 6 SELF-ASSESSMENT AND KNOWLEDGE MANAGEMENT

### 6.1 In line with quality audit, performance management and maturity or excellence models there is evidence of well-structured checklists for holistic health checks

*Poor*: There is no conscious application of structured checklists for holistic health checks.

*Fair*: Although there is no formal application of structured checklists for holistic health checks there is evidence of the application of ad hoc self-assessment processes.

*Good*: Although there is no formal application of structured checklists for holistic health checks with dedicated resources there is evidence of the application of periodic self-assessment processes.

*Very good*: Formal application of structured checklists for holistic health checks with dedicated resources is in place showing continuous improvement in processes

*Excellent*: Formal application of structured checklists for holistic health checks with dedicated resources is in place showing continuous improvement in processes. In line with quality audit, performance management and maturity or excellence models there is evidence of well-structured checklists for holistic health checks.

## 6.2 Evidence of regular self-assessment to identify and follow up areas of continuous improvement

*Poor*: Even if there is application of structured checklists for holistic health checks in place there is no evidence of regular self-assessment to identify and follow up areas of continuous improvement.

*Fair*: There is application of structured checklists for holistic health checks in place and there is some evidence of regular self-assessment to identify and follow up areas of continuous improvement.

*Good*: There is application of structured checklists for holistic health checks in place and there is good evidence of regular self assessment to identify and follow up areas of continuous improvement.

*Very good*: Formal application of structured checklists for holistic health checks with dedicated resources is in place and there is evidence of regular self-assessment to identify and follow up areas of continuous improvement.

*Excellent*: Formal application of structured checklists for holistic health checks with dedicated resources is in place and there is evidence of regular self-assessment to identify and follow up areas of continuous improvement. The improvement is also extended to suppliers.

## 6.3 Continuous education and training to share and enhance skills, process and systems knowledge of project team members and suppliers

*Poor*: There is no conscious initiative for continuous education and training to share and enhance skills, process and systems knowledge of project team members and suppliers.

*Fair*: There are ad hoc workshops for continuous education and training to share and enhance skills, process and systems knowledge of project team members.

*Good*: There are regular workshops and structured programmes for continuous education and training to share and enhance skills, process and systems knowledge of project team members.

*Very good*: There are regular workshops and structured programmes with dedicated resources for continuous education and training to share and enhance skills, process and systems knowledge of project team members and suppliers.

*Excellent*: There are regular workshops and structured programmes with dedicated resources for continuous education and training to share and enhance skills, process and systems knowledge of project team members and suppliers.

## 6.4 Well-designed and managed media such as a website, newsletter and billboards to communicate best practices and key messages

*Poor*: There is no conscious initiative for well-designed and managed media such as a website, newsletter and billboards to communicate best practices and key messages.

*Fair*: There are some ad hoc initiatives such as progress reports and occasional newsletter to communicate best practices and key messages.

*Good*: There are some good initiatives for well-designed and managed media such as a website, newsletter and billboards to communicate best practices and key messages.

*Very good*: There are some good initiatives with dedicated resources for well-designed and managed media such as a website, newsletter and billboards to communicate best practices and key messages.

*Excellent*: There are some good initiatives with dedicated resources for well-designed and managed media such as a website, newsletter and billboards to communicate best practices and key messages. The communication is extended to suppliers, stakeholders and external media.

## 6.5 There is evidence of proactive planning and communication processes to achieve longer-lasting outcomes and legacy

*Poor*: Even if there is application of structured checklists for holistic health checks in place there is no evidence of dedicated resources to focus on longer-lasting outcomes and legacy.

*Fair*: There is application of structured checklists for holistic health checks in place and there is some evidence of regular review of self-assessment and continuous improvement programmes and knowledge management initiatives towards longer-lasting outcomes.

*Good*: There is application of structured checklists for holistic health checks in place and there is good evidence of regular review of self-assessment and continuous improvement programmes and knowledge management initiatives towards longer-lasting outcomes.

*Very good*: Formal application of structured checklists for holistic health checks with dedicated resources is in place and there is evidence of regular review of self-assessment and continuous improvement programmes and knowledge management initiatives towards longer-lasting outcomes on cultural, economic and environmental objectives.

*Excellent*: Formal application of structured checklists for holistic health checks and longer-term planning with a separate group focusing on longer-lasting outcomes and legacy for cultural, economic and environmental objectives. There is evidence of regular review of self-assessment and continuous improvement programmes and knowledge management initiatives. The review is also extended to suppliers and future users of facilities.

# AN EXAMPLE OF A QUALITY MANAGEMENT PLAN

| |
|---|
| **Objectives**<br>To provide assurance that assets are safe, reliable and meet requirements. To work efficiently and effectively so that we can minimise cost and deliver on time. |
| **Scope**<br>Quality assurance of BAA capital projects. |
| **All projects shall satisfy the following requirements** |
| 1. First-tier suppliers shall implement a Quality Management System based on the 'best-practice' model BS EN ISO 9001 (or for IT/Software Engineering BS ISO/IEC 90003, IT Services ISO 20000 or the Software Capability Maturity Model ISO 15504 as applicable to their work scope). |
| 2. Computer-based systems shall satisfy the Systems Assurance Requirements Specification (SARS) produced for each system by the Systems Assurance Team. The exact requirements will be based on the BAA Generic Systems Assurance Requirements Specification and will be determined from the operational criticality, including functional safety, and the risk that the development, installation and operation may experience. |
| 3. First-tier suppliers shall set out in a plan how their quality management system integrates with BAA processes and addresses the specific project quality objectives and requirements. Supplier plans shall meet the requirements of ISO 10005 and shall include or make reference to the specific quality control and assurance activities needed to provide safe and reliable assets that are fully compliant with the project brief and any applicable regulatory or BAA Standards requirements. |
| 4. Establish forums with terms of reference to plan, deliver and assure the project quality objectives. The forum shall meet at least monthly to review progress, look ahead, anticipate and resolve issues. |
| 5. Provide quality management inductions to communicate project objectives/requirements and embed best practice and a culture to 'get it right first time'. |

6. Suppliers shall audit work at a time and frequency to ensure compliance with processes and standards and also progress against plans.
☐ Audits shall satisfy the principles and guidance set out in BS EN ISO 19011.
☐ First-tier suppliers shall set out their arrangements in an audit programme. The audit programme shall be focused and extended where appropriate to address any risks/issues identified. Audit programmes shall generally provide a six-month look ahead.
☐ Copies of audit reports(or management summary reports) shall be given to the BAA project manager.

7. Carry out systematic design and production information reviews at key stages in accordance with an agreed plan.
☐ Evaluate the ability of the results of design to meet the requirements of the design brief. Identify any production issues and propose the necessary actions.
☐ Maintain records of the results of the reviews and approvals and ensure any required actions are completed.

8. Specify, schedule, produce and agree with stakeholders and other interested parties the samples/benchmarks/prototypes/production trials and mock-ups required to verify or validate aesthetic/physical/functional acceptability (including system integration and buildability) prior to the main production activities. Ensure that, where appropriate and practical, agreed benchmarks are clearly identified, and readily accessible for quality control and briefing purposes.

9. Suppliers shall issue Certificates of Compliance/Declarations of Conformity for gateway approvals and asset/system handover. In addition Certificates of Compliance/Declarations of Conformity shall be provided to substantiate applications for payment or to confirm assurance status when requested by the BAA project manager.

10. Ensure that all approving and authorised signatories of assurance statements and certificates of compliance for critical assets are competent and pre-authorised to undertake such activities. Appropriate training, qualification and experience to demonstrate competencies shall be defined, and records shall be maintained and regularly audited. Certificates of Compliance for design shall be issued by a person with chartered status from the relevant institution unless otherwise proposed by the first-tier supplier and agreed by the BAA project manager.

11. From the start of production design onwards, develop an assured critical assets register to monitor and demonstrate that business and safety critical assets are safe, reliable and meet the brief. The register shall identify the systems to be assured, the plan setting out how they are assured and who is accountable for providing the assurance. The register shall indicate the current status of planning and assurance.

12. Ensure subcontracted laboratories/testing service providers are accredited by UKAS (or an EU equivalent) unless otherwise specified or agreed in writing by the BAA project manager responsible for the work. Testing and sampling methodologies shall be in accordance with appropriate national or international standards unless otherwise specified or agreed in writing by the designer/ technical leader. All measuring and test equipment shall be calibrated, included within a calibration system and shall be traceable to a national reference standard. Staff undertaking sampling, inspection and testing activities shall have evidence of competence to carry out the particular activities to which they have been assigned.

13. The first-tier suppliers approving and authorised signatories shall agree an inspection and test plan to validate production. The plan shall set out how compliance with the design will be demonstrated. Ensure that the plan is reviewed by any interested parties (as set out in the project execution plan/ contractual arrangements). Typically allow a minimum of four weeks prior to the start of production for this review process. Ensure inspection and test plans make clear reference, as appropriate, to:
The inspections and test activities required to demonstrate compliance with stakeholder and regulatory requirements:
☐ The procedures, checklists and instructions needed to carry out the inspections/tests
☐ Acceptance criteria/standards (such as specifications, BAA standards, national standards and applicable legislation as well as user requirement and system requirement documentation etc.).
☐ Samples, benchmarks, trials and prototypes approval needed prior to commencement of the main production
☐ The records and other assurance deliverables needed as part of the inspection and test process (including any document or form templates to be used)
☐ Responsibility for implementing the planned arrangements and any specific qualifications/training/competence required to carry out the tasks
☐ Interventions required by the project team, principal contractor, designers, technical leaders, third parties and stakeholders etc. to verify or validate at key stages. Any such interventions should be identified as hold, review or notification points as appropriate (typically allow four weeks notice for off-site activity and one week for site-based events).
☐ Protection of finished work to avoid damage. Certificates of compliance/ declarations of conformity shall be issued to confirm that the plan has actually been implemented and the work satisfies all requirements.

14. Implement documented processes to resolve any non-conformance, technical queries and concessions. Non-conformance, technical queries and concession requests shall be logged and tracked until resolution has been agreed by the relevant stakeholder, designer or project team member accountable. Any deviation from specified requirements shall be the subject of a formal concession which shall be approved by the relevant authority as determined by the BAA project manager.

| |
|---|
| 15. Provide documents and records that are clearly identifiable to the contract and systems/product. Maintain the records in an auditable and readily accessible manner throughout the project duration and store in a way that prevents loss and deterioration in accordance with the project document management policy. The records shall demonstrate satisfaction of all requirements. |
| 16. Agree and document asset handover with the appropriate stakeholders and provide the required assurance records and asset data, including O & M manual(s), 'as-built records' and maintenance integration work plan(s). |
| 17. Provide regular reports on quality management progress and performance<br>☐ First-tier suppliers shall provide reports to their project team. The report format, frequency and level of detail shall be agreed with the project team.<br>☐ Project teams shall compile a monthly summary report for the capital/ programme director. The format and date for presenting quality KPIs and measurement data shall be agreed by the capital/programme director. Standard reporting templates shall be used unless otherwise agreed. |

## KEY REFERENCE INFORMATION

ISO 10005 Quality management systems guidelines for quality plans

ISO 15504 Software capability maturity model

ISO 9001 Quality management system requirements

ISO 20000 Information technology service management

ISO 900003 Software engineering: guidelines for application of ISO 9001: 2000 to computer software

ISO 17025 General requirements for the competence of testing and calibration laboratories

ISO 19011 Guidelines for quality and/or environmental management systems auditing

BAA Systems Assurance Requirements Specification

BAA Approval of Samples and Benchmarks

# GLOSSARY

**Activity network diagram** a network analysis technique to allow a team to find the most efficient path and realistic schedule of a project by graphically showing the completion time and sequence of each task.

**APM (Association for Project Management)**, the professional body of project managers in the UK.

**Balanced scorecard** introduced by R Kaplan and D Norton in early 1990s, is a concept for measuring a company's activities in terms of its vision and strategies, to give managers a comprehensive view of the performance of a business. Typically it comprises simple tables broken into four sections of 'perspectives' which are labelled as 'financial', 'customer', 'internal business processes' and 'learning and growth'.

**Bar chart**, also known as a Gantt chart, indicates scheduling activities. Horizontal bars show the various activities with the length of the bar proportional to the duration of a particular activity.

**Benchmarking** is rating an organisation's products, processes and performances with other organisations in the same or another business. The objective is to identify the gaps with competitors and the areas for improvement.

**Best practice.** Best practice refers to any organisation that performs as well or better than the competition in quality, timeliness, flexibility and innovation. Best practice should lead to world class performance.

**Black belts** are experts in Six Sigma methods and tools. Tools include statistical analysis. Black belts are project leaders for Six Sigma initiatives, they also train other staff members in Six Sigma techniques.

**BS6079** is the British Standards Guideline to project management. It assumes a full project life cycle from inception to closure and is more suitable for large engineering projects.

**Capacity planning** specifies the level of resources (e.g. facilities, fleets, equipment, systems hardware and labour force size) that best supports the enterprise's competitive strategy for production.

**Carbon offset** is the process of reducing the net carbon emissions of an individual or organisation, either by their own actions, or through arrangements with a carbon-offset provider

**CMMI (Capability Maturity Model Integration)** is a process improvement approach that provides organizations with the essential elements of effective processes. It was developed by the Software Engineering Institute (SEI) at Carnegie Mellon University in Pittsburgh.

**CRP (Capacity Requirement Planning)** is a computerized technique to predict resource requirements of all available workstations (see also **RCCP**). RCCP balances workloads at a high level, CRP will then fine-tune the workload balance.

**Collaborative planning forecasting and replenishment (CPFR)** data and process model standards are developed for collaboration between suppliers and an enterprise with proscribed methods for planning (agreement between the trading partners to conduct business in a certain way); forecasting (agreed-to methods, technology and timing for sales, promotions and order forecasting); and replenishment (order generation and order fulfilment).

**Continuous improvement** is always looking for ways to improve a process or a product, but not necessarily making radical step changes. If the basic idea is sound then building on it will improve quality. In Japan this is known as kaizen.

**COPQ (cost of poor quality)** The cost of poor quality is made up of costs arising from; internal failures, external failures, appraisal, prevention and lost opportunity costs. In other words all the costs that arise from non-conformance to a standard. Chapter Three discusses COPQ in some detail.

**CRM (customer relationship management)**, is the development of the database and strategies necessary to have the maximum client relationships in terms of quality, cost, reliability and responsiveness.

**CTQs** in Six Sigma CTQS = critical to quality. This simply means the identification of factors that are critical for the achievement of a level of quality. CTQs in project management are also known as the 'iron triangle' of cost, time and quality.

**Cycle time** is the elapsed time between two successive operations or the time required to complete an operation.

**Demand forecast** The prediction, projection or estimation of expected demand over a specified future time period.

**Distribution channels** The selling channels supported by an enterprise. These may include retail sales, distribution partner (e.g., wholesale) sales, original equipment manufacturer (OEM) sales, Internet exchange or marketplace sales, and Internet auction or reverse auctions sales.

**Distribution requirements planning (DRP)** Process for determining inventory requirements in a multiple plant/warehouse environment. DRP may be used for both distribution and manufacturing. In manufacturing, DRP will work directly with MRP. DRP may also be defined as **distribution resource planning** which also includes determining labor, equipment, and warehouse space requirements.

**DMAIC** The cycle of Define, Measure, Analyse, Improve and Control. See Chapter 9 for detailed discussion.

**Earned value management** or **earned value analysis** is an analytical method of comparing the actual performance against the planned performance related to both time and cost in a project.

**E-business** Electronic business is more than the transfer of information using information technology. E- business is the complex mix of processes, applications and organisational structures.

**EFQM** The European Foundation for Quality Management, derived from the American Malcolm Baldridge Quality award. It is an award for organisations that achieve world-class performance as judged by independent auditors against a checklist. The checklist is detailed and extensive and covers; leadership, people management, policy and strategy, partnerships and resource, processes, people satisfaction, customer satisfaction., impact on society and business results

**ERP (enterprise resource planning)**, is the extension of MRPII systems to the management of complete business functions including finance and human resources.

**Fit Sigma**, also see **TQM**, **Six Sigma** and **Lean Sigma**. Fit Sigma incorporates all the advantages and tools of TQM, Six Sigma and Lean sigma. The aim is to get an organisation healthy (fit) by using appropriate tools for the size and nature of the business (fitness for purpose) and to sustain a level of fitness. Fit Sigma is a holistic approach.

**Flow process chart** Sets out the sequence of the flow of a product or a procedure by recording all the activities in a process. The chart can be used to identify steps in the process, value-adding activities and non-value-adding activities.

**Forecasting process** Provides a mechanism for soliciting participation from individuals who have knowledge of future events and compiling it into a consistent format to develop a forecast. The forecasting process concentrates on defining how information will be gathered and reconciled into a consistent picture of the future. In cases where a statistical forecast is used the process will also define how much weight should be given to the mathematical models versus input from participants to develop the final consensus forecast.

**Gateway review** A process that examines programmes and projects at key decision points in their life cycle. It looks ahead to provide assurance that they can progress successfully to the next stage. The process under the governance of the Office Of Government Commerce (OGC) is a best practice in UK government projects.

**Gantt chart** See **Bar chart**.

**Green belts** are staff trained to be Six Sigma project leaders, they work under the guidance of Black belts. See **Black belts**.

**Greening the supply chain** refers to buyer companies requiring a certain level of environmental responsibility in core business practices of their suppliers and vendors.

**Inventory management** The process of ensuring the availability of products through inventory administration activities such as demand planning, stock optimiaation and monitoring the age of the product.

**ISO 9000** To gain ISO 9000 accreditation an organisation has to demonstrate to an accredited auditor that they have a well-documented standard and consistent process in place which achieves a defined level of quality or performance. ISO accreditation will give a customer confidence that the product or service provided will meet certain specified standards of performance and will always be consistent with the documented standards.

**JIT (just-in-time)** Initially a manufacturing approach where materials are ordered to arrive just when required in the process, no output or buffer stocks are held and the finished product is delivered direct to the customer. Lean Sigma incorporates the principals of JIT and now relates to the supply chain from supplier and supplier's supplier, through the process to the customer and the customer's customer.

**Kanban** The Japanese word for card. The basic kanban system is to use cards to trigger movements of materials between operations in production so that a customer order flows through the system. Computer systems eliminate the need for cards but the principle is the same. As a job flows through the factory, completion of one stage of production triggers the next so that there is no idle time, or queues, between operations. Any one job can be tracked to determine the stage of production. A 'Kanban' is raised for each customer order. The kanban system enables production to be in batches of one.

**KPIs (key performance indicators)** include measurement of performance such as asset utilisation, customer satisfaction, cycle time from order to delivery, inventory turnover, operations costs, productivity and financial results (return on assets and return on investment).

**Lean Sigma** See also **JIT**. Lean was initially a manufacturing approach where materials are ordered to arrive just when required in the process, no output or buffer stocks are held, and the finished product is delivered direct to the customer. Lean Sigma incorporates the principals of Six Sigma, and is related to the supply chain from supplier and supplier's supplier, through the process to the customer and the customer's customer.

**Major projects** are substantial in value and complex in composition and involve multiple stakeholders. The project costs in a major project usually exceed £500 million.

**Major Projects Association (MPA)** is a professional forum of UK organisations to improve the initiation and delivery of major projects through the interaction of members.

**The master production schedule** Also commonly referred to as the MPS, it is effectively the plan that the company has developed for production, staffing, inventory, etc. MPS translates your business plan, including forecasted demand, into a production plan using planned orders in a true multilevel optional component scheduling environment. Using MPS helps you avoid shortages, costly expediting, last minute scheduling and inefficient allocation of resources.

**Materials Requirement Planning (MRP)** A dependent demand system that calculates materials requirements and production plans to satisfy known and forecast sales orders. MRP helps calculate volume and timing requirements to meet an estimate of future demand. There are three major types of computer-based MRP systems – MRP I, 'Closed loop' MRP and **MRP II**.

**Monte Carlo technique** A simulation process. It uses random numbers as an approach to model the waiting times and queue lengths and also to examine the overall uncertainty in projects.

**MRP II** Manufacturing resource planning is an integrated computer based procedure for dealing with all of the planning and scheduling activities for manufacturing, and includes procedures for stock re-order, purchasing, inventory records, cost accounting, and plant maintenance.

**Mudas** Japanese for waste or non-value-adding. The seven activities that are considered are excess production, waiting, conveyance, motion, process, inventory and defects. For further detail see Chapter 1.

**NEC (New Engineering Contract)** is a family of contracts that facilitates the implementation of sound project management principles and practices as well as defining legal relationships. It is suitable for procuring a diverse range of works and services.

**Novation** is the procedure of transferring the contract of a supplier employed by the client to another contractor or back to the client. In practice, this usually applies to a designer in a design and build arrangement and the transfer of surplus stocks.

**OGC** The Office of Government Commerce, responsible for the promotion and governance of PRINCE2 in the UK. At the time of writing OGC is now part of the new Efficiency and Reform Group within the Cabinet Office.

**OEE (overall equipment effectiveness)**, is the real output of a machine. It is given by the ratio of the good output and the maximum output of the machine for the time it is planned to operate.

**OPM3** Organizational Project Management Maturity Model owned by the Project Management Institute, provides requirements for assessing and developing capabilities in portfolio, programme and project management.

**PDCA** The **Plan-Do-Check-Act** cycle. Developed by Dr W.E. Deming. It refers to planning the change and setting standards, doing, making the change happen, checking that what is happening is what was intended (standards are being met), and acting, taking action to correct back to the standard.

**PEMM (Process and Enterprise Maturity Model)** promoted by Michael Hammer (2007) but not well regulated.

**P3M3 (Portfolio Programme and Project Maturity Model)** promoted by OGC as an advancement of PRINCE2 Maturity Model (P2M2) and CMMI. It aims to produce a comprehensive maturity model for apparently distinctive requirements of portfolio, programme and project management.

**PLS (partial least square)** Is an alternative estimation approach to traditional **SEM** and can provide estimates for a system of linear equations. PLS treats the constructs as individual composite scores without recreating co-variances among measured items.

**Project** A project is a unique item of work for which there is a financial budget and a defined schedule.

**Project management** involves the planning, scheduling, budgeting and control of a project using an integrated team of workers and specialists.

**Programme management** is the process of managing several related projects, often with the intention of improving an organisation's performance. In practice and in its aims it is often closely related to a common corporate objective.

**Project charter** A project charter is a working document for defining the terms of reference of each Six Sigma project. The charter can make a successful project by specifying necessary resources and boundaries that will in turn ensure success.

**Process mapping** A tool to represent a process by a diagram containing a series of linked tasks or activities which produce an output.

**PESTLE (political, economic, social, technical, legal and environmental)**, is an analytical tool for assessing the impact of external contexts on a project or a major operation and also the impact of a project on its external contexts. There are several possible contexts including ETPS, STEP, PEST and STEPLE.

**PMBOK** The project management body of knowledge published by Project Management Institute. It is a book which presents a set of standard terminology and guidelines for project management.

**PRINCE2 (PRojects IN Controlled Environments)** is a process-based method for effective project management. It is a de facto standard used extensively by the UK Government and is widely recognised and used in the private sector, both in the UK and internationally

**Product breakdown structure (PBS)** In project management the PBS provides an exhaustive, hierarchical tree structure of deliverables that make up the project, arranged in whole–part relationship. This diagrammatic representation of project outputs provides a clear statement of the scope of the project.

**Quality assurance (QA)** Covers the training and planned actions necessary to minimise failures and provide confidence that a product, process or service will satisfy given quality requirements.

**Quality audit** A systematic and independent examination to assess whether quality activities and results comply with planned arrangements and standards.

**Quality control (QC)** covers the operational activities that are used to satisfy planned quality requirements and standards, such as measuring, inspection and testing.

**Quality plan** A document setting the specific quality practices, resources, activities and responsibilities relevant to a particular product, process, contract or project.

**Quality system** An extension of a quality plan with more emphasis on organisational structure, responsibilities, resources and procedures.

**RCCP (rough-cut capacity planning)** A process that considers only the critical work centres (bottlenecks, highly utilised resources etc.) and attempts to balance longer-term workloads and demand at high level.

**Risk analysis** A risk in a project is any future event that may affect the outcome of the project. Risk analysis is the systematic process of identifying, analysing and responding to the project risk.

**RU/CS (resource utilisation and customer service)** Analysis is a simple tool to establish the relative importance of the key parameters of both Resource Utilisation and Customer Service and to identify their conflicts.

**SCOR (supply-chain operations reference-model)** A process reference model that has been developed and endorsed by the Supply-Chain Council as the cross-industry standard diagnostic tool for supply-chain management.

**SEM (structural equation modelling)** A mutivariate technique combining aspects of factor analysis and multiple regression to simultaneously examine a series of interrelated dependence relationships among the constructs.

**S & OP (sales and operations planning)** Derived from MRP and includes new product planning. Demand planning, supply review, to provide weekly and daily manufacturing schedules and financial information.

**SIPOC (supplier, input, process, output and customer)** A high-level map of a process to view how a company goes about satisfying a particular customer requirement in the overall supply chain.

**Six Sigma** Six Sigma is quality system which in effect aims for zero defects. Six sigma in statistical terms means six deviations from the arithmetic mean. This equates to 99.99966 per cent of the total population, or 3.4 defects per million opportunities.

**SMED (single minute exchange of dies)** This was developed for the Japanese automobile industry by Shigeo Shingo in the 1980s and involves the reduction of change over of production by intensive work study to determine in process and out process activities and then systematically improving the planning, tooling and operations of the changeover process. Shingo believed in looking for simple solutions rather than relying on technology.

**Supplier partnership -** An extended relationship between buyers and suppliers based on confidence, credibility, and mutual benefit. The buyer, on its part, provides long-term contracts and in return, the supplier implements customer's suggestions and commits to continuous improvement in quality of product and delivery.

**SWOT (strengths, weaknesses, opportunities and threats)** A tool for analysing an organisation's competitive position in relation to its competitors.

**TPM (Total Productive Maintenance)** Requires factory management to improve asset utilisation by the systematic study and elimination of major obstacles – known as the 'six big losses' – to efficiency. The six big losses in manufacturing are breakdown, set-up and adjustment, minor stoppages, reduced speed, quality defects and start-up and shutdown.

**TQM (Total Quality Management)** Not a system but a philosophy embracing the total culture of an organisation. TQM goes far beyond conformance to a standard, it requires a culture where every member of the organisation believes that not a single day should go by without the organisation in some way improving its efficiency and/or improving customer satisfaction.

**Value analysis** Often a practice in purchasing, value analysis is the evaluation of the expected performance of a product relative to its price.

**Value chain** Also known as Porter's value chain. According to Michael Porter the competitive advantage of a company can be assessed only by seeing the company as a total system. This 'total system' comprises both primary and secondary activities.

**Value stream mapping (VSM)** A visual illustration of all activities required to bring a product through the main flow, from raw material to the stage of reaching the customer.

**Vendor-managed inventory (VMI)** In the VMI process, the vendor assumes responsibility for managing the replenishment of stock. Rather than a customer submitting orders, the vendor will replenish stock as needed. This process is sometimes referred to as supplier-managed inventory (SMI) or co-managed inventory.

**Work breakdown structure (WBS)** A tool used to define and group a project's discrete work elements in a way that helps organise and define the total work scope of the project. A WBS also provides the necessary framework for detailed cost estimating, organisation structure, task scheduling and execution strategy. It is similar in format to **product breakdown structure**.

# REFERENCES

Abdelsalam, H.M.E. and Gad, M.M. (2008), 'Cost of quality in Dubai: An analytical case study of residential construction projects', *International Journal of Project Management*, available online from 23 September 2008.

Abidin, N.Z. and Pasquire, C.L. (2007), 'Revolutionize value management: A mode towards sustainability', *International Journal of Project Management*, vol. 25, no. 3, pp. 275–282.

Adriti, D. and Gunaydin, H.M. (1997), 'TQM in the construction processes', *International Journal of Project Management*, vol. 15, no. 4, pp. 235–243.

Ala-Risku, T. and Karkkainen, M. (2006), 'Material delivery problems in construction: A possible solution', *International Journal of Production Economics*, vol. 104, no. 1, pp. 19–29.

Algarni, A.M., Adriti, D. and Polat, G. (2007), 'Build operate transfer in infrastructure projects in the United States', *Construction Engineering and Management*, vol. 133, no. 10, pp. 728–735.

Anbari, F.T., Bredillet, C.N. and Turner, J.R. (2008), 'Perspectives on research on project management', *Academy of Management Proceedings*, Anheim, CA, USA, Academy of Management.

Andersen, E.S. (2006), 'Toward a project management theory for renewal projects', *Project Management Journal*, vol. 37, no. 4, pp. 15–30.

Ansoff, I. (1987), *Corporate Strategy*. Harmondsworth: Penguin Books.

Artto, K., Martinsuo, M., Gemundsen, H.G. and Murtoaro, J. (2009), 'Foundation of program management: a bibliometric view', *International Journal of Project Management*, vol. 27, no. 1, pp. 1–18.

Arunasalam, M., Paulson, A. and Wallace, W. (2003), 'Service quality assessment of workers' compensation health care programs in New York Sate Using SERVQUAL', *Health Marketing Quarterly*, vol. 21, no. 1, pp. 29–64.

Association of Project Management (2006), *Body of Knowledge*. Princes Risborough, Buckinghamshire: Association of Project Management.

Association of Project Management (2007), *Models to Improve the Management of Projects*. Buckinghamshire: Association of Project Management.

Atkinson, R. (1999), 'Project management: cost, time and quality, two best guesses and a phenomenon, its time to accept other success criteria', *International Journal of Project Management*, vol. 17, no. 6, pp. 337–342.

Atkinson, R., Crawford, L. and Ward, S. (2006), 'Fundamental uncertainties in projects and the scope of project management', *International Journal of Project Management*, vol. 24, pp. 687–698.

Bagozzi, R.P. (1994), *Advanced Method of Market Research*, Blackwell Publishers, Cambridge, MA, USA.

Ballard, G. (2001), 'Cycle time reduction in home building', in *The Proceedings of the Ninth Annual Conference of the International Group for Lean Construction*, Singapore, August 2001.

Baruch, Y. (1999), 'Response rates in academic studies: A comparative analysis', *Human Relations*, vol. 52, no. 4, pp. 421–438.

Basu, R. (2004), 'Six Sigma in operational excellence: Role of tools and techniques', *International Journal of Six Sigma and Competitive Advantage*, vol. 1, no. 1, pp. 44–64.

Basu, R. (2009), *Implementing Six Sigma and Lean*. Oxford: Elsevier.

Basu, R. (2010), 'In search of project excellence: A systems approach of triangulation in a mixed methodology empirical research', *International Journal of Business and Systems Research*, vol. 4, no. 4, pp. 432–450.

Basu, R. (2011a), *FIT SIGMA: A Lean Approach to Building Sustainable Quality Beyond Six Sigma*. Chichester: John Wiley and Sons.

Basu, R. (2011b), *Managing Project Supply Chains*. Farnham: Gower Publishing.

Basu, R. and Wright, J.N. (2003), *Quality Beyond Six Sigma*. Oxford: Butterworth Heinemann.

Basu, R., Little, C. and Millard, C. (2009), 'Case Study: A fresh approach of the Balanced Scorecard in the Heathrow terminal 5 Project', Managing Business Excellence, vol. 13, no. 4, pp. 22–33.

Belassi, W. and Tukel, O.I. (1996), 'A new framework for determining critical success/failure factors in projects', *International Journal of Project Management*, vol. 14, no. 3, pp. 141–151.

Bellis, P. (2003), 'Project methodologies: An introduction to PRINCE2', JISC Infonet, UK.

Birkinshaw, J., Morrison, A. and Hullard, J. (1995), 'Structural and competitive determinants of a global integration strategy', *Strategic Management Journal*, vol. 18, no. 8, pp. 637–655.

BMI. (2008), *UK Infrastructure Report Q1 2008*. London: Business Monitor International.

Boddy, D. and Macbeth, D. (2000), 'Prescriptions for managing change: A survey of their effects in projects to implement collaboration with organisations', *International Journal of Project Management*, vol. 18, no. 5, pp. 297–306.

British Quality Foundations. (1999), *'The European Foundation of Quality Management (EFQM) Model'*, London.

British Standards Institution. (2000), *BS 6079: Project Management – Part 2: Vocabulary*. London: British Standards Institution.

British Standards Institution. (2002), *BS 6079: A Guide to Project Management*. London: British Standards Institution.

Bubshait, A.A. (1994), 'Owner involvement in project quality', *International Journal of Project Management*, vol. 12, no. 2, pp. 115–117.

Burke, R. (2003), *Project Management*. Chichester: John Wiley and Sons.

Campbell, D.T. (1975), '"Degrees of freedom" and the case study', *Comparative Political Studies*, vol. 8, pp. 178–193.

Chen, H.L. and Chen, W.T. (2005), 'Clarifying the behavioural patterns of contractor supply chain payment conditions', *International Journal of Project Management*, vol. 23, no. 6, pp. 462–473.

Chew, Y.S. and Chai, L.N. (1996), *ISO 9002 in the Malaysian Construction Industry*. McGraw Hill., KL, Malaysia

Chin, W.W. (1998), 'The partial least squares approach in structural equation modelling', in G.A. Marcoulides (ed.), *Modern Methods of Business Research*. London: Lawrence Erlbaum Associates.

Chin, W.W. (2001), *PLS Graph User's Guide, Version 3.0*. Houston: Soft Modeling.

Chin, W.W. and Newsted, P.R. (1999), 'Structural equation modelling with small samples using partial least squares', in R.H. Hoyle (ed.), *Statistical Strategies for Small Sample Research*. Thousand Oaks, CA: Sage.

Cooke-Davies, T. (2001), 'The "real" project success factors', *International Journal of Project Management*, vol. 20, no. 3, pp. 185–190.

Cooper R.G. (2001), *Winning at New Products – Accelerating the Process from Ideas to Launch*. Perseus Publishing, Boston, USACooper, R.G. (2009), 'Effective gating', *Marketing Management*, March/April, pp. 12–17.

Crawford, L. and Turner, R. (2008), 'Developing project management capability of organisations', in J.R. Turner (ed.), *Gower Handbook of Project Management*, 4th edn. Aldershot: Gower Publishing.

Cronin, J.J. and Taylor, S.A. (1992), 'Measuring service quality: A re-examination and extension', *Journal of Marketing*, vol. 56, no. 3, pp. 55–68.

Crosby, P. (1992), *Quality is Free: The Art of Making Quality Certain*. New York: McGraw-Hill.

Dale, B.G. (ed.) (2007), *Managing Quality*. New York: Prentice Hall.

DeLone, W.H. and McLean, E.R. (1992), 'Information systems success: The quest for the dependent variable', *Information Systems Research*, vol. 3, no. 1, pp. 60–95.

DeLone, W.H. and McLean, E.R. (2003), 'The DeLone and McLean model of information systems success: A ten-year update', *Journal of Management Information Systems*, vol. 10, no. 4, pp. 9–30.

Deming, W.E. (1986), *Out of the Crisis*. MIT Press., Boston, USA

Descombe, M. (2003), *The Good Research Guide: For Small Scale Social Research Projects*. Buckingham: Open University Press.

Dulewicz, V. and Higgs, M. (2005), 'Assessing leadership styles and organisational context', *Journal of Management Psychology*, vol. 20, no. 2, pp. 105–123.

Edum-Fotwe, F.T. and Price, A.D.F. (2008), 'A social ontology for appraising sustainability of construction projects and developments', *International*

*Journal of Project Management*, available online from 2 June 2008. vol. 27, no. 4, pp. 313–322.

Eisenhardt, K.M. (1989), 'Building theories from case study research', *Academy of Management Review*, vol. 14, pp. 532–550.

European Foundation of Quality Management. (2003), *The EFQM Excellence Model*. Brussels: European Foundation of Quality Management.

Falk R.F. and Miller, N.B. (1992), *A Primer for Soft Modeling*, Akron, Ohio: The University of Akron Press

Feigenbaum, A.V. (1983). *Total Quality Control*. New York: McGraw-Hill.

Feng, K. and Gonslaves, G.C. (2010), 'An integrated conceptual framework for product management in pharmaceutical new product development', *Review of Business Research*, vol. 10, no. 3, pp. 100–108.

Fong, P.A. (2003), 'Knowledge creation in multidisciplinary project teams: An empirical study of processes and their dynamic relationships', *International Journal of Project Management*, vol. 21, pp. 479–486.

Fornell, C., Lorange, P. and Roos, J. (1990), 'The co-operative venture formation process: A latent variable structural modelling approach', *Management Science*, vol. 36, no. 10, pp. 1246–1255.

Gallear, D., Ghobadian, A., Liu, J. and Woo, H. (2000), 'Quality and business process synergy: key strategies promoting longevity', *International Journal of Manufacturing Technology and Management*, vol. 2, no. 1–7, pp. 83–993.

Garvin, D. (1984), 'What does product quality really mean?', *Sloan Management Review*, vol. 26, no. 1, pp. 25–43.

Gaur, S.S. and Agarwal, R. (2006), 'Service quality measurement in retail sore context: A review of advances made using SERVQUAL and RSQS', *The Marketing Review*, vol. 6, pp. 317–330.

Gilb, T. and Johansen, T. (2005), *From Waterfall to Evolutionary Development*. INCOSE, www.incose.org.

Goldratt, E.M. (1999), *The Theory of Constraints*. New York: North River Press.

Goleman, D. (1996), *Emotional Intelligence: Why it can Matter More than IQ*. London: Bloomsbury Publishing.

Grover, G., Jeong, S.R. and Segars, A.H. (1996), 'Information systems effectiveness; the construct space and patterns of application', *Information and Management,* vol. 31, no. 4., pp. 177–191.

Grude, K. and Turner, R. (1996), 'Managing change', in R. Turner, K. Grude and L. Thurloway (eds), *The Project Manager as Change Agent*. McGraw Hill.

Grude, K., Turner, R. and Wateridge, J. (1996), 'Project health checks', in R. Turner, K. Grude and L. Thurloway (eds), *The Project Manager as Change Agent*. McGraw Hill. Maidenhead, England

Haenlein, M. and Kaplan, A.M. (2004). 'A beginner's guide to partial least square analysis', *Understanding Statistics*, vol. 3, no. 4, pp. 283–297.

Hair, J.F., Babin, B.J., Money, A.H. and Samouel, P. (2003), *Essentials of Business Research Methods*. New York: John Wiley and Sons.

Hair, J.F., Black, W.C., Babin, B.J., Anderson, R.E. and Tatham, R.L. (2006), *Multivariate Data Analysis*. London: Pearson Prentice Hall.

Hammer, M. (2007), 'The process audit', *Harvard Business Review*, vol. 85, no. 4, pp. 111–123.

Hartman, L. and Ashrafi, R.A. (2002), 'Project management in the information systems and information technologies industries', *Project Management Journal*, vol. 33, no. 3, pp. 5–15.

Heisler, S.I. (1990), 'Project quality and the project manager', *International Journal of Project Management*, vol. 8, no. 3, pp. 133–137.

Hiyassat, M.A.H. (1999), 'Applying ISO standards to a construction industry', *International Journal of Project Management*, vol. 18, no. 4, pp. 275–280.

Holmes, E. and Whelan, N. (2009), 'Banking crisis', *Project*, vol. 21, no. 6, pp. 24–26.

Hulland, J. (1999), 'Use of partial least square (PLS) in strategic management research: A review of four recent studies', *Strategic Management Journal*, vol. 20, no. 2, pp. 195–205.

Hulland, J, Chow, Y.H. and Lam, S. (1996), 'Use of causal models in marketing research: A review', *International Journal of Research in Marketing*, vol. 13, no. 2, pp. 181–197.

Huin, S.F. (2004), 'Managing deployment of ERP systems in SMEs using multi-agents', *International Journal of Project Management*, vol. 22, no. 6, pp. 511–517.

Ives, M. (2005), 'Identifying the contextual elements of project management within organizations and their impact on project success', *Project Management Journal*, vol. 36, no. 1, pp. 37–50.

International Project Management Association. (2007), *IPMA Certification Year Book 2006*. International Project Management AssociationNijkerk, .

International Standard Organisation. (2000), *ISO 9000:2000 Quality management systems – fundamentals and vocabulary*. Geneva: International Standards Organisation.

International Standards Organisation. (2000), *ISO 9001: Quality management standards*. Geneva: International Standards Organisation.

International Standards Organisation. (2003), *ISO 10006: Quality management systems – guidelines for quality management in projects*. Geneva: International Standards Organisation.

International Standards Organisation. (2005), *ISO 10005: Quality management systems – guidelines for quality management plans*. Geneva: International Standards Organisation.

Jain, S.K and Gupta, G. (2004), 'Measuring service quality: SERVQUAL vs SERVPERF scales', *VIKALPA*, vol. 29, no. 2, pp. 25–37.

Jamieson, A. and Morris, P. (2008), 'Implementing strategy through programmes or projects', in J.R. Turner and S.J. Simister (eds), *Gower Handbook of Project Management*. Farnham: Gower Publishing

Jugdev, K. and Muller, R. (2005), 'Process success: A retrospective look at project success and our evolving understanding of concept', *Project Management Journal*, vol. 36, no. 4, pp. 19–31.

Juran, J.M. (1989), *Juran on Leadership for Quality: An Executive Handbook*. New York: Free Press.

Kadefors, A. (2004), 'Trust in project relationships', *International Journal of Project Management*, vol. 22, pp. 175–182.

Kano, N. (ed.) (1996), *A Guide to TQM for Service Industries*. Tokyo: Asian Productivity Organisation.

Kaplan, R.S. and Norton, D.P. (1996). *Balanced Scorecard*. Boston, MA: Harvard Business School Press.

Kaplan, R.S. and Norton, D.P. (2004), 'Measuring the strategic readiness of intangible assets', *Harvard Business Review*, vol. 82, no. 2, pp. 52–64.

Kim, J. and Wilemon, D. (2007), 'The learning organisation as facilitator of complex NPD projects', *Creativity and Innovation Management*, vol. 16, no. 2, pp. 176–191.

King, N. (2006), 'Using interviews in qualitative research', in C. Cassell and G. Symon (ed.), *Essential Guide to Qualitative Methods in Organizational Research*. London: Sage Publications.

Kirby, E.G. (1996), 'The importance of recognizing alternative perspectives: An analysis of a failed project', *International Journal of Project Management*, vol. 14, no. 4, pp. 209–211.

Kotnour, T. (2000), 'Organisational learning practices in the project management environment', *The International Journal of Quality and Reliability Management*, vol. 17, nos 4/5, pp. 393–406.

Kvale, S. (1983), 'The qualitative research interview: A phenomenological and hermeneutical mode of understanding', *Journal of Phenomenological Psychology*, vol. 14, pp. 171–196.

Levitt, J.S. and Nann, P.C. (1994), *'Total Quality Through Project Management'*, McGraw Hill, New York.

Ling, F.Y.Y., Liu, M. and Woo, Y.C. (2009), 'Construction fatalities in Singapore', *International Journal of Project Management*, Volume 27, No.7, pp 717–726

Little, C. (2005), 'BAA Terminal 5', IQA Presentation, 18 May 2005.

Lock, D. (1992), *Project Management*. Aldershot: Gower.

Luu, V.T., Kim, S.Y. Tuan, N.V. and Oguntana, S.O. (2009), 'Qualifying scheduling risk in construction projects using Bayesian beliefs network', *International Journal of Project Management*, vol. 27, no. 1, pp. 39–50.

Mankin, E. (2006), 'Is your product development process helping or hindering innovation?', *Creating Breakthrough Innovations*. The Results Driven Managers Series, Harvard Business School Press., Boston, USA

Mantel, S., Meredith, J.R., Shafer, S.M. and Sutton, M.M. (2001), *Project Management in Practice*. New York: John Wiley and Sons.

Marshall, C. and Rossman, G. (1989), *Designing Qualitative Research*. Newbury Park, CA: Sage Publishing.

McElroy, B. and Mills, C. (2000), 'Managing stakeholders', in R. Turner and S. Simister (eds), *Gower Handbook of Project Management*, 3rd edn. Aldershot: Gower Publishing.

Mengel, T. (2008), 'Outcome-based project management education for emerging leaders – a case study of teaching and learning project management', *International Journal of Project Management*, vol. 26, no. 3, pp. 275–285.

Meredith, J.R. and Mantel, S.J. (2003), *Project Management*. NJ: John Wiley and Sons Hoboken, NJ, USA. .

Millard, C. (2005), 'Make T5 Quality', *Internal BAA Document*, February 2005.

Mitchell, V. (1996), 'Assessing the reliability and validity in questionnaire, an empirical example', *Journal of Applied Management Studies*, vol. 5, no. 2, pp. 199–207.

Morris, P.W.G. (1997), *The Management of Projects*. London: Thomas Telford.

Morris, P.W.G. and Hough, C. (1997), *The Anatomy of Major Projects: A Study of the Reality of Project Management*. Chichester: John Wiley and Sons.

Morris, L.L., Fitz-Gibbon, C.T. and Freeman, M.E. (1987), *How to Communicate Evaluation Findings*. Beverly Hills, CA: Sage.

MPA. (2003), 'Learning from project failures', Major Projects Association Seminar, 13 November 2003, London.

MSP. (2007), *Managing a Successful Programme*, 3rd edn. London: The Office of Government Commerce.

Murray-Webster, R and Thiry, M. (2000), 'Managing programmes of projects', in R. Turner and S. Simister (eds), *Gower Handbook of Project Management*, 3rd edn. Aldershot: Gower Publishing.

National Audit Office (2000), *The Millennium Dome*. London: National Audit Office.

Oakland, J.S. (2003), *TQM: Text with Cases*. Oxford: Butterworth Heinemann.

O'Brien, W. (2001), 'Enabling technologies for project supply chain collaboration', NSF/ICIS Infrastructure and Information Technology Workshop, Arlington, VA, June 2001

OGC. (2005), *Managing Successful Projects with PRINCE2*. London: Her Majesty's Stationery Office with the permission of Government Commerce UK.

OGC. (2010), *Addressing Project Failures through PRINCE2*. London: Office of Government Commerce, White Paper.

Openheim, A.N. (2000), *Questionnaire Design, Interviewing and Attitude Measurement*. London: Continuum International Publishing Group Ltd.

Pallant, J. (2003), *SPSS Survival Manual*. Maidenhead: Open University Press.

Parasuraman, A, Zeithamel, V. and Berry, L. (1984), 'A conceptual model of service quality', *Journal of Marketing*, vol. 49, no. 3, pp. 41–50.

Parkdil, F. and Harwood, T. (2005), 'Patient satisfaction in a pre-operative assessment clinic: An analysis using SERVQUAL dimensions', *Total Quality Management*, vol. 16, no. 1, pp. 15–30.

Perminova, O., Gustafsson, M. and Wikstrom, K. (2008), 'Defining uncertainty in projects – a new perspective', *International Journal of Project Management*, vol. 26, pp. 73–79.

Pharro, R. (2002), 'Processes and procedures', in R. Turner and S. Simister (eds), *Gower Handbook of Project management*, 3rd edn. Aldershot: Gower Publishing.

Phillips, E.M. and Pugh, D.S. (2000), *How to get a PhD: A Handbook for Students and their Supervisors*. Buckingham: Open University Press.

Pinch, L. (2005), 'Lean construction', *Construction Executive*, vol. 15, no. 11, pp. 8–11.

Pinto, J.K. and Slevin, D.P. (1988), 'Critical success factors in effective project implementation', in D.J. Cleland and W.R. King (eds), *Project Management Handbook*. New York: Van Nostrand Reinhold.

Pither, R. and Duncan, W.R. (1998), *ISO 10006: Risky Business*. Lexington, KY: Project Management Partners

PRINCE2 (2002), London: Office of Government Commerce.

PRINCE2 (2009), London: Office of Government Commerce.

Project Management Institute (2004), *A Guide to the Project Management Body of Knowledge (PMBOK Guide)*, 2nd edn, Project Management Institute, Newtown Square., PA, USA

Project Management Institute (2008), *A Guide to the Project Management Body of Knowledge (PMBOK Guide)*, 3rd edn. Project Management Institute, Newtown Square., PA, USA

Qureshi, T.M., Warraich, A.H. and Hijaji, T.S. (2009), 'Significance of project management performance assessment', *International Journal of Project Management*,. vol. 27, no. 4, pp. 378–388.

Rail Link Engineering (2005), *Monitoring and Evaluation of Management Systems. HS1 Project internal document 000-GPP-RLEQU-00002-04,* London, November 2005.

Robson, C. (2002), *Real World Research*. Oxford: Blackwell.

Rounce, G (1998), 'Quality, waste and cost consideration in building design management', *International Journal of Project Management*, vol. 16, no. 2, pp. 123–128.

Samouel, P. (2008), *Structural Equation Modelling by Partial Least Squares (PLS)*. Workshop Handouts, Quantitative Research Techniques Workshop, Henley Business School, May 2008.

Saunders, M., Lewis, P. and Thornhill, A. (2007), *Research Methods for Business Students*. London: Prentice Hall.

Scott-Young, C. and Samson, D. (2008), 'Project success and project team management: Evidence from capital projects in the process industries', *Journal of Operations Management*, vol. 26, pp. 749–766.

Seaver, D. (2009), 'Respect the iron triangle', *IT Today*, http://www.ittoday.info/Articles/IronTriangle.htm

Sekaran, U. (2003), *Research Methods for Business*. John Wiley and SonsHoboken, NJ, USA. .

Serpell, A. (1999), 'Integrating quality systems in construction projects', *International Journal of Project Management*, vol. 17, no. 5, pp. 317–323.

Shenhar, A.J., Dvir, D. Levy, O. and Maltz, A.C. (2001), 'Project success: A multidimensional strategic concept', *Long Range Planning*, vol. 34, no. 6, pp. 699–725.

Siegelaub, J. (2004), 'How PRINCE2 can complement PMBOK and your PMP', *PMI Westchester Chapter*, Anaheim, CaliforniaSlack, N., Chambers, S., Johnston, R. and Betts, A. (2006), *Operations and Process Management*. Harlow: FT Prentice Hall.

Stanleigh, M. (2007), *Combining the ISO 10006 and PMBOK to Ensure Successful Projects*. Toronto: Business Improvement Architects.

Stuart, I., McCutcheon, D., Handfield, R., McLachlin, R. and Samson, D. (2002), 'Effective case research in operations management: A process perspective', *Journal of Operations Management*, vol. 20, no. 5, pp. 419–433.

Tabachnick, B.G. and Fidell, L.S. (2007), *Using Multivariate Statistics*. Boston, MA: Pearson Education.

Tam, C.M. (1999), 'Build-operate-transfer for infrastructure developments in Asia: Reasons for successes and failures', *International Journal of Project Management*, vol. 17, no. 6, pp. 377–382.

Tam, C.M. and Hui, Y.T. (1996), 'TQM in a public transport in Hong Kong', *International Journal of Project Management*, vol. 14, no. 5, pp. 11–15.

Taveira, A.D. (2008), 'Key elements on team achievement: A retrospective analysis', *Applied Ergonomics*, vol. 39, pp. 509–518.

Temme, D., Paulssen, M. and Dannewald, T. (2008), 'Incorporating latent variables into discrete choice model – a simultaneous estimation approach using SEM software', *Business Research*, vol. 1, no. 2, pp. 220–237.

Tennant, C. and Roberts, P. (2001), 'A faster way to create better quality products', *International Journal of Project Management*, vol. 19, no. 6, pp. 353–362.

Thomas, J. and Mengel, T. (2008), 'Preparing project managers to deal with complexity – advanced project management education', *International Journal of Project Management*, vol. 26, pp. 304–315.

Transport Select Committee (2008), *Transport Twelfth Report*. Louise Ellman MP (Chair). London: House of Commons Publications.

Tullett, A.D. (1996), 'The thinking style of managers of multiple projects: Implications for problem solving when managing change', *International Journal of Project Management*, vol. 14, no. 5, pp. 281–287.

Turner, R. (1999), *The Handbook of Project Based Management*. London: McGraw-Hill.

Turner, R. (2002), 'Managing quality', in R.Turner and S. Simister (eds), *Gower Handbook of Project management*. Aldershot: Gower Publishing.

Turner, R. and Cochrane, R.A. (1993), 'Goals and methods matrix: Coping with projects for which the goals and/or methods of achieving them are ill defined', *International Journal of Project Management*, vol. 11, no. 2, pp. 93–102.

Turner, R. and Muller, R. (2005), 'The project manager's leadership style as a success factor on projects', *Project Management Journal*, vol. 36, no.2. pp. 49–61.

Tushman, M. and O'Reilly, C.A. (1997), *Winning Through Innovation – A Practical Guide to Leading Organisational Change and Renewal*. Harvard Business School Press, Boston, USA

United Nations (1987), *Report of the World Commission on Environment and Development*. UN General Assembly Resolution, 11 December 1987. New York: United Nations.

Wateridge, J. (2002), 'Project health checks', in R. Turner and S. Simister (eds), *Gower Handbook of Project management*. Aldershot: Gower Publishing

Weinstein, L.B., Castellano, J., Petrick, J. and Vokurka, R.J. (2008), 'Integrating Six Sigma concepts in an MBA quality management class', *Journal of Education for Business*, vol. 83, no. 4, pp. 233–238.

Wetzel, M., Odekerken-Schroder, G. And van Oppen, C. (2009), 'Using PLS path modeling for assessing hierarchical construct models: Guidelines and Empirical Illustration', *MIS Quarterly*, vol. 33, no. 1, pp. 177–195.

Westerveld, E. (2003), 'The project excellence model', *International Journal of Project Management*, vol. 21, no. 6, pp. 411–418.

White, D. and Fortune, J. (2002), 'Current practices in project management – an empirical study', *International Journal of Project Management*, vol. 20, no. 1, pp. 1–11.

Whitty, S.J. and Schulz, M.F. (2005), 'And then came Complex Project Management', *The Proceedings of 20th IPMA World Congress in Project Management*, The University of Queensland, Brisbane, vol. 1, pp. 466–472.

Wild, R. (2002), *Operations Management*. London: Continuum.

Wold, H. (1985), 'Systems analysis by partial least squares', in P. Nijkamp, I. Leitner and N. Wrigley (eds), *Measuring the Unmeasurable*. Dordrecht: Marinus Nijhoff.

Womack, J.P. and Jones, D.T. (1998), *Lean Thinking*. London: Touchstone Books

Wright, J.N. and Basu, R. (2008), 'Project management and Six Sigma: Obtaining a fit', *International Journal of Six Sigma and Competitive Advantage*, vol. 4, no. 1, pp. 81–94.

Xiaolong Xue, Yaowu Wang, Qiping Shen and Xiaoguo Yu (2007), 'Coordination mechanisms for construction supply chain management in the internet environment', *International Journal of Project Management*, vol. 25, no. 2, pp 105–212.

Xue, X., Wang, Y., Shen, Q. and Yu, X. (2007), 'Coordination mechanisms for construction supply chain management in the internet environment', *International Journal of Project Management*, vol. 25, no. 2, pp. 150–157.

Yeo, K.T. and Ning, J.H. (2002), 'Integrating supply chain and critical concepts in engineer-procure-construct (EPC) projects', *International Journal of Project Management*, vol. 20, no. 4, pp. 253–262.

Yin, R.K. (2003), *Case Study Research: Design and Methods*. London: Sage Publications.

Yin, R.K. and Heald, K.A. (1975), 'Using the case survey method to analyse policy studies', *Administrative Science Quarterly*, vol. 20, pp. 371–381.

Yin, R.K. and Heinsohn, I. (1980), *Case Studies in Research Utilization*. Washington: American Institutes for Research DC.

Zeithml, V.A, Prasuraman, A. and Berry, L.L. (1990), *Delivering Service Quality*, Free Press, New York.

Zou, P.X.W., Zhang, G. and Wang, J. (2007), 'Understanding the key risks of construction projects in China', *International Journal of Project Management*, vol. 25, no. 6, pp. 601–614.

# INDEX

## ADVANCES IN PROJECT MANAGEMENT

*Advances in Project Management* provides short, state of play, guides to the main aspects of the new emerging applications including: maturity models, agile projects, extreme projects, Six Sigma and projects, human factors and leadership in projects, project governance, value management, virtual teams and project benefits.

## CURRENTLY PUBLISHED TITLES

*Managing Project Uncertainty*, David Cleden 978-0-566-08840-7

*Managing Project Supply Chains*, Ron Basu 978-1-4094-2515-1

*Project-Oriented Leadership*, Ralf Müller and J Rodney Turner 978-0-566-08923-7

*Strategic Project Risk Appraisal and Management*, Elaine Harris 978-0-566-08848-3

*Spirituality and Project Management*, Judi Neal and Alan Harpham 978-1-4094-0959-5

*Sustainability in Project Management*, Gilbert Silvius, Jasper van den Brink, Ron Schipper, Adri Köhler and Julia Planko 978-1-4094-3169-5

*Second Order Project Management*, Michael Cavanagh, 978-1-4094-1094-2

*Tame, Messy and Wicked Risk Leadership*, David Hancock 978-0-566-09242-8

# REVIEWS OF THE SERIES

*Managing Project Uncertainty*, David Cleden

> *This is a must-read book for anyone involved in project management. The author's carefully crafted work meets all my "4Cs" review criteria. The book is clear, cogent, concise and complete...it is a brave author who essays to write about managing project uncertainty in a text extending to only 117 pages (soft-cover version). In my opinion, David Cleden succeeds brilliantly...For project managers this book, far from being a short-lived stress anodyne, will provide a confidence-boosting tonic. Project uncertainty? Bring it on, I say!*
> International Journal of Managing Projects in Business

> *Uncertainty is an inevitable aspect of most projects, but even the most proficient project manager struggles to successfully contain it. Many projects overrun and consume more funds than were originally budgeted, often leading to unplanned expense and outright programme failure. David examines how uncertainty occurs and provides management strategies that the user can put to immediate use on their own project work. He also provides a series of pre-emptive uncertainty and risk avoidance strategies that should be the cornerstone of any planning exercise for all personnel involved in project work.*
>
> *I have been delivering both large and small projects and programmes in the public and private sector since 1989. I wish this book had been available when I began my career in project work. I strongly commend this book to all project professionals.*
> Lee Hendricks, Sales & Marketing Director, SunGard Public Sector

> *The book under review is an excellent presentation of a comprehensive set of explorations about uncertainty (its recognition) in the context of projects. It does a good job of all along reinforcing the difference between risk (known unknowns) management and managing uncertainty (unknown unknowns - "bolt from the blue"). The author lucidly presents a variety of frameworks/ models so that the reader easily grasps the varied forms in which uncertainty presents itself in the context of projects.*
> VISION – The Journal of Business Perspective (India)

> *Cleden will leave you with a sound understanding about the traits, tendencies, timing and tenacity of uncertainty in projects. He is also adept at identifying certain methods that try to contain the uncertainty, and why some prove more successful than others. Those who expect risk management to be the be-all, end-all for uncertainty solutions will be in for a rude awakening.*
> Brad Egeland, Project Management Tips

*Project-Oriented Leadership*, Rodney Turner and Ralf Müller

> *Müller and Turner have compiled a terrific "ready-reckoner" that all project managers would benefit from reading and reflecting upon to challenge their performance. The authors have condensed considerable experience and research from a wide variety of professional disciplines, to provide a robust digest that highlights the significance of leadership capabilities for effective delivery of project outcomes. One of the big advantages of this book is the richness of the content and the natural flow of their argument throughout such a short book....Good advice, well explained and backed up with a body of evidence...I will be recommending the book to colleagues who are in project leader and manager roles and to students who are considering these as part of their development or career path.*
>
> Arthur Shelley, RMIT University, Melbourne, Australia, International Journal of Managing Projects in Business

> *In a remarkably succinct 89 pages, Müller and Turner review an astonishing depth of evidence, supported by their own (published) research which challenges many of the commonly held assumptions not only about project management, but about what makes for successful leaders.*
>
> *This book is clearly written more for the project-manager type personality than for the natural leader. Concision, evidence and analysis are the main characteristics of the writing style...it is massively authoritative, and so carefully written that a couple of hours spent in its 89 pages may pay huge dividends compared to the more expansive, easy reading style of other management books.*
>
> Mike Turner, Director of Communications for NHS Warwickshire

*Strategic Project Risk Appraisal and Management*, Elaine Harris

> *...Elaine Harris's volume is timely. In a world of books by "instant experts" it's pleasing to read something by someone who clearly knows their onions, and has a passion for the subject...In summary, this is a thorough and engaging book.*
>
> Chris Morgan, Head of Business Assurance for Select Plant Hire, Quality World

> *As soon as I met Elaine I realised that we both shared a passion to better understand the inherent risk in any project, be that capital investment, expansion capital or expansion of assets. What is seldom analysed are the components of knowledge necessary to make a good judgement, the impact of our own prejudices in relation to projects or for that matter the cultural elements within an organisation which impact upon the decision making process. Elaine created a system to break this down and give reasons and*

logic to both the process and the human interaction necessary to improve the chances of success. Adopting her recommendations will improve teamwork and outcomes for your company.

Edward Roderick Hon LLD, Former CEO Christian Salvesen Plc

## *Tame, Messy and Wicked Risk Leadership*, David Hancock

*This book takes project risk management firmly onto a higher and wider plane. We thought we knew what project risk management was and what it could do. David Hancock shows us a great deal more of both. David Hancock has probably read more about risk management than almost anybody else, he has almost certainly thought about it as much as anybody else and he has quite certainly learnt from doing it on very difficult projects as much as anybody else. His book draws fully on all three components. For a book which tackles a complex subject with breadth, insight and novelty - its remarkable that it is also a really good read. I could go on!*

Dr Martin Barnes CBE FREng, President, The Association for Project Management

*This compact and thought provoking description of risk management will be useful to anybody with responsibilities for projects, programmes or businesses. It hits the nail on the head in so many ways, for example by pointing out that risk management can easily drift into a check-list mindset, driven by the production of registers of numerous occurrences characterised by the Risk = Probablity x Consequence equation. David Hancock points out that real life is much more complicated, with the heart of the problem lying in people, so that real life resembles poker rather than roulette. He also points out that while the important thing is to solve the right problem, many real life issues cannot be readily described in a definitive statement of the problem. There are often interrelated individual problems with surrounding social issues and he describes these real life situations as 'Wicked Messes'. Unusual terminology, but definitely worth the read, as much for the overall problem description as for the recommended strategies for getting to grips with real life risk management. I have no hesitation in recommending this book.*

Sir Robert Walmsley KCB FREng, Chairman of the Board of the Major Projects Association

*In highlighting the complexity of many of today's problems and defining them as tame, messy or wicked, David Hancock brings a new perspective to the risk issues that we currently face. He challenges risk managers, and particularly those involved in project risk management, to take a much broader approach to the assessment of risk and consider the social, political and behavioural dimensions of each problem, as well as the scientific and engineering aspects with which they are most comfortable. In this way, risks will be viewed more holistically and managed more effectively than at present.*

Dr Lynn T Drennan, Chief Executive, Alarm, the public risk
management association

*Sustainability in Project Management,* Gilbert Silvius, Jasper van den Brink, Ron Schipper, Adri Köhler and Julia Planko

*Sustainability in Project Management thinking and techniques is still in its relatively early days. By the end of this decade it will probably be universal, ubiquitous, fully integrated and expected. This book will be a most valuable guide on this journey for all those interested in the future of projects and how they are managed in a world in peril.*

Tom Taylor dashdot and vice-President of APM

*Project Managers are faced with lots of intersections. The intersection of projects and risk, projects and people, projects and constraints ... Sustainability in Projects and Project Management is a compelling, in-depth treatment of a most important intersection: the intersection of project management and sustainability. With detailed background building to practical checklists and a call to action, this book is a must-read for anyone interested in truly implementing sustainability, project manager or not.*

Rich Maltzman, PMP, Co-Founder, EarthPM, LLC, and co-author of Green
Project Management, Cleland Literature Award Winner of 2011

*Great book! Based on a thorough review on existing relevant models and concepts the authors provide guidance for different stakeholders such as Project Managers and Project Office Managers to consider sustainability principles on projects. The book gets you started on sustainability in project context!*

Martina Huemann, WU-Vienna University of Economics and
Business, Vienna Austria

*While sustainability and green business have been around a while, this book is truly a "call to action" to help the project manager, or for that matter, anyone, seize the day and understand sustainability from a project perspective. This book gives real and practical suggestions as to how to fill the sustainability/ project gap within your organization. I particularly liked the relationship between sustainability and "professionalism and ethics", a connection that needs to be kept in the forefront.*

David Shirley, PMP, Co-Founder, EarthPM, LLC, and co-author of Green
Project Management, Cleland Literature Award Winner of 2011

*It is high time that quality corporate citizenship takes its place outside the corporate board room. This excellent work, which places the effort needed to secure sustainability for everything we do right where the rubber hits the road – our projects – has been long overdue. Thank you Gilbert, Jasper, Ron, Adri and Julia for doing just that! I salute you.*

Jaycee Krüger, member of ISO/TC258 a technical committee for the creation
of standards in Project, Program and Portfolio Management, and chair of
SABS/TC258, the South African mirror committee of ISO/TC258

*Sustainability is no passing fad. It is the moral obligation that we all face in ensuring the future of human generations to come. The need to show stewardship and act as sustainability change agents has never been greater. As project managers we are at the forefront of influencing the direction of our projects and our organisations. Sustainability in Project Management offers illuminating insights into the concept of sustainability and its application to project management. It is a must read for any modern project manager.*

Dr Neveen Moussa, Project Manager, Adjunct Professor of Project
Management and past president of the Australian Institute
of Project Management

## ABOUT THE EDITOR

Professor Darren Dalcher is founder and Director of the National Centre for Project Management, a Professor of Project Management at the University of Hertfordshire and Visiting Professor of Computer Science at the University of Iceland.

Following industrial and consultancy experience in managing IT projects, Professor Dalcher gained his PhD from King's College, University of London. In 1992, he founded and chaired of the Forensics Working Group of the IEEE Technical Committee on the Engineering of Computer-Based Systems, an international group of academic and industrial participants formed to share information and develop expertise in project and system failure and recovery.

He is active in numerous international committees, standards bodies, steering groups, and editorial boards. He is heavily involved in organising international conferences, and has delivered many international keynote addresses and tutorials. He has written over 150 refereed papers and book chapters on project management and software engineering. He is Editor-in-Chief of the *International Journal of Software Maintenance and Evolution*, and of the *Journal of Software: Evolution and Process*. He is the editor of a major new book series, Advances in Project Management, published by Gower Publishing which synthesises leading edge knowledge, skills, insights and reflections in project and programme management and of a new companion series, Fundamentals of Project Management, which provides the essential grounding in key areas of project management.

He has built a reputation as leader and innovator in the area of practice-based education and reflection in project management and has worked with many major industrial, commercial and charitable organisations and government bodies. In 2008 he was named by the Association for Project Management as one of the top 10 influential experts in project management and has also been voted *Project Magazine's* Academic of the Year for his contribution in "integrating and weaving academic work with practice". He has been chairman of the APM Project Management Conference since 2009, setting consecutive attendance records and bringing together the most influential speakers.

He received international recognition in 2009 with appointment as a member of the PMForum International Academic Advisory Council, which features leading academics from some of the world's top universities and academic institutions. The Council showcases accomplished researchers, influential educators shaping the next generation of project managers and recognised authorities on modern project management. In October 2011 he was awarded a prestigious Honorary Fellowship from the Association for Project Management for outstanding contribution to project management.

He has delivered lectures and courses in many international institutions, including King's College London, Cranfield Business School, ESC Lille, Iceland University, University of Southern Denmark, and George Washington University. His research interests include project success and failure; maturity and capability; ethics; process improvement; agile project management; systems and software engineering; project benchmarking; risk management; decision making; chaos and complexity; project leadership; change management; knowledge management; evidence-based and reflective practice.

Professor Dalcher is an Honorary Fellow of the Association for Project Management, a Chartered Fellow of the British Computer Society, a Fellow of the Chartered Management Institute, and the Royal Society of Arts, and a Member of the Project Management Institute, the Academy of Management, the Institute for Electrical and Electronics Engineers, and the Association for Computing Machinery. He is a Chartered IT Practitioner. He is a Member of the PMI Advisory Board responsible for the prestigious David I. Cleland Project Management Award; of the APM Group Ethics and Standards Governance Board, and, until recently; of the APM Professional Development Board. He is a member of the OGC's International Reference Group for Managing Successful Programmes; and Academic and Editorial Advisory Council Member for PM Today, for which he also writes a regular column featuring advances in research and practice in project management.

National Centre for Project Management
University of Hertfordshire
MacLaurin Building
4 Bishops Square
Hatfield, Herts.
AL10 9NE
Email: ncpm@herts.ac.uk